To Robert Christmas '86
Some memories of your misspent youth. Will Squibs be sporting mast stunts soon?
(see p 112)

Bryan.

THE MERLIN ROCKET BOOK

COMPILED BY

JIM PARK, IAN HOLT & JIM LOWDEN

Foreword by Ian Proctor

Published by Jim Lowden
10 Denham Drive, Yateley, Camberley, Surrey GU17 7LQ   Tel. 0252-872161
in association with the Merlin Rocket Owners Association
1986

Generously sponsored by the following:
M.R.O.A., Alan Warren (H. D. Tribe Ltd.), Dick & Gill Batt (Batt Sails), Chris Andrews
Jim Robinson (Robinson Buckley Insurance Brokers Ltd.), Alan Chaplin
Stuart Gurney (Gurney Triggs Partnership, Architects, Surveyors)
Guy Winder (Guy Winder Boats), Robin Judah

ALL RIGHTS RESERVED

ISBN 0 9511186 0 9

© J. LOWDEN

Printed in Great Britain by
Stones Printers, High Street, Milford-on-Sea, Hampshire

COVER PHOTOGRAPHS
Front   Phil King and Andy Neal in the highly successful *Bananas*, No. 3211, at Salcombe in 1980
Photograph by R. O'Neill
Rear   Ian Holt and Tony Cole in the early "wide beamed" *Broad Minded* at Salcombe, 1977
Photograph by R. O'Neill

FOREWORD

It is the people who sail the boats that really make a class, not the boats themselves. This book is a fine example of the enthusiasm and dedication to a class that some may give to a class to help keep it moving, interesting and alive. The original concept of a "development class" lays down a framework for the future and prototype boats are built in the knowledge that designers, spurred on by competitive owners, will use the rules to what they believe to be maximum advantage. The whole motivation of a development class is to develop as far as possible within the limitations laid down by those rules.

I believe that the three principal development classes in the UK, the International 14s, National 12 and National Merlin Rockets, have led the world with examples of class rules which give designers sufficient freedom to allow and encourage the innovation and evolution that keeps these classes ever fresh, yet at the same time providing a basis for continuity and avoidance of expensive and destructive rapid outclassing of older boats. There is a great responsibility resting with the class committees and their technical advisors to ensure that the rules steer the class in the right direction and hold the right balance.

It is rule-makers, rather than designers, who probably bring about the more profound changes in design. The designers are naturally always searching for better performance in one way or another and if they are skilful, or lucky, they will make progress. But any "big bangs" in the evolutionary process are likely to be influenced by the rules – or new materials or fittings. It is inevitable that astute designers will very quickly exploit the potential of rule changes, and often the long-term effects of what appear to be quite trivial rule amendments are quite far reaching and well beyond the imagination of many of those who vote upon them.

The influence of rules has been profound in the Merlin Rockets, but has often exerted itself in a subtle manner. The Merlins started out with a "power" question mark; the original rig extended a lofty 25ft above deck and was far from easy to hold up. Early rule amendments brought a fairly massive reduction in maximum permitted height to 22ft 6ins, and many boats subsequently went down to 21ft 6ins or even 20ft 6ins. But the hulls also became more powerful, with more flare for sitting out power, slimmer bows for driving through choppy water and long flat runs for planing ability. Then terylene sailcloth came in, leading eventually to the characteristic mainsail with long top batten and roughly 22% more sail area high up in the sail plan. An efficient, driving sail, but one which demanded more sitting-out power from the hull. This was when the beam was successfully increased from 5ft 3ins to over 7ft and the new era of really wide hulls was established.

I mention this because it may be interesting as a classic example of how a new material or fitting in one sector, with apparently limited significance within that sector, can ultimately have far reaching influence on some seemingly quite unconnected aspect of the boat. The length and position of a sail batten influenced trends in hull shape. It has happened many times, with even such things as self-bailers nudging hull design towards different shapes.

The Merlin Rocket class has been steered very successfully through all the progress that has taken place in the sphere of dinghy sailing in the past forty years. When the class was first introduced, it was in the forefront of dinghy development. It still is.

To sort out and record the great amount of detail that goes to make up the story of so active a class as this demands a vast amount of research and dedication. The thanks of all those who have sailed in and so much enjoyed the Merlin Rocket class naturally goes to all involved in the compilation and production of this record. Perhaps even more thanks will be due from future generations of Merlin Rocket sailors many years from now, who will now be able to read of what happened in the otherwise dim, or lost, past.

The Merlin Rocket spirit is, and always has been lively. The boats are intriguing and challenging. Competition is keen, but friendly. All the ingredients for a very long life are there, so why should I be conventional and say "Here's to the next forty years"? Why limit our toast to only forty years?

So here's to the future of the Merlin Rocket class and may it extend far into the next century.

Duncannon   July 1986   IAN PROCTOR

CONTENTS

			PAGE
CHAPTER 1	*The Post-War Pioneering Days, 1946–1955*		1
CHAPTER 2	*The Dinghy Sailing Boom, 1956–1965*		17
CHAPTER 3	*The Developing Years, 1966–1975*		26
CHAPTER 4	*Surviving the Hard Times, 1976–1986*		40
	Chronology of Historical Events		57
CHAPTER 5	*Designers and Their Designs*		58
CHAPTER 6	*The Rig*		89
CHAPTER 7	*The Builders*		120
CHAPTER 8	*The Silver Tiller Series*		139
CHAPTER 9	*Salcombe Week*		149
CHAPTER 10	*The 1970 Championships at Pwllheli*		159
CHAPTER 11	*Where Merlin Rockets Sail*		167

INTRODUCTION

The idea of commemorating the 40th Anniversary of the Merlin Rocket Class by publishing a book tracing the Class's history was first put forward by Jim Park, a past chairman of the Class Committee, in 1981. However, it was not until 1985 that the Committee formally invited Jim Park and Ian Holt to write such a book, with Jim Lowden, a member of the Committee, taking responsibility for the co-ordination, financial backing and publication.

No history of a Class as active as the Merlin Rocket can be truly comprehensive. We can only hope that we have done justice to this entertaining and challenging subject. A great deal of work has gone into ensuring that the contents are accurate, and only first-hand accounts or publications have been used to recount memorable events and in describing the development of the boat itself.

We would like to thank everyone who has helped us in our task and, in particular, the following, who merit a special mention.

Ian Proctor, whose designs dominated the Class for fifteen years, has kindly written the Foreword to the book, as he did for Robin Steavenson's history of our sister Class, the National 12, and Ian's writings as a yachting journalist have provided further sources of information. Jack Holt, Beecher Moore and Group Captain Haylock have each recalled the early days of the Merlin, while Dr. Robin Steavenson has shed light on the launching of the Rocket. Cliff Norbury and Ken Rose, managing directors respectively of Proctor Metal Masts and Bruce Banks Sails, have supplied details of the developments in masts and sails.

Phil Morrison and Michael McNamara have provided information on latter day boat design and rig development, whilst the views of Spud Rowsell, Jon Turner, Dick Wyche and Jack Chippendale on the changes in building techniques have been invaluable. Additional information was supplied by Dennis Ellis, David Robinson and John Harris.

The task of putting the chapters together was greatly eased by the sub-editing efforts of Berry Ritchie and Peter Fryer. Factual checking and editing was assisted by Dick Batt, Chris Haworth, Alan Warren, Neil Thornton, Pat Blake, Tom Booth, Keith Callaghan, Peter Greatrex and Michael Jackson.

Exceptional photographic assistance was given by Robert O'Neill and Guy Gurney, while the line drawings were redrawn by Mark Nicholson and Marcus Owen. Much of the typing was carried out by Ruth Reid and Annette Chapman.

Finally, the authors wish to express their thanks to Jim Lowden, without whose efforts this book would not have appeared during this 40th Anniversary year and to Mr. E. W. Lowden for having the faith to provide the initial loan necessary to finance the project.

Four Glorious Decades . . .

CHAPTER 1
The Post-War Pioneering Days 1945-1955

World War II found many dinghy sailors in the Services with time to think of the type of sailing they would want once hostilities ceased. At that stage your choice was pretty limited compared with today. Most dinghies were very heavy and the only one which could be relied upon to plane was the International 14. However, if that splendid dinghy capsized, that was the end of your race because the absence of decks allowed the boats to fill, there was only a small amount of buoyancy, no transom flaps and no self-bailers. In short, the ethos of the Class was that anybody unseamanlike enough to capsize did not deserve to continue racing. This attitude governed the thinking of the YRA (now the RYA), perhaps because many International 14 sailors went on to become members of the RYA Council, and this was for many years to inhibit the plans of Classes to allow self-draining hulls.

The National 12 Class had been started shortly before the war in 1936. Although these boats were decked, they did not have a spinnaker and were a little cramped for two full-size adults. Whilst the manouverability of a 12 was much admired, the overall length was still felt to be too short to punch efficiently into the short chop you encountered off the English coast and which had led so many designers to compromise on an overall length of 14ft. This certainly was the view of eight National 12 owners at the Ranelagh Sailing Club whose clubhouse at Putney was virtually on the starting line for the University Boat Race. Sitting at the bar of the Ranelagh SC with a pint of beer in one hand and a pencil in the other, indicating how a design might be improved, had always been one of the great traditions of that Club. The Merlin Class owes its existence to the eight members – Tony Howard, Noel Jordan, Beecher Moore, Bernard Leigh, Richard Stafford, Jack Holt, Veri Wagner and his brother-in-law (who had access to heavily rationed timber), who decided to transform an idea into a reality.

World War II had only ended that summer, but it had had the effect of conditioning the minds of those who had served in it, that disciplined thinking could make things happen in a very much shorter time than had previously been thought possible. Applying the principles learned when delays could cost lives, this group formed itself into a Syndicate, agreed the desired qualities they sought and resolved to commission the designer of the fastest National 12 to put these ideas into a design for perusal. If accepted, a prototype would be built.

As it happened, one of their own members, Jack Holt, was building some of the fastest 12s around at the outbreak of the War and he had spent much of the wartime building lifeboats for the Merchant Navy and models of warships for aircraft recognition. With Jack's yard only a short stroll away from the clubhouse, he was the obvious choice for the commission.

The Syndicate thought of the various qualities they required. The hull must be light and this could be achieved by using the new marine plywood which had been developed during the War; the length must be long enough to plane easily (nobody in the post-war age would buy a non-planing dinghy); there must be decks – the new marine plywood could be bent into curves at the side decks which would enable a boat to heel 90 degrees before allowing water in, this would also stiffen up the hull; the sail

The original Syndicate on a cold November day in 1945, at Camper & Nicholson's boatyard. From here Merlin was first tested using an International 14' as a trial horse. From left to right: Veri Wagner, Beecher Moore, Jack Holt, Noel Jordan, Tony Howard and Bernard Leigh. *Photograph courtesy of Jack Holt*

area for such a light easily driven hull should also be much reduced, thereby enabling the boat to be crewed by women. The Syndicate had correctly foreseen that after achieving so much during the War, women were no longer going to be content to be passive spectators, and much of the Merlin's original ideas were planned with women crews in mind. There was to be a spinnaker, but of a moderate size to assist running against the current at Putney. A running spinnaker could be set from a halyard just below the forestay, making gybing easier. This also effectively precluded spinnaker reaching and the need for greater physical strength.

With the disappearance of the Club Boatman, the boat must be easily handled on shore. This could be facilitated by placing four wooden carrying handles at strategic points. At this time, it should be remembered that galvanised launching trolleys were still a thing of the future. Finally, the mast must rotate so that it maintains a constant angle of attack to the mainsail as it is released downwind. These ideas were extremely advanced for the 1940s and had there been a greater availability of wood in post-war Britain, the Merlin as the first post-war dinghy, would have been better placed to benefit.

Whilst others celebrated the end of the War and looked to their personal futures, the Syndicate put its specifications to Jack Holt and asked him to produce the dinghy which would combine the best features of the National 12 and the International 14 without the shortcomings of either. Jack said that he had spent many hours in the wartime considering the demands of future customers. Clearly the boat had to plane and would therefore require a flatter floor.

The eventual dinghy produced was named *Kate*, after the Syndicate. With low freeboard, *Kate* was flatter than the design eventually adopted, and had a higher mast than the National 12 (24ft against 20ft), although 6ins shorter than the rig eventually agreed. The freeboard was cut down to reduce wind resistance, but, to compensate for this, the hull was almost completely decked. Even at this early stage, Jack was thinking of a hull where a knockdown from the sort of gust which so frequently blasted through gaps in the trees or buildings on the river bank at Putney, would not full up the boat and put it out of the race.

Jack Holt and Beecher Moore sail the original *Kate*, No. 1.

Photograph courtesy of Beecher Moore

There were many new ideas on this boat and the Syndicate decided that *Kate* needed some changes to achieve the wide popularity needed to successfully launch the first post-war class. The boat was purchased by Charles Leafe, but Jack was asked to try again. The second boat was slightly less radical and was accepted. Originally christened *Wizard*, this name was changed by Group Capt. Haylock, who had tired of this RAF slang word, to *Merlin* after King Arthur's wizard, and given an insignia in the shape of Merlin's hat. This boat is regarded as the founder of the dynasty. She should perhaps have been given the first number allocated, but out of deference to the prototype, this was given to *Kate* and *Merlin* has always borne the number "2".

Compared with *Kate*, *Merlin* had a 25ft mast and more rocker to assist in the quick tacking needed on the Thames. Recognising that this was to be a development Class, the Syndicate deliberately left the tolerances for mast height, centreboard depth and decking very wide so that other designers (and of course Jack himself) could experiment with the variables with a view to improving the boat. The Syndicate wisely recognised, no doubt with the benefit of wartime experience, that it was unreasonable to expect any designer to achieve perfection first time and there had to be an opportunity to improve faults found by experience. As National 12 owners they were aware that their Class rules were formulated around the successful *Uffa King* rather than Uffa Fox's design built to pre-existing rules.

Although *Merlin* was generally regarded as having made her debut at Ranelagh's Easter regatta 1946, *Yachting World* recorded her sailing in January, watched by proud members of the Syndicate. Unquestionably therefore she was the first of the post-War dinghies. After a long career during which she even competed against the 6ft 8ins wide *Wotnots* in the 1969 Ranelagh Silver Tiller Meeting (causing even the legendary calm of Alan Warren to be disturbed when she overtook him at one stage), *Merlin* was honourably retired to the National Maritime Museum at Greenwich in 1971, the year of the Class's Silver Jubilee.

That *Merlin* was able to make that vital transition from a good racing dinghy to the founder of a thriving Class, owes much to the then Editor of *Yachting World* – Group Captain Haylock, RAF Rtd. Good publicity in this magazine (now considered very much more a keel boat journal) together with pressure for efficient organisation, led to the formation of the first Class Association in this country, with the worthy Group Captain as its first Chairman.

The Merlin gradually spread along the Thames, its extra speed advantage over the National 12s often making the difference as to whether the current could be stemmed. The extra room in the boat was much appreciated by crews who, in the light and variable breezes of a tree-lined river, have to spend most of their time crouched in the bottom of the boat and moving quickly from side to side. With a large crew himself (Beecher Moore), Jack designed a high rig with plenty of room under the boom. This also lifted the rig further above the bushes which obstruct the wind on the river bank. In fact, the Merlin was such an efficient river boat that International 14s with considerably greater sail area were frequently beaten over the line and almost invariably on handicap. The Merlin was very light, only 10 lbs heavier than National 12. However, the Class had to prove itself on the sea if it truly was to be a boat for all waters. With this purpose in mind, the Class's first ever National Championship was organised at one of the windiest spots on the South Coast, Hayling Island. Fittingly, it was won by the designer, Jack Holt, crewed by the ebullient Beecher Moore, in a boat called *Gently*, No. 16. *Gently* has for the last few years been perched precariously on the rafters of the Waveney & Oulton Broad Yacht Club's boathouse, waiting for someone to restore her

Yachting World's cover for January 1946 shows Merlin already sailing and clearly England's first post-war class.

Reproductions courtesy of *Yachting World*

Yachting World
14ft RESTRICTED CLASS

Introduction

SOME three years ago eight dinghy helmsmen, who felt that the ideal racing dinghy had yet to be produced, got together with the idea of starting a new class. With a good deal of experience in the 12ft. National and 14ft. International Classes, they drew up a set of rules which embodied the best points of both, as well as many new features making for greater safety and enhanced performance.

They wanted a craft comparable with a 14 footer but costing little more than a 12, but of a more advanced design than either. A length of 14ft. was adopted, as being the smallest hull which could be designed for the required displacement of 600lb., (including crew), without the lines becoming unduly coarse, while, at the same time, anything larger could not be handled conveniently out of the water, and trailed behind a private car. This last consideration was felt to be important, for the ability to convey his boat easily to any part of the country would open up great possibilities for the keen dinghy helmsman.

A light hull was to be the keynote of the design, the required stiffness being attained by means of a light plywood deck which was to have the additional function of enabling the boat to capsize without filling. The light hull was to be driven by a small but extremely efficient sail plan, and, so that the mast could be made with a deep fore and aft section to give the necessary rigidity without setting up undue turbulence, it was to rotate upon a ball fitting mounted on the deck. To this general plan, to which there were a number of minor restrictions, Mr. Jack Holt was commissioned to design and build an experimental boat.

After tests lasting for many months, a second boat, also designed by Mr. Holt, was built, in which various refinements were incorporated, one of which was an increase in the height of the sail plan from the original 24ft. to the new limit of 25ft. The high aspect ratio rig is by no means a freakish experiment but a natural development of very thorough research.

Merlin, the new boat, satisfactorily passed her trials in the Solent under exacting conditions, and now stands as the prototype for the new Yachting World 14ft. Restricted Class. She is a delight to sail, perfectly responsive and feather light. In spite of her tall mast she is surprisingly stiff and has proved herself to be a good seaboat—she is therefore admirably suited to the conditions normally associated with British waters. Mr. Holt is to be congratulated upon his achievement.

In a sea way she is dry, not only by reason of her wide decks but because the design of the hull itself tends to throw the bow wave well clear. Being extremely light, no heavier than a National 12, she planes readily and fast and is most exciting to sail on a reach. By no means designed only for the young sportsman, Merlin's wide side decks, curving down at their inner edges to fit the legs of her crew, provide a far more comfortable seat for the middle-aged helmsman than the sharp gunwale of an open dinghy, while her boom, being set well above the deck, makes it unnecessary for the jib hand to duck whenever she goes about. Safety has also received a good deal of consideration for, as the drawings show, Merlin can be hove down until her mast head touches the water, while she retains several inches of freeboard in calm water. As all dinghy sailors know, an open boat rarely capsizes completely, but is inclined to heel over until the water begins to come in over the lee gunwale, and then proceeds to fill, very often without wetting her sails. It will be realised, therefore, that with a boat such as Merlin, which can be heeled very much farther without filling, even in something of a lop, the helmsman will usually be able to regain control and bring her upright again long before the mast reaches the horizontal and should only fill if handled incompetently.

Class rules have been most carefully framed, the best points of the 12ft. National rules being adopted wherever appropriate, and it is hoped that they will prove sufficiently close to prevent some striking innovation from outclassing the fleet. At the same time there is room for experiment as it is a bad thing to rule out all initiative.

By ruling out single-handed sailing much of the crew trouble, which is due to some keen youngster being left ashore in light weather, will be eliminated. Pleasure is given to the greatest number of people, with disadvantage to none. The inclusion of a spinnaker was intended to add to interest from the crew's point of view as well as making crew drill and teamwork a race-winning factor.

A price limit of £130 is about fifty per cent. above the present-day cost of a National 12, which is considered to be a fair figure both for builder and purchaser.

Scope has been left for the development of moulded plywood technique without putting boat-builders out of business, for the rules permit the use of a moulded plywood skin which it is hoped will be available to the small boatbuilder who will, by its use, be able to construct boats of a variety of shapes. It will be seen that plywood boats have to carry

YACHTING WORLD 14ft RESTRICTED CLASS

lead ballast. This is a temporary measure only and it is felt that after a year or two a preference will show itself for one form of construction or the other, and the rules can then be modified accordingly.

Efficient, in spite of its small area, the sail plan gives a performance which compares favourably with that of the average 14ft. International, having, in addition, other advantages which are not, at first, apparent. The short foot of the mainsail permits a single purchase mainsheet and the sail can be spilled by paying out only a few inches of sheet.

The Merlin design which we are making available to readers has one unique feature, which, although not inherent in the Class rules, is regarded as a very important contribution to dinghy design. The centre board, although extending 4ft. 6in. below the keel when fully down, is withdrawn into the boat through a slot only 2ft. 6in. long, which means that the hull is not unduly weakened.

When reaching, the centre plate can be hauled back to an angle of approximately 45 degrees, before it begins to retract into the hull, and this has been found to be about the best position for close reaching. On a run, or a broad reach, the plate can be retracted to any desired degree without the centre of area moving aft with a result that the boat remains under full control of the helm and can be put about with greater ease than usual.

It may be thought that the weight of the plate, being carried farther forward than usual, would require an even greater change of trim on the part of the crew than that required in the average International 14. This clever design runs and planes, even in a stiff breeze, with her crew sitting in the normal position, which is something of an achievement on the part of Mr. Holt. These points are well exemplified in the photographs appearing on the front cover and on P. 12.

All correspondence should be addressed to the Hon. Sec., W. Noel Jordan, 22, Union Road, Clapham, London, S.W.4.

MERLIN

Designed by

JACK HOLT

Brief Description

IT was very interesting to have the opportunity of designing to the Yachting World 14ft. Restricted Class Rules, since they permit an advanced type of craft, which, nevertheless, should be within the capacity of any boatbuilder.

Merlin's clench-built hull is in many ways similar to that of a National 12, but since it has only to bear the strains of sailing and not those of the crew moving about, and because the decking contributes a good deal of strength, planking is slightly lighter and other scantlings proportionately reduced.

The rise of floor is between that of the National 12 and the International 14, but the boat is stiffer than the former by reason of the greater length and wider transom. The water-line forward has been kept fine, but above this there is considerable flare to keep the bow wave clear of the deck and spray away from the jib.

Apart from the plywood deck and the forward placing of the centre-board case, construction is orthodox. From the drawings it will be seen that the plate is supported by two wooden rollers which rest on the top of the case, while its forward edge bears against a roller at the front end of the slot. When the plate is raised, the top is pulled forward; it first tilts, and then retracts in an upward and forward direction; when the rollers pass over the hump on the case at the end of their run, the tip passes up between the two strips of rubber, the purpose of which is to seal the slot.

When in this position the weight of the plate is taken by the hull, and there is no strain on the tackle. To lower the plate the protruding trailing edge is grasped and pressed down and backwards. The plate then overbalances and may be lowered on the tackle in the usual way.

The plywood deck is fastened to the inwales and centre stringer, but I do not think it is necessary to fasten it to the deck beams or side stringers. The rubbing bead should be fitted after the deck, so that it covers the edge of the plywood. The side decks, being mounted on their own stringers and beams, form separate units from the fore and after deck, and their curvature may be adjusted to suit the preference of the owner. The centre stringer under the foredeck is wide enough to allow the mast step to be moved fore and aft, and the twin king-posts which support it should be adjusted in conformity whenever the mast step is moved.

A metal fitting which passes through a slot in the deck takes the pull of the jib down to the stem and makes the rig all inboard. The revolving mast step is quite a simple affair, and consists of a ball on the foot of the mast resting in a cup in the step. The amount of rotation is limited by stops. The arrangement of the jib halyard is intended to allow the mast to rotate, and has the advantage of reducing the sag of the luff of the jib by half. It also takes some of the compression strain off the mast.

Gently, winner of the first two Championships and then winner again in 1949 and 1950. A record which has never been equalled.

Photograph courtesy of Ranelagh SC

to her former condition for presentation to the Lowestoft Maritime Museum. Happily, in the Class's 40th anniversary year, *Gently* is being brought down to Upper Thames YC to sail in a parade of past Class Champions.

Having established herself as a dinghy with the manouverability of the National 12 but which could plane, and as a fast dinghy like the International 14 which did not need to reef her mainsail upwind, the next stage was to persuade clubs on good stretches of water that the Merlin was the dinghy they should adopt as a Club Class. Jack Holt reports that the tactic was to approach the Club concerned with a request that they put on a race for Merlins at the end of their sequence of starts. About 25 Merlins would turn up and sail through the Club's own classes and then leave their boats available for inspection whilst the helmsmen and crews retired to the Club bar to build up goodwill and the Club's bar profits.

The Class's reputation gradually spread and much was achieved when the Class went to Cowes for the 1949 championships. At first sight, Cowes was a tide-dominated stretch of the Solent more suited to keel boats. However, to the newcomers whom the Class were seeking it was the Mecca of yachting. It was also the home of Frank Beken, the most famous yachting photographer of all time. The magnificent photographs which Beken took, appeared not only in yachting magazines, but also in calendars, other magazines, greetings cards and the many outlets for Beken's talents. It was a publicity exercise of enormous value, just at a time when a new market was opening up.

Had the Class adopted a cautious approach, it would have been very easy to become the "one-design 14ft dinghy," in contrast to the developing International 14, and grow fast as the one-design Firefly. Had this happened, the Class would have enjoyed a short-term success and then died as newer designs appeared. It was to the credit of the Class Committee that it looked at the Merlin's handling qualities on the sea and decided that improvements must be made to the rig. Excellent though a 25ft rig was on a river, it was a handful to hold up in the stronger winds of the sea, particularly when there was a sea running. Uffa Fox, the dominating influence at the time, had always maintained that on the sea you wanted the power as low down as possible. For this reason he had designed

Before trolleys were availables, boats had to be carried – hence the carrying handles.
Photograph courtesy of Grp. Captain Haylock

The incomparable Frank Beken's photography of *Dilly*, sailed by Ken Mollart and Tom Nisbet in the 1949 Championships at Cowes, helped publicise the Class.

Photograph by Beken

the Firefly rig to be a foot lower than the National 12. Uffa had a great admiration for the Merlin's ability to avoid reefing and the suitability for crewing by women who, in the post-war years, were taking up dinghy sailing.

Clearly the rig needed to be lowered, but this was a major step when the Class was sufficiently well established to have had four National Championships and some 200 boats registered. Nonetheless, trials were carried out and the rules allowing a lower rig height passed. These trials also showed that to compensate for loss of luff height to windward, a small increase in area along the boom was needed. This led to a sliding scale of rig heights/sail areas and much fun was had with pencil and squared paper trying to find an optimum formula.

At about the same time a group of dinghy sailors from Northumberland and a separate group in the West country (an area which had had much to do with the emergence of the International 14) decided that they were unhappy with the 14. The Northumbrians were led by Jack Liddle, Commodore of the Tynemouth Sailing Club which did so much in the post-war years to boost the sport of dinghy racing in the North. Discussing the matter with fellow club member Dr. Robin Stevenson, already by then a winner of the National 12 championships, he sought a lightweight clinker-built 14-footer with a moderate sail area which would not require reefing upwind in normal sea conditions but which would have enough sail power to plane fast. Since Robin was friendly with Dick Wyche of the well-known National 12 boatbuilders, Messrs. Wyche & Coppock of Nottingham, he asked him for his views.

Dick Wyche's reply outlined details of his clinker-built International 14 *Robin Hood* which was a serious attempt to produce a 14 at about half the cost of the traditional carvel hull which, with post-war labour costs, had become very expensive. Dick thought that this hull could be decked and given a rig of 110 sq ft on a mast no higher than a National 12. The weight would be only 200 lbs. This 14 (appropriately for a Nottingham boatbuilder) called *Robin Hood,* formed the basis of the new design called Rocket. The plans were offered to the interested parties and comments invited.

The Rocket syndicate did not like the open decks of the 14s, but they were not impressed with the rolled side-decks of the Merlin either. The trouble with these was that although in smooth water, you could heel a Merlin right over until the mast touched the water without getting any water in, once you were sailing on the sea or on any open waters, you were bound to take water in over the foredeck and the Merlin decks operated like an unspillable inkwell and they prevented efforts to bail the water out.

Wyche & Coppock's solution was to have decks like the National 12. To make the dinghy lighter, Wyche defied the accepted wisdom of Uffa Fox and provided a wooden centre-board. This was a major step, saving some 40 lbs. At the time most people believed that the idea was dangerous because in a capsized position, a metal plate would tend to sink, thereby righting the boat, whereas a wooden board would float up to the surface, thereby inverting the boat. Practical experience showed that although the difference was minimal, the weight gain was significant.

Once the plans were completed, they were made available to other builders such as Chippendales of Fareham, and the Rocket quickly gained adherents in widely dispersed areas such as the Hamble, (Ian Proctor spent most of 1950 in one and it provided inspiration for many of his later ideas), and Northumberland where the first Rocket was ordered by Jack Liddle, Commodore of Tynemouth SC.

In 1950, Dick Wyche altered a Rocket to comply with the Merlin rules and put her in the hands of one of the foremost dinghy sailors of the day, Bruce Banks, later to win the International 14's Prince of Wales Cup four times. Winning a Merlin Open Meeting at

Hayling Island, Bruce could well have won the Merlin Championships at Burnham had he not strained his back. Even then, he was able to show that the Rocket had clear advantages over the Merlin in heavy weather, her flatter floor not only increasing stability, but markedly improving planing performance. In light airs however, the Merlin maintained its superiority.

Yachting World photographs compare the Merlin and the Rocket.

Reproduction courtesy of *Yachting World*

Clearly there was not room for two such similar dinghies and in 1951 the YRA got the two classes together and promised them National status if they would merge and reconcile their rules. The Rockets were happy to join a well-organised Class, but there were some diehards amongst the Merlin owners who felt that whereas they had a supremely efficient light-weather boat, they were being compelled to merge with a "cut-down 14" and would lose their individuality. This attitude continued for quite some time and some consider that the Holt designs continued the Merlin theme whilst the emerging Ian Proctor (designing for those sailing mainly on the sea), followed the Rocket line. Certainly southerners tended to talk of Merlins and northerners of Rockets for a long time after the merger, which actually took place in the Savile Row offices of Graham Donald, one of the diehards. For a Class which was to pride itself on being tailored to the individual requirements of the owner, the site of the historic merger was a happy choice.

Oddly enough, this was not the first attempt which had been made to merge the Merlins with another Class. The YRA (as it then was) was conscious that the International 14 had evolved from a merger of the West of England Conference 14ft dinghy and the Norfolk dinghy to form a National 14ft dinghy class, later to be given International status. Clearly the YRA had in mind a new National 14 class which would take in the Redwing (designed in 1938 by Uffa Fox for rough seas off the Cornish coast), the Irish 14ft dinghy and any other 14ft dinghy they could find. The laudable intention was to standardise classes so that people from different areas could sail against each other on level terms. Beecher Moore had taken Merlin to a few trials, but she had proved too fast for the others to see any benefit in a merger. The advantage of the Rocket was that not only was she similar in design but also in performance.

To Graham Donald then, as so often since, the Class was indebted for his painstaking work in drafting the necessary rule changes. The first amalgamated Championships took place at Torquay in 1951 and was attended by the boat which had caused the merger, *Rockettoo*, now given the Merlin Rocket number 227. Sailed by Howard Williams (whose son Francis was to win the Championships twenty years later) she came third. Neither dominant nor outclassed, the Rockets fitted comfortably into the Merlin's new Silver Tiller Open Meeting circuit and this country's first (and perhaps only) merger involving a major Class ended happily.

Clearly the amalgamated Class was going to attract new designers and new ideas. South Devon Boatbuilders had carried the Merlin idea of rolled decks to the extreme in a boat called *Mayfly* by rolling them right down to the floor so that no water could be trapped. This had enormous advantages for sea sailors because virtually no water would stay in the boat after a capsize. Others however, felt that a collision where the boat was holed could have disastrous consequences, because the boat would sink. The idea was rejected and *Mayfly* went off to form her own One-Design Class. This Class still exists in a small way, but one look at that very full bow makes one realise how lucky the Class was, that its then Committee did not succumb to a not unreasonable temptation to let the Class become One-Design, after the amalgamation.

The main feature of 1952, however, was a boat designed and helmed by Ian Proctor and crewed by Cliff Norbury, *Cirrus*, No. 290. Ian was designing both National 12s and Merlin Rockets with an eye to the wave formation caused by their passage through the water. He was also pursuing a theory which was later to make his fortune, that extruded metal masts with a predictable bend would enable a better match to be made between mainsail and mast. With its metal mast *Cirrus* was a convincing winner of these Championships and was generally regarded as the boat which proved that alloy masts worked. The history of alloy mast development is recorded elsewhere but to the Merlin Rocket Class must be given the credit for paving the way.

The 1950s saw dinghy sailing extend from rivers and sea to reservoirs and lakes. These easier conditions, frowned upon by some, enabled many new sailors to start in conditions they could manage and then progress on to the Silver Tiller circuit. Leslie Brain from Birmingham broke the Thames/South Coast domination of the Class by twice winning the Championships and the Silver Tiller.

In 1954, The Class held its Championships at Falmouth, a venue with strong International 14 connections. Somebody asked Brian Appleton if these Merlin Rockets were really seaworthy or only good for the Thames. Brian's reply was to sail, on the rest day the Championships then had, to the Scilly Isles and back, a round trip of some 60 miles into the Atlantic.

This was the year when a building improvement devised by Dick Wyche appeared, which was to substantially benefit clinker hulls,d glued clinker ply. No more would hulls need those transverse ribs which hindered bailing and cleaning the boat and which were sources of leaks. No longer would you need a bucket, just a duster!

Cirrus, sailed by the designer, Ian Proctor, and crewed by Cliff Norbury, won the 1952 Championships at Poole and proved the efficiency of metal masts.

Photograph courtesy of Ian Proctor

Another improvement which appeared was the first self-bailer ever seen in England. Although of the probe type, subsequently superseded by the wedge, crews could see that in the future they would no longer have to spend downwind legs bailing out spray which had come in upwind. This Merlin Rocket "first" was installed in Ian Proctor's boat by his crew Peter Cook, now Editor of *"Yachts & Yachting"*. Peter tells an amusing story how they had to retire from the Practice Race when he found that he had fitted them the wrong way round!

When the Championships returned to Cowes in 1953, Frank Beken's camera was there to catch Jack Holt and Beecher Moore's *Trinket*.

Photograph by Beken

Many look back to the mid-1950s as a golden age. There was enough wood to build boats, interesting designs from which to choose and fittings to take much of the toil out of crewing. Roads to Open Meetings were not so crowded because less people had cars, there were very few classes, therefore the sailing talent was channeled into these. Increased leisure and a decline in church attendance had made people look for a sport which operated on Sundays, and the end of petrol rationing in 1952 had made it an adventure to explore. Merlin Rocketeers put up visitors to their Open Meetings on a reciprocal basis.

At the heart of this was the Silver Tiller Series which, by requiring helmsmen to count two Sea and two Inland results, encouraged designs and sailing skills which would be successful on widely different stretches of water. The pioneering days were over, there were exciting times ahead!

CHAPTER 2

The Dinghy-Sailing Boom 1956-1965

The Second Decade takes us right through the boom years of dinghy sailing in this country. To put matters into historical perspective, this was the time when Harold Macmillan came to office and increased the money supply to expand the economy, leading to the affluent days of the '60s. Instead of restoring old boats made with inferior post-war timber, there was money for new boats, new sails, and a car to trail the boat to the increasing number of Open Meetings on the Silver Tiller Circuit.

Ian Proctor, whose designs had already won the 1952 and 1954 Championships, was now starting upon an unbroken run which was to bring his designs thirteen consecutive Championship wins and many other leading places in spite of a growing number of designers trying to dislodge him. Jack Holt was still designing Merlins for particular customers, boats to succeed on the Thames such as John Harris' *Passing Cloud* and Adrian Fearnley's *Flinkidink*, but he had realised that his future lay in the mass-produced hard-chine One-Designs.

The decade opened with a feat which has never been equalled – John Oakley's three successive Championship wins from 1956 to 1958. Oddly enough, although John O stayed with Merlin Rockets until transferring to the Olympic Flying Dutchman Class in 1963, he never looked like winning the Championships again. Since he later became World FD Champion, there was clearly no decline in his skills, rather a catching up by the rest of the Class.

John O's first win was in the Proctor "Mk VI" which was rated the best design as the decade opened. Easy to handle, it could be driven hard without fear of an unexpected capsize. However, John O had had a mighty struggle to win the 1956 Championships from Proctor's prototype "Mk IX", *Crewcut*, sailed by John's old National 12 rival Cliff Norbury. In fact, had not only four races counted in those days, Norbury would have won. Some discreet discussions with the boat's owner and crew Tony Fox (sadly to die prematurely in a car accident) led to John O being at the helm of *Crewcut* next season.

In one of those splendid confidence tricks, by which those in possession of a fast boat discourage others from acquiring one similar, John O fostered the impression that the "IX" was more difficult to sail. To be fair, the "VI" was such an easy boat to handle that the distinguished helmsman Robin Judah (twice runner-up in the Championships, winner of the Silver Tiller and later Olympic representative in the Dragon Class) was still campaigning a "VI" at the end of 1962. However, the long straight planing run gave the "IX" such speed through the water that Oakeley had an advantage until the rest of the pundits acquired them as well.

In 1959, the Class adopted terylene sails and this gave many newcomers a fresh chance. Old boats went off-tune with the extra power available from these sails. Those willing to try new sailmakers, frequently found that their products were better than those from traditional sail lofts who were unwilling to alter time-honoured sailmaking techniques to take advantage of the new material.

Crewcut, No. 684, J. Oakley and A. Fox sailing a Proctor "Mk IX," winners of the Merlin Rocket ▶
  Championships at Torquay 1957 and Plymouth 1958. Note the barber's pole mast stripes
Photograph courtesy of J. Chippendale

Ian Proctor and Cliff Norbury sail a "Mk XII" in the 1960 Championships at Weymouth – a favourite ▶
  venue. Terylene sails were starting to take advantage of unmeasured area on the roach

The Class had by now been in existence long enough for those who had campaigned vigorously against the forces of reaction which would have strangled the Merlin at birth, become themselves resistant to change. It seems quite incredible now that at the start of the '60s, Merlin Rockets still had to sheet their spinnakers inside the forestay and to have the halyard sheave sited below the hounds. The forces who sought to retain this were the river sailors who frequently had to gybe spinnaker on a winding river and whose girls crews found the existing system easier to manage. To those who asked how you could be expected to reach properly under this system, their answer was that once you had the spinnaker round the front of the forestay to leeward, you would need stronger crews and this would kill off female crews, one of the advantages the Merlin Rocket Class enjoyed over the International 14s.

It was these arguments at the 1960 AGM (which in those days was always held at Ranelagh SC as the Class's home) which prevented the adoption of a 6ft spinnaker pole. The Class had to wait another 19 years for this, putting up in the meantime with a 5ft pole, the same length as that of a Mirror dinghy! To be fair, the same forces of reaction also kept down for many years the length of the International 14 pole.

The voices of reaction might have prevented the sheeting of the spinnaker outside the forestay and the raising of the halyard above the hounds had not there been a dramatic improvement in the art of cutting spinnakers, pioneered by the Merlin Rocket helmsman Ken Rose (now Managing Director of Bruce Banks Sails Ltd) and the International 14 designer and crew Austen Farrar, who started up in business as Seahorse Sails. By applying engineering principles based upon circular geometry rather than copying the "proper" way of cutting spinnakers, they revolutionised the art of downwind sailing.

Up until this time, the "culture" of crewing had derived from the National 12s and the International 14s. Put simply this involved working hard up the beats and taking a rest downwind. Spinnakers were flown on the runs and broad reaches, but since International 14s had no decks and were difficult to recover after a capsize, few people risked spinnakers if the wind was anywhere near the beam. The availability of better cloth and better sailmakers encouraged the more enterprising to try spinnakers in a wider range of conditions. This led to a rethink of the uphaul/downhaul systems and a new generation of helmsmen coming to the fore. Many good helmsmen found difficulty in adapting to the new importance of the spinnaker downwind – a problem noted in Europe as our top Flying Dutchman helmsmen and crews (including Merlin Rocket men Stuart Jardine and James Ramus and John Oakley and Tony Fox) powered through opponents whose equipment and techniques were outdated.

The old guard did not of course disappear. There were, and are still, some clubs where the spinnaker is not much help. However, there was a pleasing flood of new helmsmen, who had succeeded in other classes, wanting the freedom of the Merlin Rocket class rules to try ideas banned in their own classes and, in particular, to benefit from the spinnaker techniques being developed here.

As the Class lost top-rate helmsmen such as John Oakeley, Robin Judah, Stuart Jardine, Brian Saffery Cooper and Mike Astley to the Olympic Classes (and every one of these represented Britain at the 1964 or 1968 Olympic Games) and those such as Nick Truman (later to win both the Dragon Gold Cup and the Edinburgh Cup), Bob Hoare (to become the leading FD builder in the world and personally win the World FD Week) and Brian Southcott to become Chairman of the RYA, new blood emerged to maintain the very high sailing standards of their predecessors. Some of the new helmsmen would succeed for a few years and then move on to Olympic Classes

Restless III sailed by B. Southcott and A. Legg, a Proctor "Mk XI". Winners of the Merlin Rocket Championships at Whitstable in 1959.

Photograph courtesy of J. Chippendale

themselves, or be snapped up by the owners of off-shore keel boats who were now increasingly turning to the leading dinghy classes for "jockeys". To others, such as Pat Blake, Chris Andrews, John Harris, Alan Warren, Spud Rowsell, the pleasure of racing with the Merlin Rocket Class meant that they would stay, even when past their youth.

One of the most noticeable features of this decade was the development of boat fittings and the willingness of the new generation to look not just at what the pundits of this or that British Class was doing, but what was being tried in Europe and even further afield. Frequently it was found that the requirements of the Merlin Rocket differ from those of the Olympic classes, but there was considerable thought put into every aspect of the boat. In this respect the Class was very fortunate to have a strong following at the Hamble River SC amongst those employed by Proctor Metal Masts Ltd. Ideas came from this company and their Merlin sailors quickly seized upon the good ideas they saw on other people's boats whether at home or abroad.

Some ideas had consequences far beyond their original purpose. In the 1965 Championships at Plymouth, gales reduced the racing to three days. Experiments were carried out with letter-box type flaps in the transom to help empty a boat after a capsize. One of the Class's characters, better known at the bar than on the water, was sent out in a Force 6 and told to capsize, and then use the flaps. Ned Sparrow capsized with a skill born of long practice, righted his boat and then emptied it so quickly that the flaps were adopted at the AGM without argument. The intention was to make Merlin Rockets self-rescuing, partly to help the helmsmen and crews, partly to reduce the number of rescue boats needed, and partly to encourage Race Officers to send out fleets in stronger winds.

Designers had always been aware that there was no maximum restriction on the width of a Merlin Rocket, but had not dared to design too wide a hull because of the amount of water it would hold after a capsize. The ease with which Ned had emptied his boat with the now permitted transom flaps unquestionably led to the major development of the next decade – wider and wider hulls.

The other development which was to have a profound influence upon the Class from now on was the success of Alan Warren (Silver Tiller winner in 1964 and joint Champion in 1965) with a centre mainsheet.

Centre mainsheets were nothing particularly new. Larger boats such as FDs had always had them (the European helmsmen, sailing on large lakes or the sea, used nothing else) and they were gradually taking over the 5-O-5 and Osprey Classes. However the Merlin Rocket had been considered by most people as too small to divide up with a trade. Further, the usual problem with centre mainsheets was that the boom sagged off to leeward, ruining the pointing of a boat to whom windward performance was vital. Where a boat did not have a trapeze to keep it upright to windward, the accepted wisdom of the time was for it to point high enough to prevent wind and waves combining to push it further off to leeward. For this reason, owners opted for "V" section bows which would slice through a chop. To point high, the boom must be kept nearer the centre (only rarely was the full width of the transom track used), and this was not possible with centre mainsheeting.

To get round this problem, various ideas were tried:–
1. *The high take off point.* This idea (analogous to the hoops which the Class has regularly used since 1977) reduced the distance between the boom and horse, but was thought to suffer the disadvantage that the boom could not move out evenly as it would with a track. The theory then was that the whole sail should move out like a barn door.
2. *The strop.* This was a triangle of rope or wire upon which a block ran taking the mainsheet. Again the object was to reduce the distance between block and boom and to avoid providing an obstruction to fore and aft movement. The advantage of this system was that it could be adjusted for height – low for strong winds so that the boom could move and spill wind and then return, high for light winds tio to keep the boom in the middle for pointing. The supposed disadvantages were the same as for the high take-off point.

At Putney you usually have to judge the start carefully because the flood tide is often pushing you over the line. A typical Open Meeting at Ranelagh SC, 1963. Merlin No. 2 is well placed.

Photograph courtesy of Ranelagh SC

3. The conventional track. Unlike Ken Rose's system of 1960, which was at deck level and doubled as a kicking strap but which required a chorus girl kick to cross it, tracks were usually laid along the thwart – operating as a bacon slicer for the seated crew. If you tried to overcome the problem of the boom sagging to leeward by pulling the traveller up to windward on a slackened mainsheet with a control line, the line had to be freed off before a tack (otherwise the traveller would be pinned down to leeward on the next tack). This control line would then be loose on the following tack and the boom would slide right off to leeward to the accompaniment of complaining oaths from the helmsman.

At an early stage this problem rarely arose because the traveller rollers frequently jammed (causing further problems of their own), but once Ian Proctor brought out his ball-bearing traveller, it slipped far too easily. At Wembley, where quick tacking on the shift was at a premium, two travellers were used so that one never had to be uncleated. This gradually became the standard system, although some people elsewhere joined the travellers with bars which seemed to defeat the object of the exercise. Others opted to cleat the mainsheet and play the traveller. The skilful, such as Pat Blake, did extremely well with this arrangement because they were then able to control the leech tensions. Others (and Pat) capsized whenever a gust was more than anticipated because they could not let out enough sail.

Brian Southcott sailing *Restless IV,* Championship winner 1961 and 1963. A Hoare-built Proctor "Mark IX," seen here at Wembley SC. Note the light touch on sheet and kicking strap which always kept Brian's boat moving when others stopped.

Photograph courtesy of Guy Gurney

Whatever system you used, there was still the problem of tacking. Merlin Rockets had always been rolled round by a fluid movement which involved throwing the forward leg diagonally back over thwart and platecase (to prevent the transom dragging, most helmsmen sailed to windward with one leg either side of the thwart), resting the bottom on the thwart briefly as hands on tiller and sheet were changed and then throwing the other leg diagonally forward in front of the thwart.

One of the problems of adjusting to centre mainsheet (which older members found harder than newcomers) was to keep the boat rolling as they manouvered round the system. Tacks took longer and the whole way of sailing was more geared to gaining power out of the sail rather than flicking round under an opponent's lee bow. Boat speed rather than tactics was starting to be the prime requirement.

As the second decade ended, the old guard were convinced that the Class was now firmly set on a course which would take it ever further from the ideas of the founding fathers. To an extent they were right. Although that splendid helmsman, Brian Ellis, won the 1966 Championships with transom mainsheet, he was the last person to do so and the quest for power would dominate the thinking from now on. Transom mainsheets would still continue to be profitable on the small reservoirs and rivers where many Merlin Rockets were sailed, but the next decade would see the new system gradually take over on every kind of water.

A big leap forward was clearly coming in hulls and rigs, but which path would be the one to follow?

CHAPTER 3

The Developing Years 1966–1975

To most Merlin Rocketeers, the Third Decade is the one in which the boats developed from being 5ft wide (the Proctor "Mk IX") to anything up to a hastily imposed maximum of 7ft 2½ins. The idea of a wide boat was not new. In the very early days of the Class, one of its "founding fathers" was a very large helmsman named Tony Howard who was crewed by his petite wife. In the very narrow (4ft 7in wide) Merlins of the day, Tony used to complain that in light airs when he was trying to induce enough leeward heel to fill the sails, he had to double himself up in the middle of the boat because his crew could not get far enough away from him to counterbalance his weight. Jack Holt, therefore, designed the first "wide" boat, not to give greater leverage upwind but to give the crew more leverage downwind in light airs!

Attempts to design wide had been seen in the International 14 class, but the Committee had very quickly stamped upon it and settled upon a maximum beam of 5ft 6in. The National 12s had seen a history of steady increase in width, but this was, perhaps, because that Class had never enjoyed a splendid yardstick such as the 5ft wide Proctor "IX" against which all new designs had to prove themselves. In this connection it should be noted that the "IX" had shown itself the fastest boat of the 1956 Championships (deprived from winning only by less races then being counted), had won outright the 1957, '58, '60, '61, '62, '63 Championships and shared those in 1965.

One of the first to take the positive step of commissioning a wide boat instead of just talking about it was Royston Comport, a leading helmsman who worked for Ratsey & Lapthorn Sailmakers. His first move was to ask the Adur Boatyard to produce a wider version of their highly successful "Mk VII". Unfortunately, simple scaling-up produced a waterline beam which was too wide to be efficient in all but the strongest of winds. Virtually all successful Merlin Rockets have had the narrowest waterline beam of the day. David Robinson used to say, on his endless quests for a "Magic" design, that unless he had to have a stand-up fight with the measurer to get the rise of floor measurement accepted, he had no confidence in that particular design.

Others followed: the amateur designer John Aveston from Ranelagh and Hamble River's Martin Jones, whose "Lucky Number" had the previous year dominated the National 12 Championships. Both produced designs which kept to the same waterline beam as the successful boats, but flared out the hull just where helsman and crew sat out on the beat. This, they reckoned, was the only place where the extra power would be needed. John built only for himself, free from the worry whether his design would be accepted professionally by a builder. Martin, however, was fortunate to find a builder, already a growing force in the National 12s, who wanted to break into Merlin Rockets but could not get a licence to build to Proctor designs. Building the new Jones design with a pronounced bulge in the middle (the boat was aptly named "Xpectant") for Royston Comport was the builder who was to make his mark on the Class right up to the present day – Spud Rowsell.

Gradually, other designers began to get in on the act: Nick Truman widened his successful "Surf Scooter" to a "Sooper Scooter"; Tom Booth produced some designs to individual requirements, the wider than average "Star Rocket" and "Sugar Plum"; designs of Mike Nokes and Mike Jackson respectively, started to become popular again. Finally Ian Proctor, who had tried to "think wide" three years before with his "Mk XV" and "XVI" but only enjoyed limited success, produced a 5ft 6in version of his "Mk IX". Since Proctor's designs after "Mk XII" had not been so successful, he called this the "IXb" – the "IXa" having already applied to various builder variations on the "IX" theme.

The 1966 Championships were held at Weymouth, an excellent testing ground for new ideas since a wide variety of wind conditions can be expected during the course of a week. As it happened the first race was won by Mike Jackson in one of his new designs, for no better reason than that the wind shifted unexpectedly and, with the experience of many Burton Weeks there (Weymouth is the National 12's favourite venue), Mike went the right way.

Other days of the week, designs would look impressive only for the boat to capsize in a cloud of spray as another helmsman found himself not wholly in tune with his recently installed centre-mainsheet system. As stated in the last chapter, centre-mainsheets were just beginning to appear in reasonable numbers as the Second Decade ended. Those who had set their mainsheet jammers so that the sheet went in effortlessly, found that when a gust came, the sheet took that vital second longer to release and they were swimming. Quickly they learned that it was better to be compelled to put a foot on the mainsheet to get it in if, in consequence, it could be released with a simple jerk.

Already with a few year's centre-mainsheet experience under his belt, Alan Warren might have been expected to win. However, mishaps apart, it was clear that his "Star-Rocket" no longer held any heavy weather advantage over the newer wide boats and they were better in all other conditions. "Xpectant," although suffering from several capsizes, proved fast enough in between for Warren and others to decide that this was to be the boat for them next year. Others reckoned that Proctor's expertise as a Naval Architect and his track record was enough to go for the "IXb", and this was to be the most bought design for the following two years.

But who won? Well, for what proved to be the last time, a transom-sheeted 5ft wide Proctor "IX" sailed by the experienced 1964 Champions, Brian and Ken Ellis (oddly, no relation) won their second Championships, with three more "IXs" in 2nd, 3rd and 6th places. Centre-mainsheets were to be found on Tim Hockin's 2nd place "Mk. IX", David Potter's "Adur 7" and David Thomas' "Mk IX", whilst David Child's 4th placed "Surf Scooter" and Graham Leech's 6th placed "IX" remained faithful to transom sheeting.

Clearly, much thought had taken place over the winter, for at next Spring's Hamble Warming Pan (the Merlin Rocket equivalent of the Easter Parade) David Potter was to be seen in a new "Mk IXb", Alan Warren in a new "Xpectant," David Thomas in another "IX" and Brian Ellis defending his title in a "Sugar Plum" he had bought previously but not used. David Child, a most promising young helmsman who had already won the past two Silver Tiller Series was, not surprisingly, remaining faithful to his "Surf Scooter," whilst in a narrow "IX" was the 9½ stone frame of David Robinson who had joined the Class as National 12 Champion.

That David Robinson had got to Poole for the Championships at all says much for his strength of purpose. Having spent all his limited financial resources on buying an "IX" hull from Bob Hoare and completing it himself, David proudly took his new creation (for which he had been lucky enough to be allocated the sail number 2000) to the Lymington Easter Regatta.

Lymington faces on to the confused waters of the Solent opposite the western end of the Isle of Wight. At Easter, the strong winds combine with spring tides to give some extremely difficult sailing conditions, especially to anyone getting accustomed to a new boat. David had a bad capsize, was separated from his boat, and taken ashore in a rescue boat. *Tantrum* was later recovered several miles downwind and down-tide in a very damaged state. Thinking, as he arrived home, that not very much more could go wrong, David discovered on the hall table an unposted envelope containing the boat's insurance proposal form and premium!

Bob Hoare, who had built the boat for David, took pity on him and did the difficult structural work for a generously low figure. David almost lived at Bob's Christchurch yard (in fact the garden of Bob's house), doing all the other jobs necessary to restore *Tantrum* to what had been so recently her brand-new condition. David's equal 4th position in the Poole Championships that summer (and in those days the Championships were held mid-June) was rightly applauded as one of the outstanding feats of the year.

There was, however, plenty else to attract attention. Alan Warren won the first two races and looked set to secure his first ever outright Championship win when he followed this up with 6th, 4th and 3rd places. Improving steadily, however, was David Potter after an initial 18th place with 4th, 2nd and 1st places. This year the Class was celebrating its 21st birthday, so the Ranelagh SC donated 21 bottles of champagne for the first 21 boats home in a special race on Thursday, apart from the Championships. Alan Warren and Barry Dunning (one of the greatest partnerships in Merlin Rocket history) won the Champagne Race and would no doubt have preferred it to count for the Week as it now does. As it was, all depended on the last race. The Warren/Dunning team had 5½ pts and the Potter/Brixton team 6¾ pts and a worse discard. Potter needed to win with Warren no better than 3rd. In a fleet of 153, a good start would be vital. At that time the Parkstone YC Race Committee believed that it was quite sufficient to have a buoy as the Outer Distance Mark with the secondary Committee Boat neither on transit nor at anchor. With a port-biased line (in itself a good idea to encourage competitors away from the starboard end so many favour), it was not surprising to see Potter up by the Outer Distance Mark at the starting gun and many still swear that he was several lengths over beforehand in an effort to keep clear wind. His number was called by the Secondary Committee Boat but was subsequently reinstated by the Race Officer as the second boat was not on transit. There was too much doubt to disqualify Potter who went on to win the race. Warren made a great effort to secure the second place which would have given him the Championships, but was thwarted by that most experienced campaigner, Brian Southcott – 1959, 1961 and 1963 Champion and sailing in his last Championship Week.

Third was the consistent David Child, who that year was to win the Silver Tiller for the third year running. David Thomas, later to become an extremely successful designer of racing keelboats, came joint 4th with David Robinson, whilst the retiring Champion, Brian Ellis, could only manage 6th place. Brian promptly emigrated to Australia, where he subsequently proved a championship winning Sydney Harbour 16ft skipper.

Falmouth was the venue for the 1968 Championships. Once again there was to be seen a fine duel between the Potter/Brixton team in their "IXb" *Shenanigan* and the Warren/Dunning duo in the first of the designs to exceed 6ft 6in beam. However, unlike the "Xpectant" which had broken the 6ft "barrier", the Tony Watts designed "Wotnots" did not attempt to keep the waterline beam to a minimum. Conditions at Shoreham, where both Tony and Alan sail, are usually fairly blustery and local conditions have a decided effect upon a designer's thinking. Tony belonged to the school of thought favoured by Proctor – a boat which is easy to handle in a blow gives the helmsman more time to think of tactics. The boats were built by local builder John Freeman and laid out exactly to Alan Warren's requirements.

David Robinson and Chris Law sailing Alan Warren's "Wotnot" at Shoreham.

Photograph by R. Hutchings

This year it was Potter who set the pace with an early win and Warren who was always struggling to catch up. Winds could vary markedly during the race, sometimes nullifying a hard-earned lead or bringing back-markers up into company to which they were rarely accustomed. Never was this clearer than on Monday when sea-mists persuaded the Race Officer to hold the race inside the Estuary – known locally as the Carrick Roads.

Faced with a strong ebb-tide, the fleet stayed on the Falmouth shore where they had been started. Just two helmsmen, Jim Park and a man named Locke, opted to cross the estuary to the St. Mawes side where the windward mark had been laid, before the ebb got stronger. In splendid isolation, they watched the fleet being swept back as they rounded the mark and welcomed the tide taking them to the next mark. For an hour they enjoyed an uninterrupted cruise together, until Jim hit a flat patch and stopped. Locke, seeing his stationary boat, was able to sail round the spot. As the wind shifted, the rest of the fleet caught up and formed, round the wing mark off Flushing, one of the largest "rafts" ever seen at a Merlin Rocket Championships. Locke, who had never even won a race at his home club (Tamworth) before, went on to win the race.

To some backmarkers, a win of this kind (albeit in a race which would now never be allowed to count for Championship points) would have been a stimulus to achieve great things. Poor Locke, however, spent the rest of the season trying to recapture his one moment of glory and, when he could not, gave up sailing altogether – a sad example of Icarus who flew too close to the sun, burned his wings and fell.

After a magnificent Champagne Race, which sadly, did not count for the Championships, and could have had a major effect otherwise, all depended upon the last race. Alan Warren had a good chance of winning both race and Championships, but contrived to break both centreboard and stem fitting for the jib. The Potter/Brixton team in *Shenanigan* won again – but without the controversy this time. The original "Xpectant", sailed now by one of the Class's delightful eccentrics, Chris Andrews, scored 3rd place ahead of another eccentric, Graham Leech, whose crew, Jenny, showed that women crews still had a place in the new power sailing age. Both Leech and the 5th placed John Harris in the 1966 Champion *Stringbean* used transom mainsheets, but the 6th placed David Child in a new Jackson "Superstition" design, had now decided that centre-mainsheets were the thing of the future.

It was at Whitstable in 1969 that Alan Warren, after two years coming a close second, finally secured his first ever outright Championship. Once again a helmsman who won the first two races failed to win the Championships. This time it was Michael McNamara, with some impressive pre-Championship successes to give him the confidence he always needs, who made the pace. Had not two days been lost to gales, it is possible that Michael, who had only joined the Class the previous year from the National 12s and Albacores, would have gone on to win. However, two days waiting played havoc with Michael's nerves and when racing did resume, he tacked without looking and collided with another boat three minutes before the start. As one of sailing's honest men, he immediately retired in a race which Warren won.

The winds got up again and if the last race was not sailed Warren, by virtue of a better discard, would win. At the fancy dress party that evening an unhappy Mike Mac was to be seen pointing up at the darkened sky muttering "There's a ring round that moon, there's going to be storm." He was right – there was. The race was cancelled, Warren was champion and Michael McNamara was never to come so close to a Merlin Rocket Championship again, although, happily, he was to win the Championships of the National 12, Albacore, Lark and Enterprise classes and become a much sought after sailmaker.

That year saw Alan Warren win the Silver Tiller and bring to an end David Child's record of four years in a row which still stands. It also saw the start of another team-racing event for the Class, the South-East Area Team Championships. This joined the Topmast weekend which had started in 1964, as another event to satisfy the growing interest in the sport of team-racing (the RYA National Team Championships also started that year) and the Topmast weekend was now designated the Class's National Team Championships. Area Championships were encouraged, the first being for the South & East Areas to be held annually at the Welsh Harp, Wembley. The Nationals, on the other hand, were to be held at a different venue each year, moving round the country on a five year cycle.

At the end of this year, the Class Committee undertook a major rethink of the Class Rules. Metric money was due to come in two years' time and if that came, could metric measurement be far behind? Robert Harris and Tom Booth shouldered this considerable task, taking the opportunity to permit an interesting idea, noted on the British Flying Dutchman which had so convincingly won a Gold Medal at the 1968 Olympic Games, the spinnaker chute.

The effect of the spinnaker chute at sea is described in a special chapter upon the remarkable Championships held that at year at Pwllheli, but their effect inland can best

Krakawot, No. 2258, returning to shore at Whitstable during the 1969 Championships, sailed ▶ by the champions, Alan Warren and Barry Dunning. Michael McNamara, sailing *Emotion*, is in the far distance

Photograph by Guy Gurney

be described in a conversation between Race Officer and Assistant during the Team Championships, held at the Welsh Harp that summer. "Now do you see this boat coming down under spinnaker? He's got a problem, because if he takes it down before he gets to within two lengths, the boat behind will catch up, gain an overlap and force him wide round the mark and the third placed boat (which is in his team) will go through both of them, converting for the leader a winning score into a losing one. If, on the other hand, the leader keeps his spinnaker up until he reaches two lengths, he will have left it too late to make a close rounding and the fellow behind will gybe inside him." At this stage the leading boat entered the two length circle, called "No water" quite properly, his spinnaker disappeared and he was able to make a tight rounding of the mark. From that moment, many converts were made. It is interesting to note that nobody can recall a Merlin Rocket being built after 1970 without a spinnaker chute.

The end of the 1970 season saw many familiar faces from the '60s disappear. For some it was the usual reasons of infirmity or young families. These were known as the "Census" group, "broken down by age and sex." Some, such as David Child and Alan Warren, went off to campaign Olympic Classes. Happily, Alan Warren was to return. To others however, "the Class had changed." In fact, this criticism had been made at various times: when it amalgamated with the fast-planing Rocket – when ending the sheeting and halyard restriction made spinnaker handling a race-winning feature – when centre-mainsheets ushered in a different way of sailing, and now – the need for a wide boat and the demise of the trim little 5ft-beamer which was so easy to handle in a tight situation.

Some of the riotous characters of the early '60s were growing into respectable middle-age. The survivors of the famous storming of the Imperial Hotel, Torquay, were now Race Officers muttering about the new young members in the Class. The competitors in a climbing race up the ornamental palm trees at a Weymouth hotel were now senior executives in the clothing industry or contesting Wills in the Chancery Division of the High Court. Was the Class getting too professional in its approach to racing and was some of the fun going out?

Perhaps an ideal antidote to the cold Force 6 gales at Pwllheli in 1970 was the warm breezes at the Plymouth Championships the following year. Compelled by a local Race Committee to sail inside Plymouth Hoe in waters where the judgement of tides was crucial, this was a chance for the older style boats to come back. Winds barely reached Force 4 all week, staying for the most part around Force 2.

Spud Rowsell, who had looked the fastest at Pwllheli in the prototype "Courageous" and who had spent all winter building them for his customers, surprised everybody by turning up with a boat some 5ins narrower – the 6ft 5ins wide "September Girl." The designer, Phil Morrison, another successful National 12 designer, was aiming for minimum waterline beam and was prepared to sacrifice sitting-out power to achieve it. Phil was to sail the prototype, built by his amateur builder friend (and later business partner) Bill Twine.

Francis Williams (whose father Howard had sailed the famous *Rocketoo* 20 years earlier) and the well-known Midland helmsman Harry Haynes had both been sufficiently impressed by David Robinson's "Ghost Rider" to order copies from Rowsell. David Spiers, upon whom Northern hopes rested, had been very impressed at Pwllheli with the performance of the wide version of the Jackson "Superstition." Spiers' main rival on the Silver Tiller Circuit, Pat Blake, had opted for another new designer with an idea about reducing waterline beam, Keith Callaghan, and would have Keith crewing for him. There was a clutch of "Courageous" designs in the hands of good helmsmen and finally Alan Warren, taking time off from his Olympic campaign to sail his championship-winning *Superwot* from the previous year, even keeping the same sails.

No time to look at the scenery as Ranelagh SC and Oxford SC start a race in the 1971 Team Championships at Bristol Corinthian YC.

Spud Rowsell won both the Practice Race and the first of the 1971 Championship races. As so often, such early success was fatal and it was Francis Williams who came through to win the Week from his Exe SC colleague Spud. Phil Morrison's 3rd place established the new "September Girl" as a potent new design. Spiers and Warren never had enough wind to propel their "Wide Superstition" and "Superwot" properly, but sailed well to gain 4th and 5th places. However these designs were not to be seen in the hands of top helmsmen again. The message from Plymouth was that Morrison and Gregory ("Ghost Rider") were the new designers to watch.

The Championships usually provide at least one bizarre story and this was no exception. Alan Chaplin and Stephanie Whitcher from Sussex Motor YC at Shoreham were one of those teams which could easily have won other Class Championships, but preferred Merlin Rocket company and trying to make the top 40 in a really competitive championships. On the Wednesday they debated whether to launch, since Alan's wife was expecting a baby and Stephanie's grandmother was not expected to live more than a day. Deciding that there was really nothing they could do, they only just reached the starting line in time for the gun and at what appeared to be the wrong end. A massive windshift made it very much the right end and they shot off in a fair breeze with everyone else almost becalmed. Each time their pursuers seemed likely to catch them, another windshift came to their aid and they just held on to score their first (and so far, only) Championship win. Dashing ashore to the telephones, they found that during the race, Stephanie's grandmother had died but Alan had become the father of a healthy daughter.

This Class's 25th anniversary year ended with a raffle for a new Merlin Rocket which had already been allocated the number 2500. Tickets sold at £1 each and the cost allowed for was £500. Enough tickets were sold to include a suit of sails. At the Annual Dinner the winning ticket belonged to Francis Williams' crew, Derek Sheffer. As Francis had accepted a very favourable offer for his Championship-winning boat (although oddly enough the boat was never seen at a Championship or Silver Tiller event again), he ordered an identical boat from Spud Rowsell, *Silver Ghost*, a pleasant pun on the "Ghost Rider" design and the famous Rolls Royce.

One of the pleasing features of this period was the way in which the different clubs had their years at the top. Ranelagh SC had always had a strong fleet of London based helmsmen who competed on the Silver Tiller Circuit. Hamble River SC had from Ian Proctor and John Oakeley right up to the Potter/Hockin/Thomas/Pike/Robinson era, a fleet which had been powerful for 20 years. Sussex Motor produced Warren and Andrews and now it was Exe SC with Williams, Rowsell, McNamara, Colin Rowley, Chris Ellis and Paul Seddon all in the top 11 at the Championships.

The 1972 season saw the Rowsell order book full. Much in demand was the "September Girl" design, which had succeeded at Plymouth, and the flared out version (to 6ft 10in) which Morrison had drawn to demand. For the heavyweights, Morrison had designed a boat which many feel to be the best light airs boat ever, the original "Satisfaction." There was obviously an interest in the "Ghost Rider" whilst Pat Blake's Silver Tiller win in a Callaghan design brought orders for Callaghan's next mark, the "Hornblower."

However, Rowsell was not the only builder. Chippendale may have closed (a sad loss), and Bob Hoare may have been devoting more time to the Flying Dutchmen for which Rodney Pattisson's Gold Medal had brought him a full order book, but there were some soundly built Merlins from Arnott Dobson's Aln Boatyard in Northumberland, the home of the Rocket. With an awakening interest in wide boats with narrow waterlines, the old average of 120 new boats a year suddenly jumped to 146. With the fear of VAT, the following year saw the number of new registrations jump to 170, the highest this Class of individually made boats has ever known. In retrospect, the two years 1972/73 which produced 316 new boats may take many years to equal, for in many ways 1973 was to represent the end of the "affluent sixties".

Still, to be around in 1972 was exciting. Exe SC narrowly failed to repeat their convincing win of the previous year's Team Championships when Spud's spinnaker halyard jammed in the sheave leaving it neither up nor down. A revitalised Silver Tiller Series (described in a separate chapter) was attracting entries of quality and quantity, with more areas now taking an interest and feeling they could compete. Much of this was due to more new boats being available.

The Championships at Falmouth in 1972 provided a variety of sailing conditions. With the exception of Alan Warren (away winning the final Olympic Trials in the Tempest Class and on his way to a Silver Medal at Kiel), and David Robinson, the Olympic coach, most of the Class's major names were there.

Francis Williams looked a likely winner, but hit another boat in a rainstorm, always a risk for a bespectacled helmsman. Spud Rowsell won a race but was not consistent, finding his new "Satisfaction" unusually tippy. Pat Blake allowed an over-the-line disqualification in the first race to make him feel that the gods were against him again. All these contenders suffered on Champagne Day (the Thursday race and now part of Championship Week points) when the wind backed so much that, with a weather going tide, spinnakers were set at some time on each leg of the course. The one person to keep cool amongst the series leaders was David Spiers in his "Phantom Kipper". His win proved critical when the Championships points were added up next day. Second was Colin Rowley, one of the Exe SC squad in his "Ghost Rider" whilst the new "Satisfactions" of Richard Davis, Paul Seddon and John Harris filled three of the remaining top six places, the other going to Pat Blake's "Hornblower".

The year 1973 is generally remembered for the introduction of VAT and the enormous increase in the rate of inflation following the oil price rises. A new boat with sails, all the up-to-date fittings and cover which, before April 1st, was costing under £700 was, by the end of the season, costing over £1,000. The big scramble to get boats ordered before the VAT date, made for a record increase of new boat registrations and 180 boats assembled at Poole for the Championships.

Poole Bay is usually blessed with warm sunshine and light breezes. Coupled with ideal beach conditions for the families, it is not surprising that an unusually large proportion of the 180 boats came from the inland clubs, who had now had three years to get over the traumas of the 1970 Championships at Pwllheli. However, those who sail inland only, are liable to get caught out by a weather-going tide and forget that if they make their favourite start, right up on the line with sails flapping, they can be carried over by the tide. Poole 1973 was the type of Championship which gives line starts a bad name. One day there were 11 false starts before the fleet got away on the 12th, just as the Race Officer ran out of cartridges. On another day, he became so exasperated that after 7 false starts he sailed home and cancelled the race!

Many people had their moments. Tony Lane, later to become Class Chairman, won the first race. Alan Warren, back with Spud Rowsell's *Philistine,* runner-up in 1971, was going better in light airs than ever before. Pat Blake, crewed once again by Keith Callaghan, looked very fast in Keith's latest design, the "Hexagon," whilst John Harris, who always prefers it when the conditions are tricky, was showing how right the "Satisfaction" is for light airs. One person who was decidedly not going well was local helmsman Rodney Pattisson, just back from a second Olympic Gold Medal, who was struggling in the thirties each day. This was his second Merlin Rocket Championships, the first having been at Pwllheli, and he found more good helmsmen that he had expected.

With Francis Williams winning the last two races, the final results were very close and Alan Warren won his third Championship outright, by just one-quarter of a point from Pat Blake. John Harris was so close behind, that with luck in the last race, he could have won the Week.

The variable breezes (which enabled Robert Trickett to win a race with a substantial margin by doing the opposite to everybody else) left no clear message as to the relative performance of designs. The new full-length top battens had proved a nuisance in the light airs and more research was needed. The most significant news from the AGM was that the Class did not want to go four-plank like the National 12s, particularly if this was to be a transitional step towards smooth skins like the International 14s and an outclassing of so many recently-purchased new boats. The same AGM abolished the price limit as unenforceable.

The year ended happily at Oulton Broad at the National Team Championships where 22 teams took part. South Yorkshire's Harry Haynes beat Cookham's Pat Blake on the finishing line to give South Yorks their second successive win. In a preliminary round, Cookham had beaten South Yorks in an amusing manner. Tacking in the water of a South Yorks boat on the starting line, Cookham's Peter Flanagan quite properly retired. However, the course had been changed over lunchtime and the remaining 5 boats all sailed the wrong course. All were disqualified with 9 pts, except the honest Peter Flanagan who earned 7 pts for a timely retirement. Was ever virtue in a team race more

35

properly rewarded? Peter makes rather a speciality of winning team races for his side. Sailing at the Welsh Harp in the SE Area Team Championships for a rather elderly London Pirates team on a particularly windy day, the Pirates decided that, with nothing much to gain or lose they would not sail the last race but let Ranelagh get cold and wet sailing over and winning by default. Two of Ranelagh's members decided that they preferred the Wembley SC bar and sent out their youngest team member, Pip Hudson, to sail round the course and claim victory. As the wind increased to Force 7, Pip Hudson spent so much time flattening his sail and checking all his fittings that he was still on the pontoon at the 3 minute gun used for team races and therefore was disqualified. As a disqualified boat, he scored 9 pts whereas non-starters scored 7 pts. From the warmth of the Wembley clubhouse, Peter led the Pirates to another splendid victory!

At the start of 1974, there was keen interest in the drawing-boards of Phil Morrison and Keith Callaghan. The previous year had produced some decidedly unsuccessful designs. Morrison's "Infidel" would only go for very light weights sailing in very strong winds, Tony Watts "Rapidity" wouldn't go even for Alan Warren (the reason why he had borrowed "Philistine"), Gregory's "Echo" wouldn't go for anybody (unlike his "Ghost Rider" which went fast for everybody). Callaghan, whose "Hexagon" had been the only successful new design in 1973, produced a modified version, the "Hysteria," and now dealt principally with Aln Boatyard although he, along with Phil Morrison, was still making his designs available for purchase by the amateur builder. The considerable increase in home building throughout the '70s owes much to Morrison and Callaghan.

Just as everybody waited in the Second Decade to see what Proctor would bring out, the question now was what would Morrison produce after a dull year for new designs? As so often, Phil thought along two separate lines. He produced a modified "Infidel" (named the "Hooligan" for lightweights like himself), and the anticipated flared-out "Satisfaction" (to be known as the "Smoker") for well-built helmsmen such as Rowsell, who was now building only to his designs. There was an immediate rush to order the "Smoker" and this proved the most popular design for years to come. It was perhaps the excellent light airs performance coupled with real weight carrying ability which appealed, but they were in demand on every type of water.

This year the Class returned to Pwllheli. Once again the winds blew, although not quite as hard as in 1970. This time, however, the boats, helmsmen and crews were very much better prepared. Those four years saw a large-scale change to boats which were substantially the same as those sailed today. The fleet was a more usual 135 now, instead of the 1970 record at 227. In consequence there were none of the dramas of 1970, just a large fleet of modern boats enjoying some splendid racing, wherever they finished. Spud Rowsell and Jonathan Turner were popular and thoroughly deserved to win for their first time. In second place was Lawrie Smith, later to win the Championships and later still to become helmsman for two America's Cup challenges. Crewing him was Neil Thornton, later to helm with some success, his own Merlin and to win the European Fireball Championships. Pat Blake slipped to 3rd place overall, although he received some consolation in winning (as described elsewhere) the Silver Tiller for the third time. In 4th place was the rising figure of John Patterson with the consistent Paul Seddon 5th.

The decade ended with the "Satisfaction" and its widened version, the "Smoker" dominant. In the absence of Pat Blake, who had now started his Olympic Flying Dutchman campaign, Harry Haynes achieved the double of Championships and Silver Tiller, but John Harris (also now in a "Smoker") sadly finished the season with nothing, despite almost winning every race he entered but somehow blowing up and retiring or

In 1974 the duo of Spud Rowsell and Jon Turner finally succeeded in becoming National Champions, sailing *Fadeaway* at Pwllheli.
Photograph by Robert O'Neill

coming second. His major tragedy was to achieve the result he needed in the last race to win the Championships, only to be disqualified for having been seen over the line before the start.

The Championships in 1975 were held in Weymouth Bay. More and more boats were changing over to twin spinnaker poles, after some years experimenting with single poles along the boom and up the mast. Jerry Rook, who had crewed Alan Warren when they won the 1973 Championships, was a worthy runner-up. It was at Weymouth this year that Jerry, in an attempt to restore the fun to Merlin Rocket Week, acquired some sugar tongs and founded the Tongs Trophy for activities off the water. The precise rules governing the award of this Trophy have never been laid down and have led even to protests, so strong have been the feelings aroused, but older members of the Class who have occasionally felt that the new generation was taking its Championships too seriously, can be assured that not all the Week is devoted to serious racing.

Richard Davis and Geoff Worsdale proved that the original narrow "Satisfactions" could succeed against their wider brethren by coming 3rd and 4th. The lightweight Ian McLuckie came one place higher than the previous year's 6th in an "Infidel" and then moved off to the Lark Class where there would be more lightweights. At this stage, there was still a belief that in most conditions you had to be heavy to win in the Merlin Rockets at sea. The real point was that in so many other classes, fittings to enable lightweights to keep up with heavyweights in a blow meant that you had to be light to be competitive. In the Merlin Rockets, however, a choice of design and mast section could do much to enable the heavyweight to remain competitive. In consequence the Class was attracting able heavyweights from other classes.

Brave attempts to break the "Satisfaction"/"Smoker" monopoly came from Graham Pike and David Robinson. Graham went to former Merlin Rocket pundit David Thomas, by now succesfully designing keel boats. Thomas noticed that the rule which allowed the planks to be fared in at the stem, did not state precisely how far back they were allowed to go. His startling conclusion was that there was nothing in the rules to prevent a smooth-skin Merlin Rocket. Mindful that the Class had indicated very clearly only two years earlier that it did not want smooth skins, which would outclass traditional clinker hulls, Graham and his crew/partner, Patrick King, instructed Spud Rowsell to confine the smooth skin to the area up to the mast. Rowsell glued some ply to the frames in this area and built the rest traditionally. A certificate was granted and the boat *Nitro*, appeared on the Open Meeting Circuit, beautifully finished (as all Graham and Patrick's boats were) not in the usual primrose paint but in battleship-grey.

A hastily summoned Class Committee Meeting agreed that Graham had not broken the rules as drawn, but they would not allow any other boat to be built the same way. This initiative came from the former Class Chairman, Ken Ellis, who was now Chairman of the RYA Centreboard Committee. Had he delayed, several more similar boats could have been built leaving the Committee the unpleasant choice of allowing to remain, boats which could have (or be thought to have) a substantial advantage, or revoking their Certificates and nullifying a substantial capital outlay. Fortunately for the Class, the hull, although attractive to behold and with a very fine and smooth entry, was not a success. In spite of being obviously well sailed by the Pike/King team, Graham had not acquired a weapon which others were denied.

The other bold shot in the dark came, more predictably, from Graham's Hamble River SC colleague, David Robinson. David went to Stephen Jones, a successful radical in the Quarter-Ton and other small keel-boat classes. Stephen's boat, *Shaft*, is described in detail elsewhere, but suffice to say that David hastily ordered a "Smoker" for the

Championships and lent *Shaft* to a club colleague, Chris Rhodes, then at the top of the British OK fleet. Perhaps the best service which this boat did was to bring Chris into the Merlin Rocket Class whose Championships he was to win in 1979. Lovers of the ironical will also appreciate that David, in his replacement conventional "Smoker", had a worse Championship result than *Shaft*, the boat he had discarded!

Also at the Championships was the prizewinner of another raffle for a new Merlin Rocket with the pre-allocated number 3000, Peter Rainey. Having had the misfortune to have had a boat which he had commissioned from Martin Jones written off in an accident, Peter used his raffle prize to have another "Admiral Benbow" design built by Aln Boatyard.

By the end of the Third Decade, the sail numbers had reached 3000, one hundred a year, although the graph was an erratic one. New registrations were, in common with other classes, beginning a downward trend. However, with some 180 boats at the Weymouth Championships, 22 teams at the Team Championships and 100 at the Inland Championships, the Class was attracting keen helmsmen and looking forward to the Fourth Decade.

CHAPTER 4

Surviving the Hard Times: 1976 - 1986

The Fourth Decade started on a note of controversy, always a good thing to have in a Development Class, when the March 1976 edition of the Merlin Rocket magazine published an article calling for a new spinnaker and a longer pole. The reasons given for the change were these:-
1. The existing spinnaker, probably the only feature of the boat which had remained substantially unchanged since 1946, was completely outdated.
2. An increase in mid-section width would improve close reaching qualities on restricted waters.
3. The improvement in size would help to promote planing on the broader reaching legs of Olympic triangles.
4. Due to the advent of the quadrilateral mainsail over ten years earlier, the greater sail area in the mainsail needed to be balanced downwind by a larger spinnaker.
5. Wider boats gave their crews more leverage to hold the boat level.
6. With so many devices available to help lightweights sail upwind in a blow, heavyweights needed something to redress the balance.

The magazine itself had been developed by Ken Ellis (Class Chairman, 1971/73, and Art Editor for *"The Readers' Digest"*) from the old Chairman's Newsletter into a lively publication which encouraged members to write in with their views – and they did! Speculating upon the effect which rule changes might have on design is a hallowed Merlin pastime. Some speculations on the effect of a larger spinnaker – for example that it would depress the bows downwind so that designers would have to make them fuller, thus making the boat less suitable for cutting through waves, were clearly misconceived. Those who knew more about the forces involved said that the spinnaker would lift the bows earlier on to a plane and, of course, they were right.

Some said that the new spinnaker would kill off the girl crews – an argument which, it will be recalled, had been used before to justify the retention of the rule requiring spinnakers to be sheeted inside the forestay. Some complained that a longer pole would be more difficult to stow, at a time when more and more boats were going over to stowing the pole (or twin poles) along the boom. Others complained that they had just worked out their correct lengths of line for twin 5ft poles and did not want to start again measuring for twin 6ft poles. Good helmsmen at the top muttered that they had got there by learning to master the present system, why should they give away their advantage and start level with the others? Such an argument could, of course have been used against any new idea. Was the Merlin Rocket Class about to get into one of its periodic ruts?

The Class Committee ordered a detailed survey into the ideal spinnaker for the Merlin Rocket under the chairmanship of Chris Ellis. Differently shaped spinnakers were commissioned from a variety of sailmakers – some of whom submitted two alternative designs, and poles were obtained 6ft long (as for the GP14), 6ft 3ins (the Scorpion) and 6ft 7ins (2 metres) as for the Fireball. These were sent out to individual clubs and trials held at Queen Mary Reservoir SC in the south and Hollingworth Lake in the north. The Queen Mary trials were conducted in a blizzard, the spray turning to ice on the spinnakers. Nobody fancied capsizing on the coldest day that winter and therefore the boats were not driven hard under the new spinnakers and very little was learned. Jim Park's view, having spent the previous winter using the largest spinnaker and the 2 metre pole, was that it was like the existing spinnaker in one force more wind, except that on a close reach the spinnaker was easier to keep from collapsing. He remained convinced that whatever shape was chosen, the 2 metre pole opened up the slot between spinnaker and mainsail, without having to move the spinnaker sheet fairleads back.

At Hollingworth Lake they had other ideas. The fashion in spinnaker pole stowage there was to push it under the foredeck. It was found that a 6ft pole could be pushed right up to the front and the aft end be clipped on to the shroud lever. It was something as small (and as irrelevant, after everybody started stowing poles along the boom) as this which carried the day and made the official proposal a 6ft pole. Now, ten years later, there are thoughts that a 2 metre pole might have been better after all, because the 6ft length is too small for the maximum size spinnaker permitted under the rules and heavier helmsmen are compelled to use a smaller size intended for lightweights.

So far as the size of the new spinnaker was concerned, it is perhaps significant that all the members of the Sub-Committee were small in stature and light in weight. There was a real fear that too big a spinnaker would destroy the very Merlin Rocket art of close spinnaker reaching and in the end a spinnaker was chosen almost identical to the one which Neil Thornton of No. 1 Sails had designed for the winner of the previous year's Scorpion Championships.

The Committee went to referendum, which had not been needed for the far-reaching developments in hull beam, centre mainsheets or quadrilaterial sails. The result was a massive vote, 81% to 19%, in favour of the new spinnaker and pole. These were allowed from the beginning of the 1979 season – three years after the article was published.

Not all measures took that length of time. In 1978, the same year as the new spinnaker and pole were passed at the AGM, Barry Dunning (for so long Alan Warren's expert crew, and an Olympic Soling crew at the 1972 and 1976 Games) decided to copy a very successful National 12 idea and replace the centreboard case with a narrow-slotted daggerboard case and daggerboard. The advantages had been well proved in the National 12s. Less water is carried in the plate case, there is less drag and there is a constant centre of lateral resistance in a board which comes straight up downwind rather than swinging aft.

The National 12 Class Committee reacted slowly and over a dozen boats had been built by the time a resolution was passed to prevent this idea. The objections were that to be successful, owners needed a boat which could easily break its daggerboard if it ran aground, and that crews put their masculinity at risk as they moved quickly from one side of the boat to another.

The Merlin Rocket Committee was aware that crews need to move even more often across a boat which has a spinnaker. The Committee referred the matter to the Centreboard Committee of the RYA where the same Chairman who had moved quickly three years before to ban smooth skinned hulls, Ken Ellis, stepped in again to ban

Spud Rowsell working on an Omega foam sandwich "NSM" hull in 1980. Notice how the bulkhead ▶ at the shrouds ties up with the bow tank and the centreboard case capping, giving a rigid "box" section to withstand the transverse compressive loads from the shrouds and the vertical loads from the mast

Photograph by John Bickford

Graham and Tessa Pike sailing *Gringo*, the first competitive GRP foam-sandwich boat, ▶ on the Exe estuary

Photograph by John Bickford

daggerboards before the building process could get any further. For this he received some rather unfair criticism, but only one boat had to be altered. Unlike the National 12s we did not have the ridiculous situation where some boats with a built-in if uncomfortable advantage had a licence to compete. Oddly enough, daggerboards have been allowed in the International 14 Class. Pat Blake, who sails in both 14s and Merlin Rockets, says that using a daggerboard when sailing in Chichester Harbour makes him very grateful that the Class Committee and the RYA moved quickly to ban it for Merlin Rockets.

The other measure on which a very quick decision was taken was the new GRP hull and the low front buoyancy tank needed to stiffen the hull. Glass reinforced plastic had been tried in the late 60s by both Bob Hoare and South Yorkshire Boatbuilders. The trouble was that the fibreglass then available was much heavier than wood, so the boats were either as strong as plywood and heavier, or as light as plywood and weaker. In consequence they were either slow, or broke up, or both!

Robert Inglis, a member of Wembley SC, was a Naval Architect lecturing at London University and is described in the chapter on our Designers. He tested some new honeycomb GRP which had been sent to him by Spud Rowsell. Robert satisfied the Committee that this would produce strong, light hulls which would not absorb water. The Committee approved the material and Spud was able to build without delay.

At the same time, it was thought necessary to stiffen up the hull in the area where it is subject to the stresses impossed by mast and shrouds. The easiest way to do this was to bring the bow tank back to the mast and lower it. At a stroke this would stiffen the hull, ensure that all the tank was below the water level after a capsize (and therefore ensure that all of it produced a lifting force) and provide easier stowage for the spinnaker. Although a previous Committee had been advised not to adopt this idea, in case a broken jib halyard might result in a falling mast pucturing the bow tank, the new Committee permitted the improvement with nothing more than a formal resolution at the 1980 AGM.

It should not be thought that the first four years of the new decade were entirely spent in improving the boat. The racing standard in the Merlin Rockets has always been one of the highest in the country and the '70s had seen a substantial increase in the number of competitive helmsmen from the North and the Midlands. Two changes had assisted this. One of these was the revival of interest in the Silver Tiller events by permitting very large reservoirs to be designated "Open Waters." This has substantially increased entries from Midland helmsmen who had never been keen on travelling to race on the sea. Although the sea requirement was later restored, only one (instead of two) sea results was needed as a minimum and this encouraged the able helmsmen to think of wider horizons than the Midland Circuit.

The second factor to bring top helmsmen from all parts of the country together sprung from an idea of Graham Pike (then sailing with the coastal club Hamble River SC) that an Inland Championships should be held over a long weekend. The first event was held in 1973 at Queen Mary Reservoir, near London Airport, which had been opened for dinghy racing the year before. This was one of the new breed of reservoirs which could offer Olympic triangular courses with legs of nearly a mile. The first winner was the Exmouth-based Francis Williams, but in the two succeeding Inland Championships at Grafham Water and Draycote Water, the winners were Harry Haynes and David Liddington, excellent inland sailors who had enjoyed only limited success on the sea. Clearly this was a highly suitable event for the Class's growing number of reservoir sailors, who by now constituted a majority of the Class.

One of the new breed of "Open Water" reservoirs, Queen Mary SC, has the reputation of producing the best sea sailing in London. Sometimes it lives up to its reputation. The winter Merlin fleet here has produced some excellent racing out of the Silver Tiller season.

Photograph by Ian Holt

The first three Inland Championships at the end of the third decade all attracted entries in excess of 100 boats. With entries of 150 plus at the Nationals and up to 22 teams for the Team Championships at the Welsh Harp, the fourth decade started in a mood of confident optimism. However, the crippling imposition of 25% Value Added Tax plus the increased cost of materials was having its effect on the number of new boats built. The old annual average of 120 boats shrank to 54 in 1976 and has been shrinking annually since. Since the first thing the owner of a new boat does is take it to the National Championships, it is perhaps not surprising that Championship entries started to fall.

The summer of 1976 was one of the hottest on record. Competitors at the Queen Mary Reservoir Silver Tiller Meeting spent the hottest day ever known in London sluicing water over themselves as they drifted round the reservoir. The Championships were due to be held at Whitstable, noted for strong and bitterly cold winds straight down from the North Pole. As it happened, competitors enjoyed a pleasant Force 3-4 all week which took the edge off the sweltering heat and made for almost ideal Championship conditions. This, however, is not what the Whitstable Championships would be remembered for.

When a new Merlin Rocket is first weighed, if it scales under 98 kilos (217 lbs) it must be brought up to weight by lead correctors. If, in course of time, the boat takes up moisture and thereby becomes heavier, it can be reweighed and some, or all, of the correctors be removed. Keen helmsmen are always reweighing their boats to see if they can rid themselves of useless lead! With less new boats being built, more keen helmsmen were sailing older boats that year and some had already removed correctors because they maintained (and had a measurer's certificate to prove it) that their boats had "taken up." It may well be that the very hot summer had removed the moisture (and the accompanying weight) acquired, it may be that some measurers had been using spring balance scales where the spring had slackened with age, or it may have been that some measurers had themselves got slack with age, but the abiding memory of Whitstable was the leading boats coming ashore to be met by Dennis Ellis, the founder of the RYA Measurement Scheme, and a set of very accurate beam scales!

Dennis is the most punctilious and least corruptible of measurers. Patiently he weighed each boat exactly in accordance with the rules and, with courteous regret, disqualified boat after boat. All this was carried out in the dinghy park in front of the clubhouse with most of the fleet sitting on the sea wall watching, like spectators at the Grand National, to see who would fall next.

It is not an exaggeration to say that the 1976 Championships were not won but lost by most of the principal contenders. In addition to those ruled out of races on the scales (and who spent evenings searching for lead piping to fit under the thwart), Spud Rowsell managed to lose a Championships in which he won the first 2 races and came 2nd and 1st in the last two. How? In the third race, Spud came into a mark on port, tacked quickly to avoid a starboard boat and hit the mark. Merlin Championships rules do not permit you to re-round. In the 4th race, his discard gone, Spud sailed inshore to avoid an adverse tide and tore off his rudder pintles. He had only borrowed Chris Andrew's "Smoker" *Fantasia* because he was dissatisfied with his new experimental design and yet he could so easily have won.

Another helmsman under a handicap was Pat Blake, just back from the Olympic FD trials with the recently launched *Aftermyth* which had scarcely been sailed before the Championships but which was going very fast. Overtaking Graham Pike to windward, Pat decided to hoist spinnaker and drifted on to Pike. The resultant disqualification plus a further disqualification on the scales put paid to his chances.

It was perhaps not a bad thing for a Class which was being called "expensive" by the yachting press that the winner was *Satisfaction*, which had first appeared at the 1972 Championships in Spud Rowsell's hands. Sailing her was one of the many Merlin helmsmen who has successfully moved on to bigger boats, Lawrie Smith, the 12 metre skipper for *Lionheart* in 1980, *Victory '83* in 1983 and a leading 470 and Admirals' Cup skipper over the past ten years. Lawrie had been runner-up at the 1974 Merlin Championships and now showed himself able to keep his head while many older and more experienced helmsmen were losing theirs.

Second was a home-built boat, albeit by that very experienced home builder, Bill Twine. Apparently, from his record, equally at home in the front or back of a Merlin, Bill showed great downwind speed in his home-made "Mustard Seed" design *Oberon*. Third was another boat sailing in its fifth Championships – *Chuft*, a "Satisfaction" design sailed by one of the Class's longest standing members, Geoff Worsdale.

It was, in fact, a good year for older boats. After many years crewing for his father Harry, Kevin Haynes took the 1971 boat *Phantom Rider* to a windy Inland Championships at gorgeous Bala Lake, won convincingly, and then went on to win the Silver Tiller.

The following year, 1977, saw considerable trouble spent on accurate weighing of boats, perhaps not unconnected with the knowledge that Dennis Ellis was running the Nationals at Hayling Island. As it happened, not a single boat was underweight. A cooler summer or more careful measuring? In 1977, Pat achieved the still unique treble of winning the Nationals, the Inlands and Silver Tiller.

The Championships were held during this Silver Jubilee year at Hayling Island, with the Royal Navy Spithead Review only a few miles west. Sailing conditions were again ideal, a steadily increasing wind throughout the week in bright sunshine. Could one ask for more? To many people Hayling Island is an almost ideal venue and it was very nice to have Jack Holt return to present the prizes thirty years after the first two Championships at Hayling Island. A somewhat riotous party followed as it gradually dawned on Pat Blake that after so many years he had finally won his first Merlin Rocket Championship.

The pressure off, Pat easily won the Inlands at Grafham and the Silver Tiller to end a memorable year. Perhaps his sole regret was losing in the final of the Team Championships. Facing old rivals Nottingham, Pat was unselfishly helping his team, quite happy to let Kevin Haynes finish first if Cookham could achieve the winning combinations. All seemed safe as his team-mate Mike Fowler, on port tack, covered a Nottingham boat right up to the jetty in front of Waveney & Oulton Broad YC's picturesque clubhouse. As the wind slid round the clubhouse, Fowler got a header and tacked for the line. The Nottingham boat (sailed by the extremely competent National 12 sailor Tony Edwards) held on, unwilling to move from Fowler's lee to his dirty wind. Tacking later, Edwards was just able to lay the line on starboard whereas Fowler had to tack on to port. There was not quite enough room for Fowler to cross and Cookham missed the title by inches – just as they had done at the 1973 Team Championships, also held at Oulton Broad!

For many Merlin Rocket helmsmen and crews, the winter period is for serious racing. With stronger winds, less counter-attractions such as the Silver Tiller series, holidays and other family commitments, racing at such clubs as Ranelagh, Bristol Corinthian, Queen Mary or Wembley is even keener than in the summer. For others, however, the winter period is a time for thinking, for deciding upon a new hull, finishing it off and preparing for the new Silver Tiller season.

Whilst many considering a new boat would have asked for nothing more than a carbon copy of Pat Blake's treble-winning *Aftermyth*, the perceptive thinkers had looked at the boats of the Class's two main sailmakers, Phil Morrison and Neil Thornton. Each had separately concluded that the hoop system for centre-mainsheets was inherently preferable to the track. The system was not new, it had been seen on an English 505 and an American Fireball, each World Champions. It certainly had the advantages of simplicity, cheapness and the elimination of a track upon which one tore trousers and wasted time getting a traveller to the right position. Clearly, if the sail was to be controlled by the kicking strap more than the traveller, sails would have to be cut differently, but the helmsmen trying this system were the Class's main sailmakers!

The immediate impression created by the crop of new boats in 1978 was that metal was taking over from wood. This, of course, was an old criticism heard when first "tin" masts and then booms took over. It was the combination of the metal hoops and the metal struts which created this impression, but whether or not they would be successful was another matter. The thinking behind this development is recorded in the chapter on Rig Development. On the design front, there had been obvious interest in Phil Morrison's "Summer Wine" and the boat itself had been bought by the promising young helmsman from Bolton, Paddy Atkinson, who had finished 6th the previous year. The general view, however, was that "Summer Wine" was an extreme boat built for the lightweight Phil Morrison to sail in the predicted strong winds of Hayling Island.

It was for this reason that Phil had designed a modified version, halfway between the "Summer Wine" and the "Smoker," the "NSM," standing for "New Smoking Material." This was a palliative issued by the Health Education Council to encourage people to give up the smoking habit and obviously appealed to Phil's offbeat sense of humour. Rowsell, John Harris and Michael Fowler had these with a special "NSM" rig consisting of hoop, strut and "Morrison Wires" to pre-bend the mast in light airs. Since Morrison was also a highly respected sailmaker, he could offer a package of boat, rig and sails. Many accepted this although Pat Blake and Lawrie Smart stayed with the "Smokers" which had stood them in such good stead the year before. Harry Haynes had shaken off a bad attack of glandular fever and ordered his last boat, a Robert Inglis-designed "Bad Company" for flat water speed. Nigel Waller was there with an attempt to "Merlinise" a successful National 12 design with tremendous two-sail reaching speed, and John Patterson had re-rigged his "Winderbox" design in the belief that this lake boat could achieve sufficient speed in the relatively sheltered waters off Abersoch, 1978 Championship venue.

The bay at Abersoch is more sheltered than Pwllheli, with surrounding headlands which can cause pronounced windshifts. Whereas Pwllheli favoured the power sailing of Rowsell, who had dominated the 1970 and 1974 Championships, Abersoch's flatter waters and windshifts would give the lake sailors a better chance. Was this a dastardly plot to end the South Coast domination of the Championships?

The pattern for the Week was established in the first Championship race. With an offshore wind, those who sailed a long starboard tack up to St. Tudwals Island, picked up a massive header and fetched the weather mark on port. Two spinnakers were hoisted instantly, one a red band on a white background, Rowsell's colours, the other a dark green band on a white, Patterson. Whether Abersoch Bay was supposed to suit Rowsell less than Pwllheli is not known, but two opening races in Force 4 gave Rowsell two wins, each from Patterson.

The history of the Class Championships is littered with those who have won the first two races and then blown the Championships, Rowsell himself had done so only two years earlier at Whitstable, and three years earlier at Weymouth, so all Spud would admit on Tuesday was that he had no worse chance than anyone else.

Tuesday produced a Force 5 and several capsizes. It produced some exciting bursts of speed on reaches, too close for spinnaker in that wind, from Nigel Waller's *Meglo*, which hitherto had found that two-sail reaching ability was not much help when the rest of the fleet is expertly handling spinnakers. At the front, the order remained the same. Rowsell gained his third win and Patterson his third second place. The fascinating battle between the latest in technology and a lake boat sailing its third Championships continued into the 4th race, sailed in a rainstorm. Like another distinguished Merlin helmsman, Francis Williams, John Patterson wears spectacles. The warmth generated from sailing in a strong wind causes the glass to steam and reduce vision. Just as Francis had had the odd collision, John completely missed seeing a tailender half a lap behind and retired following a collision in which he did not have right of way. Rowsell went on to score his fourth successive win to equal Warren's record eight years earlier at Pwllheli.

Spud Rowsell and Jon Turner, in the days when the duo were supreme. The boat is the "NSM" *Foot Loose*, in which they won the Championships in 1978.

Although the wind strength was falling in the 5th race, Rowsell could probably have won that as well and achieved the first ever "perfect score" of 5 wins in the 5 countable races. However, he was being covered with extreme care by Patterson, who was determined to secure at least one win that week. Aware that Patterson had a considerable reputation as a team racer, Spud did not push his luck and risk disqualification. With light airs for the last day, Spud still managed 3rd place to achieve probably the best Championships record of all time. The race was won by Pat Blake, making a rare appearance in Merlins that year as his priority was his Flying Dutchman campaign for the 1980 Olympic Games. The tragedy of the last race was Patterson's disqualification for being over a starting line which caught many others. So close to Rowsell for so long, Patterson had two retirements and, therefore, a final place well down the rankings.

Patterson was clearly out for revenge when the Class gathered for the Inland Championships at the recently opened Datchet Reservoir near Windsor. Rowsell was there and the wind was blowing Force 5 and upwards. Patterson sailed well, but once again the Rowsell/Turner team powered their way to 4 successive wins, taking the title with a "perfect score." Patterson won the last race (when Rowsell broke his mast) and this time achieved the second place he should have had at the Nationals. Good results on the Open Meeting Circuit brought the Patterson/Cheetham team the Silver Tiller from the dominant names of the '70s, Haynes and Blake.

The demands of the medical profession and those of the Silver Tiller circuit have never been compatible, so Patterson decided to move on to the 505 Class where, instead of many one day events, there are a few major weekends.

Third at Datchet (and 6th at the Nationals) were the brother and sister team of Mike and Mandy Fowler. To come 3rd in the survival conditions at Datchet suggests the type of girl the Russians produce to putt the shot or throw the discus. Those who know Mandy find it difficult to believe that she would be able to survive races in which she and her brother excel, since there is nothing aggressive or "butch" in her delightful personality. Her quiet determination plus an able helmsman and a well-organised boat proves what can still be achieved by female crews in all conditions.

As the thinking season approached, prospective purchasers thought of larger chutes to take wider spinnakers, hoops and struts were clearly here to stay, the new "West" system of saturating the planks in epoxy resin – or at least using it as a glue – was obviously going to make the boat last longer, but which design?

It is a truth universally acknowledged that people are not built One-Design. Less obvious is the point that, given a fleet of helmsmen and crews of differing weights (and different distribution of even the same weight between two different boats), a choice of design and mast flexibility, far from dividing the fleet, actually enables helmsmen to compensate for the physical differences between them. Lightweights sailing on the sea were opting for "Summer Wines," medium weights went for "NSMs", heavyweights sailing inland went for "Bad Companies," or remained faithful to the "Smokers" which had proved so sound in such a variety of conditions throughout the '70s.

For the 1979 Inlands, the Class gathered at Rutland Water, near Stamford in Lincolnshire, and just off the A1. Formed by flooding most of the county of Rutland, this is a beautiful stretch of water with no suggestion of the "concrete bowl" of most man-made reservoirs. Grazing sheep and cattle on the steep banks seem to have one leg longer than the other, and there was plenty of time to examine them! In some of the lightest wind of any Class major event this decade, Roger Harris from Hollingworth Lake won in a "Disguys." Kevin Haynes, new "Bullett," a modified "Bad Company," came second from the Fowlers, who proved as competent in light airs as they had been in the strong winds at Datchet the year before.

For the Nationals, the Class trailed to a spot for which it has always had a great affection, Falmouth. Although fears of petrol shortages kept down the entry to just below 100 for the first time in 25 years, the keen members were all there.

Falmouth bears little resemblance to a seaside resort. It is a working port (like another Class favourite, Whitstable) set amidst beautiful scenery and large areas of sailing water. The sail out to the starting line, past St. Mawes, the black rock at the mouth of the Carrick Roads, and Pendennis Point into a partly sheltered bay, is an experience in itself for inland sailors. The Bay has enough waves to promote surfing downwind, but they are not so steep as to stop a boat beating to windward through them. With easier sailing conditions, there is more time to think of tactics. Will the configuration of the shifts make it pay to go inshore and risk less wind under the headlands? Is the tide subject to back eddies just outside the mainstream as it ebbs out of the Carrick Roads? This is a thinking sailor's venue.

A variety of names came to the fore during the Week with the last race won by the now veteran (eligible for the over 45s Cup) Alan Warren in a boat he had picked up cheaply because someone had not taken delivery. The winners, Chris Rhodes and Patrick King, became Champions without actually winning a race. Chris joined the Class after having been lent David Robinson's unsuccessful design "Shaft" at the Weymouth Championships four years earlier, while Patrick was sailing in his 15th Championships as a crew.

Patrick's winning the City of Plymouth Cup for the crew of the Champion boat was all the happier in retrospect for, after one more Merlin Championships, he was to suffer a stroke which would deprive him of the use of one arm. Being Patrick, he would not give up sailing, or even racing, but would be pushed into crewing boats without spinnakers until acquiring his own keel boat.

Chris and Pat were sailing a "Summer Wine" with a lightweight C-section mast, sleeved to give stiffness in the right places. Both ideas were not in vogue at the time, but they would be something to chew over that winter. Second were Phil Morrison and Bill Twine (crewing this year) in a Lawrie Smart "NSM," *Second Chance*, which was to finish in the first 3 overall for three consecutive years, but third was to be a Guy Winder boat, borrowed for the Week by Graham Pike and crewed by his fiancée Tessa. Although of more athletic build than Mandy Fowler and bigger than Jilly Blake, Tessa's achievement in keeping Graham's boat at the front in spite of some strong winds again proved that women crews are competitive in Merlin Rockets. This was the second time Tessa had crewed the 3rd placed boat at the Championships, the other occasion being at Weymouth in 1975.

The Haynes family were dominating the Silver Tiller Series, Harry winning more meetings, but Kevin winning the series because he could count a crucial win at sea gained on a rough day at Lowestoft. In their Inglis-designed "Bad Company" and "Bullett" respectively, the '70s ended with a wider choice open to prospective purchasers than for some years. Which design would prevail at the 1980 Championships?

The chosen venue was Weymouth, a Bay regarded by the British Olympic Yachting Association as the best in England for international racing. Like Falmouth, it has headlands which can give rise to certain windshift configurations, but it has a much more predictable tide. Launching is from a sandy shallow shelving beach into calm water with an unobstructed sail out to the start. Unlike Falmouth where the wind came in like a lion and went out like a lamb, the wind the next year was to start light and gradually increase to survival conditions.

An unexpected and rather sad entry was received from the 1977 Champion, Pat Blake. Having proved himself the first British helmsman faster than Rodney Pattisson in Flying Dutchmen by winning the final Olympic Trials at Weymouth a month earlier, Pat had been deprived of his place in the Olympic Yachting team by the Royal Yachting Association's unilateral decision to withdraw from the Moscow Games in protest against the Russian invasion of Afghanistan. Pat got over his disappointment in the best possible way. Unable to borrow his treble-winning *Aftermyth* because the new owner was competing in her, Pat borrowed from his clubmate, Bob Deacon, a "carbon copy" and triumphantly won the Championships. It was a popular victory, albeit a narrow one.

Those who had said that "Smokers" were now only competitive inland found that the new Champion was sailing one. For the rest, however, "NSMs" occupied many of the leading places. Graham Pike's 5th place in the prototype GRP boat showed that this method of construction gave neither advantage nor disadvantage – an ideal situation, perhaps reflected when the decision to adopt went through the AGM with barely a dissenting voice.

The Championships ended with one of those wild races which live on in the memory. A strong offshore wind was realised to be a Force 6 as soon as boats drew clear of the area sheltered by the cliffs. The wind increased in strength and the clear win by Gavin Willis and Bob Taig was a tribute to masterly skill in the most difficult of conditions.

The Inlands were held at a venue by now established as the last Silver Tiller Meeting of the year, Draycote Water SC, near Rugby. Easily accessible via the motorway system from North, South or Midlands, Draycote Water SC was started by Merlin Rocket owners and has remained popular in the class as a result, even if, for some strange reason, Midlanders have shown a preference for smaller waters than this magnificent reservoir. With splendid facilities on shore, Draycote is well equipped for major events. Phil King, a Draycote member, won the Championships with freelance sailmaker Richard Estaugh coming a creditable 2nd in a borrowed boat from the consistent David Griffiths. David is one of those many helmsmen in the Merlin Rocket Class whose name regularly appears in the top 6 at both Nationals and Inlands and was a member of the South Yorks team which won the Topmast Trophy 5 times in 9 years.

The availability of an "NSM package" of the a GRP "NSM" hull for £400 less than its wooden counterpart, plus matched mast and sails, was no doubt the inspiration which reversed the downward trend of new boat registrations. Just as many helmsmen at the start of the '70s had been tempted by the twin attractions of wide hulls and spinnaker chutes to change their boats, at the start of the '80s it was the cheap package and the new tank layout. With a new Championship venue at Exmouth, there was much to attract entries.

In fact, the Championship entry at Exmouth in 1981 was singularly disappointing, not quite making the 100. There were various reasons put forward; the counter-attraction of Salcombe Week, the tendency for tailenders not to want to come for a week's racing, the decline in the number of helmsmen based at coastal clubs, youth not liking to face realities at a Championship. There is no doubt that in a normal Championship Week, people find their level pretty soon, and many do not like what they find!

Two people blissfully free from all such worries were Andy Street and Andy Pickrell. The two Andies were members of the same club as arch-designer Phil Morrison. Phil reckoned that the "NSM" would not take heavyweights in moderate to light airs. Before the suspicion that "NSMs" would not carry weight became too well known, the two Andies joined a group of people who commissioned Jonathan Turner to build to a new design, the "NSM II."

The "NSM II" was not only to bring a Championship victory to the two Andies, but was to win a total of 4 Championships in succession. This feat has only been achieved in modern times by the "Proctor IX" and some variations on the "Satisfaction" hull shape. Phil Morrison did his usual trick of nearly winning the Championships easily. This time he would have won if he had not let slip a minor place in the teens he thought did not matter: that place cost him the Championship! The next 3 places were filled by helmsmen from one of the Class's early strongholds. Bristol Corinthian YC sail on Axbridge reservoir and are liable to lose water in hot summers when it does not rain much. This has had an inhibiting effect upon the growth of its home Merlin fleet, although it has encouraged Bristol men to support the Silver Tiller Series. The extension of the M5 to within easy reach of Axbridge has made the Winter Series a much more practical proposition and in the '80s has attracted a nucleus of top-line helmsmen.

Exmouth put on such an excellent Championships that it would be asked to hold them again three years later in 1984. The warm sun which seems to persist longer on the Exe than elsewhere and the delightful surroundings made Exmouth a popular venue from the start.

1982 was World Football Cup year and of course the Class returned to North Wales. By now some Lancashire members enjoyed weekends away from the mills so much they had joined the South Caernarvon YC and were thus able to ensure that the Class returned to Abersoch. The Championships were won by Pat Blake, who was finding it all so much easier now that he had already won them twice, crewed by his brother-in-law Roger Taylor who had crewed the Champion boat 10 years earilier for Pat's arch rival David Spiers. In the meantime, Pat and Roger had married the Henderson sisters from Leigh SC. When Jilly and Debbie crew they do so with distinction, but while they were occupied in bringing up the next generation of Merlin Rocket sailors, their husbands joined forces and won the 1980 and 1982 Championships.

The Abersoch Championships of 1982 produced a surprise which was to have substantial repercussions. Derek Hanrahan had bought one of the first Turner-built "NSM IIs" on the understanding that it would be helmed at the Championships by Lancashire's leading helmsman, Lawrie Smith. But as skipper in the *Lionheart* challenge for the America's Cup and signed up for the *Victory '83* Syndicate, Lawrie could not be spared by Peter de Savary. Derek's loss of a "jockey" was resolved when Jonathan offered to helm and signed up Richard Parslow to crew. The third place they achieved in his first Merlin Championships (although he had been doing some crafty practice in the Scorpion which he also builds with distinction) showed Jonathan ready to take his place as one of the Class's top boat tuner/helmsmen.

Jonathan and Richard won the following year after a close battle with Spud Rowsell. They went even better the following year at Exmouth, winning the Championships with a day to spare, with Phil Morrison again second, this time in the prototype "Gnome." By now somebody else had decided to help Jonathan, this time to get to the Los Angeles Olympic Games. It seemed a task entered too late in the day, but Jonathan quietly got down to preparing a very advanced Flying Dutchman from the American builder Lindsey. At the final Olympic trials, Jonathan came second and went out to Los Angeles as tune-up helmsman to the British representative. His performance there has already marked him out as the strongest contender for the Flying Dutchman place at the 1988 Games. Jonathan's sponsor was another Merlin Rocket helmsman, Graham Northway.

Jonathan and Richard continued on form, winning the Inlands at Leigh and sailing for the victorious Bristol Corinthian team in the Topmast Trophy at Queen Mary Reservoir. They could well have won the Silver Tiller had there not been a rule requiring the competitor to own the boat. This still belonged to Derek Hanrahan!

The fourth decade ended in the best traditions of the Class, a heavy-weather Championships and an unexpected winner. It blew "old boots" at Shoreham in 1985. In similar conditions at the Queen Mary Open Meeting, Gavin Willis had dominated a very strong fleet and was a hot favourite to win. Jonathan and Richard had borrowed a competitive boat and were out to "do an Oakeley" by winning the Championships three times in a row. Nick Aubrey and Chris Rutter from the North had shown heavy weather form at Queen Mary when they came second. Everybody agreed that the winners would be big muscular fellows.

Nigel Appleton might justly be regarded as one of the great Merlin crews of all time since he brings out the best of every helmsmen with whom he sails. He was due to race with Phil Morrison in *Gnome* with which they had been runner-up at Exmouth. When Phil (no doubt fed up with so regularly coming second in the Merlin Nationals), opted instead to race in the 505 Nationals the same week, Nigel invited David Robinson.

David has woven a thread through the Merlin Rocket Class ever since, as a young helmsman, he nearly wrote a new boat off at the Lymington Easter Regatta and then restored it in time to come 4th at the 1967 Championships. He would disappear and then return, sometimes with a dazzlingly successful new design such as "Ghost Rider" at Pwllheli in 1970, sometimes with spectacular failures such as "Shaft" in 1975 or "Batty Bat" (the Merlin that was going to plane to windward but just sagged off to leeward) in 1980. Sometimes David would turn up with a conventional boat, sail well but not make the top 6. In between David would go off and become Olympic Coach, found a successful sailmaking firm, sail a Quarter Tonner to win the Championships or Cowes Week, or merge his sailmakers firm with an American multi-national and become much sought-after among Admirals Cup contenders. However, the Holy Grail of the Merlin Rocket Championships was always just out of reach.

At the Class's 40th Championships however, pitting his spare 9½ stone frame against Shoreham's strong winds and steep seas that taught Alan Warren once how to become the best heavy weather helmsman in the country, David finally achieved the prize which had eluded him for nearly 20 years. In conditions in which nobody would have backed him, he beat all the fancied contenders to end the fourth decade as Class Champion. Nobody who has followed his determined effort to be different could begrudge him this supreme reward.

Jonathan and Richard came second, so close to the elusive hat-trick of Championships, but the favourites, Gavin Willis and Bob Taig lost 3rd place to Chris and Nigel Haworth in the first "NSM IV," which they had completed themselves from a Rowsell hull. Those who think that top-rate helmsmen don't bother to have "pretty boats" should look at the Haworths' *Shadowfax*. This boat would win prizes at a Concours d'Elegance anywhere and yet look at the Haworths' record that year, 3rd in a heavy weather Championships, 3rd again at the Inlands and runner-up in the Silver Tiller.

Gavin Willis salvaged his pride by deservedly winning the Silver Tiller. Nick Aubrey marked steady improvement over the years by taking the Inlands at Lake Bala from Dick Batt, crewed by his wife Gill, another lightweight girl crew who was justifying the belief of the Class's founding fathers that women should be able to compete at the highest level.

As the Class started the round of 40th birthday celebrations with the Ranelagh SC Silver Tiller meeting, a slight figure with grey hair was to be seen near the prize table. His eyes appeared to be searching for faces no longer there and then casting a surprised but admiring glance at some beautiful "state of the art" boats. Quietly he moved from one group to another, unwilling to intrude, for all the world like an elderly relative from abroad returning for a family reunion, glad to see the new generation but fearing that few would remember him. A certain look about the eyes suggested memories of earlier Merlins stretching right back to *Merlin* herself. Was this really the boat he had designed?

As the Commodore announced that the prizes were to be presented by the original designer, Jack Holt, warm applause showed that the Class remembered and appreciated his sound parenthood. His careful guidance in the formative years, leaving the Class to mature on its own and benefit from outside influences, had produced a racing dinghy which is as modern after 40 years as it was in 1946.

Epilogue

What of the future? While the clinker-ply method of building may be unusual these days, it is singularly appropriate for a development Class because moulds can easily be altered in a small way to improve a design. Sails are highly developed for a two-man boat without trapeze and even now experiments are taking place to assess the worth and longevity of Mylar fabric. The Class has always been at the forefront of development in mast technology where the variety of mast sections as well as hull design has enabled helmsmen and crews of vastly different weights to compete in all wind-strengths on equal terms.

The Silver Tiller series still offers the most varied Open Meeting competition in this country. Fourteen feet overall is an excellent length for a sailing dinghy racing on a variety of waters. It is long enough to go through a coastal chop yet short enough to be tacked quickly on the windshifts one finds on rivers or small reservoirs. Wide beam rather than trapeze has prevented heavier helmsmen ceasing to be competitive. The fine slicing bow which makes the Merlin Rocket such a joy to sail upwind remains a distinctive feature.

Compared with some One-Designs mass-produced in fibreglass, the Merlin Rocket may seem expensive. However, the quality of craftsmanship which produces such a magnificent boat when new (and many people will always prefer a well finished wooden boat to one in GRP) also makes Merlin Rockets so strong that they have a long competitive life and a good resale value. Damage to a wooden boat is easier to repair and, without doubt, many boats racing in the Class's 40th anniversary celebrations will be racing competitively in the year 2000.

The 40th anniversary was celebrated by the "Day of Champions" at Upper Thames SC, held on the Saturday after Bourne End Week. Sailmaker Dick Batt and Class Chairman Stuart Gurney spent many hours tracing as many ex-National Champions and their boats as could be brought to Bourne End. *Gently*, winner of the first two Championships, was carefully lowered from the rafters of the Waveney & Oulton Broad YC where she has remained for some years, waiting to be restored for presentation to the Lowestoft Maritime Museum. Many other historic boats were there and the list of past Class Champions included Jack Holt and Beecher Moore, Jim Ledwith, Tom Nisbett, Ian Proctor and Cliff Norbury, Brian Southcott and Dick Pratt, Bob Hoare, George Slack, David Potter and Duggie Brixton, Alan Warren and Barry Dunning, Francis Williams and Derek Sheffer, Spud Rowsell, Harry Haynes, Chris Rhodes and Patrick King, Andy Street and Andy Pickrell, representing every era in the Class's history. Many of these sailed in the informal race and none with greater enthusiasm than Ian Proctor in No. 579, *Candy*, which was built in 1955! The old boats were not all that far behind some very much more modern craft, on a beating/running course sailed in a force 2/3. The ever competitive Brian Southcott had even bought back his famous "Mark IX" *Restless IV* and equipped her with brand new sails from Dick Batt for the event. Had there been a handicap based upon a boat's age, Southcott would almost certainly have won with Proctor a close second. As it was, Southcott's superb skills inland kept him in front most of the way round the course until the wind increased at the end and the "Two Andies" used their youth and their 1981 Championship-winning *The Feet*, to win. The Upper Thames SC were splendid hosts, the weather was fine, old friends met again, on a day in which many members and Champions came, saw, and remembered.

Anthropologists define the art of survival in a species as the ability to adapt successfully to changing circumstances. The Merlin Rocket has had plenty of challenges to face when it has been vital that the Class's custodians steered a proper course between the Scylla of fashionable trends outdating existing boats and the Charybdis of stultifying the progressive elements which make it such a live force. A straight course having been steered, avoiding both the whirlpool and the rocks, and the Merlin Rocket Odyssey moves on towards the 21st century, confident in the belief that those seeking a "boat for all seasons" will continue to travel with it.

Upper Thames SC at its best. Hordes of spectators watching the Fortieth Anniversary Champions race.
Photograph by Jim Lowden

An historic line-up of early Merlin Rockets preparing for the race
Photograph by J. Lowden

Fortieth Anniversary Champions Regatta. In the foreground is Ian Proctor and Brian Southcott keeping up with some more modern boats.
Photograph by J. Lowden

Chronology of Historical Events

1945	Trials of *Kate*, and later *Merlin* in preparation for the formation of a new class.
1946	January. Official launch of the class and its rules, followed later in the year by the first championships at Hayling Island.
1949	The 25ft mast designed for the River Thames is replaced by lower rigs as Merlins are sailed more on the sea and the new reservoirs. The Rocket Class design is commissioned from Wyche & Coppock.
1950	The Silver Tiller series is started.
1951	Merger between the Merlin and Rocket classes.
1954	The first glued plywood boat appears and the first self-bailers.
1959	Terylene sails are adopted. Sail numbers pass 1,000.
1962	Spinnaker sheets are allowed outside the forestay. New style spinnakers designed for reaching.
1964	Class Team Championships started.
1965	Transom flaps introduced to make capsized boats self rescuing. First gaff styled mainsails appear.
1966	"Xpectant" design appears – the first design with over 6ft beam.
1967	Optional built-in buoyancy approved.
1968	GRP construction approved. The Midland circuit founded. First appearance of a design with over 6ft 6ins beam, "Wotnot."
1969	Class Committee steps in to place a maximum beam of 7ft 2.5ins to prevent excessive width breaking the then road trailing limits. S.E. Area Team Championships started.
1970	Championships at Pwhlleli produce the highest entry ever – 227 boats. Wide designs dominate in a heavy weather week. Rules and measurement changes to allow spinnaker shutes and the acceptance of the metric system.
1971	Silver Tiller rules change to reflect the large lakes now available for sailing.
1972	Design change begins to stabilize with 6ft 10ins width, maximum rise of floor and minimum waterline beam.
1973	Price limit lifted as country enters major period of inflation. Inland Championships started. Full length top batten adopted for mainsails.
1976	Extensive trials begin on new larger spinnaker design.
1978	New spinnaker adopted at AGM. Mainsheet hoops (first seen in 1977) become standard on new boats.
1980	New GRP sandwich construction boats appear and meet with general approval. Low front buoyancy tank layout approved.
1986	Trials of Mylar/Kevlar sailcloth begin.

CHAPTER 5

Designers and their Designs

Ever since the conception of the Merlin Rocket class, it has been, along with the National 12 and the International 14, the hotbed of hull and rig design and development. Many eminent designers have tried their hand at designing a Merlin Rocket and introduced many new ideas into the class, though not all have met with success. As with all restricted, or development classes, hull shape has consumed a great deal of the effort, thought and money. There will always be the question as to whether the rig or the hull is the more important contributor to boat speed, but it is fair to say that while both have received equal consideration from those racing in the class, there have been more variations in hull shape than in rig configuration.

Hull shapes can be divided into two generations; those designed before 1968 and those after. Up until 1968, Ian Proctor designs reigned supreme, after an initial domination of the class by Jack Holt. The classic Proctor "Mark IX", although not popular when first introduced, became for many years *the* Merlin Rocket shape.

The major change that overtook the class was the sudden increase in beam, a trend set by Mike Jackson. His National 12 *March Hare* dominated the Burton Cup Week at

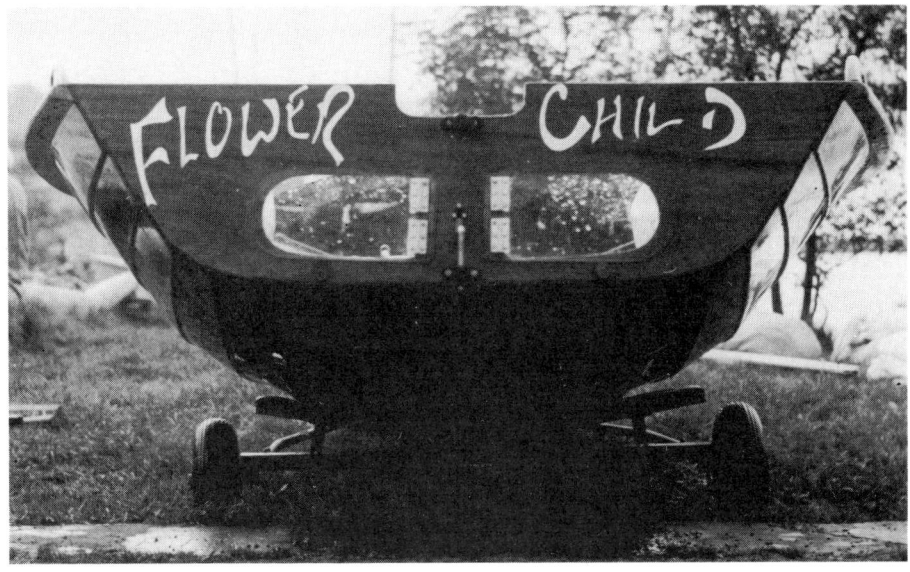

Flower Child, built to the "Superstition" design of Mike Jackson. In the hands of David Child, this boat won the Silver Tiller in 1968, and came 6th in the Championships.

Photograph by Guy Gurney

Weymouth (1963). Tom Booth, who measured Mike's rig was convinced that it was the hull rather than the home-made rig that was responsible for the success. Although Mike's Merlins never had the same success, everybody was applying his ideas to their own designs. The traditional 14 foot dinghy, established by Uffa Fox and developed by Jack Holt, Digby Coppock and Ian Proctor, was well "V'd" forward (to knife through the sea), blending into a fairly flat transom. The latter, combined with a long run achieved by having the deepest part of the keel forward of mid length, provided a surf board for good planing.

The conventional wisdom was to keep the beam down to the minimum permitted, both at the sheerline (the minimum beam at the sheerline has since been abolished) and at the waterline at mid-length, in order to present the minimum obstruction to the waves, and, in the original Merlins, to go into the Ranelagh SC boathouse!

Mike Jackson stood this concept on its head. "U'd" sections, which gave minimum wetted surface area for a given displacement, were blended into a completely flat transom, for easy, stable planing. At mid-length the waterline beam was kept to the minimum, but above the waterline the topsides were flared out to provide a much wider boat at the sheerline, for greater sitting-out power. Compared with a "V" section, the "U" section gave displacement lower down, thus floating the boat higher. The measurement point for waterline beam was raised above the actual waterline, so the actual waterline beam was reduced.

Mike's boats were well behaved, but, if minimum waterline beam was retained, excessive beam at the sheerline forced the turn of the bilge inward and downward, resulting in a boat which was narrow in the bottom and very tippy. The boat would also ship water at a smaller angle of heel. One of the most extreme examples of this was the "Xpectation," designed by Martin Jones. Whilst maintaining the same transom and rocker line as the earlier "Xpectant," the overall beam was considerably increased to 7ft 3ins. The resultant extreme hull shape was not popular, and subsequent designs had a maximum beam of around 6ft 6ins, some 18ins wider than the "IX".

The general trend in hull shapes has always been influenced by the sailing waters. Jack Holt predominantly designed for Ranelagh, which for years was the stronghold of the class. The demand was for boats that could tack quickly and accelerate in gusts. While the National Championships were held on the sea, the majority of sailing was inland. With the advent of the Silver Tiller circuit however, the class found it necessary to produce designs that were a better compromise for sailing in all conditions, whether inland or at sea.

It has often been commented upon that in spite of the many supposedly different hull shapes in the class, the racing is very close. It seems strange that some supposedly one-design classes fight over a millimetre or two in the beam or on the rocker, while in the Merlin Rocket, differences can be measured in inches! The truth is that today's Merlin Rocket, or even the Merlin Rocket of the 1970s, is an efficient hull shape that has evolved over the years. More important, however, is that the class has been fortunate in the last decade to have had designers who have generated designs which have all made progressions along the learning curve. The refinements to the basic shape have often been extremely small, necessitating in some cases only the addition of a strip of ply on sections of some of the frames over which the previous design was built.

In this way, the class has benefited from the confidence of knowing that the hulls were not quickly going out of date, while development has continued at a steady pace.

To date, sixty-one designers have tried their hand at designing Merlin Rockets. Some have met with a great deal of success, while others have produced disasters. It is extremely likely that some very fast designs have vanished into obscurity for reasons other than their hull shape. Many one-offs were amateurly built. Innovative helmsmen/designers often could not justify the risk financially of having a one-off hull built professionally and with the best rig available. As a consequence, such boats may never have had the vital edge in boat-speed to bring them to the front of the fleet.

Beat-Nik, one of the Debenham & Truman designed "Surf Scooters," which David Child raced successfully at four consecutive Championships in the 1960s.

Rowan Ayres' *Zigger Zagger,* a standard Proctor "Mk. IXb". Note the softer turns on the bilge compared to the "Mk. IX."
Photograph by Guy Gurney

Restless IV and Brian Southcott, one of the reasons for the popularity of the Proctor "Mk IX," the design which dominated the class for ten years.
Photograph by Guy Gurney

The wide transom and flat sections of Joe Richard's "Dumper Truck" design.
Photograph by David Eberlin

It is impossible in this book to mention and comment on all the designs, for reasons of lack of space and information. More than one design has been significantly altered during construction, with the result that only the boatbuilder really knows what shape it is. Not all boats are even symmetrical! However, included in this chapter is a review of some of the better known designs and their background, along with a few of the stranger one-off creations, which gives a good indication of how the shape of the boat has been conceived, and changed in subsequent designs. It is interesting to note that many of the designers have very similar aims, but have different interpretations of the required hull shape. One hopes it will be ever thus!

Glossary
Before we become too involved in explanations of the designers' variations and creations, a few definitions of the terms used may well help to unravel a few of the mysteries that surround boat designing.

Bilge. The bilge of the boat is basically the point on the hull where the flat bottom section of the hull becomes the side of the hull. If a boat is constructed with a single chine (such as the "Mirror" or "Hornet"), the chine is the bilge. On a Merlin Rocket, this definition point on the hull is not so apparent but when viewing a hull's transom, it is usually possible to discern a "kink" somewhere between two planks. If a bilge is described as "slack" or "rounded" then the change is gradual, indeed the hull may be a very fair curve from the keel to the gunwhale. If a hull is described as powerful, then the bilge is usually more prominent (or "firm"), producing a flatter bottom to the boat.

In the last ten years there have been a few one-off Merlin Rockets created by National 12 designers. Rob Peebles' contribution was "Radical Posture," which had the appearance of a big National 12, having a very small jib and mast positioned well forward. In its time it has caused a few upsets at Open Meetings in the hands of Nick and Rob Martin, but has also given Nick a few surprises in return!

Photograph by Ian Holt

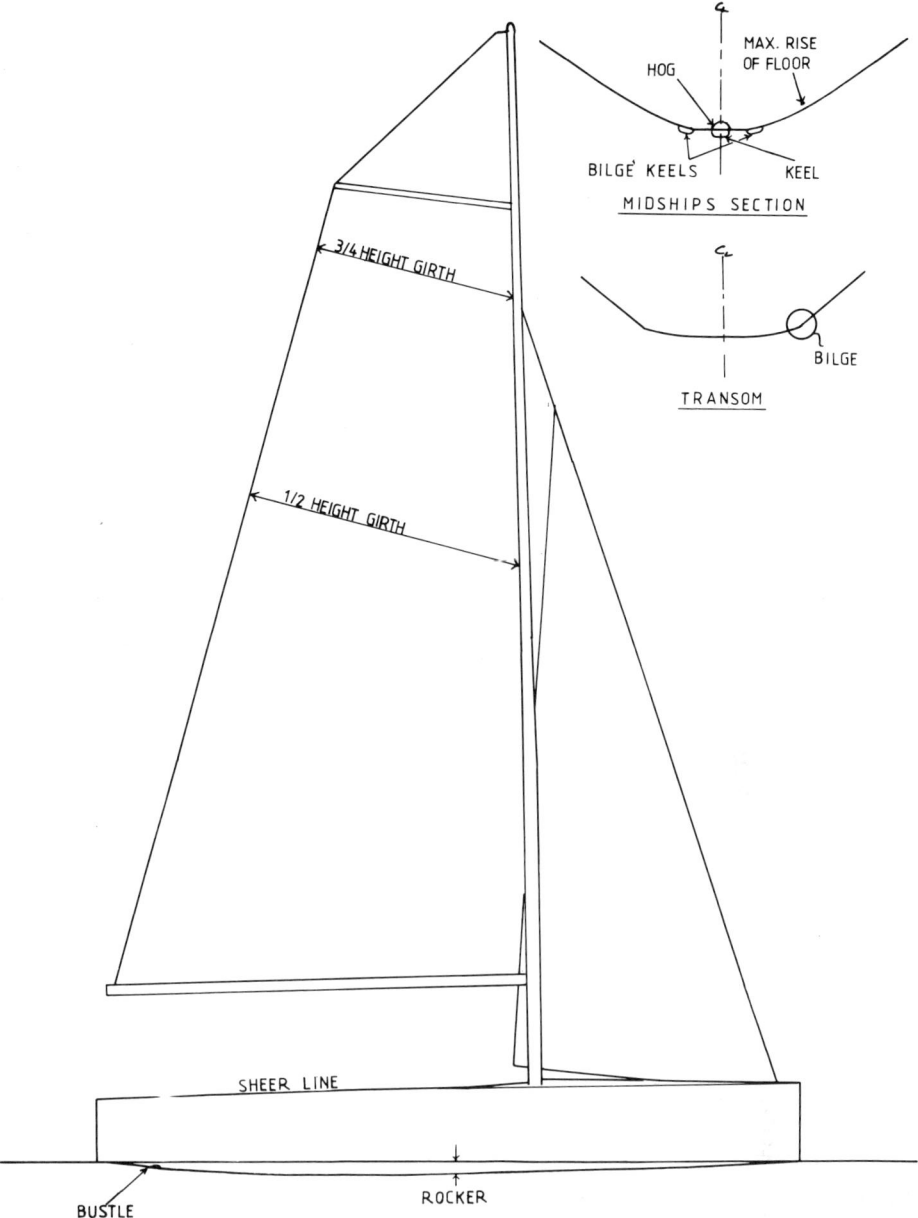

Rocker. The rocker of a boat is a measure of the curvature in the keel line, between stem and transom, when viewed from the side. If an imaginary line is drawn from the bottom of the stem to the bottom of the transom, then the amount of rocker in the boat is the measurement from this line to the deepest part of the keel line. As a guide, this is typically in the order of 6 inches. The position of this maximum value is also important to the design, as it affects how curved the keel line is on either side of this point. If the maximum rocker point is under the mast, then the keel line up to the bow will have more curvature than the run to the transom. This is typically the case in Merlin Rockets, as most designers have aimed at a straight run to the transom to help planing.

Bustle. If a boat is described as having a bustle, this means that the hull has fuller underwater sections near the stern of the boat, which has the effect of increasing the displacement, or weight-carrying potential of the hull. When viewing such a hull from the side, the keel line will appear more curved at the aft end than on other boats.

Rise of Floor. The rules of the Class state that the midships cross-section of the hull (a view of the hull when it is sliced open 7 feet from the transom) must pass outside an imaginary point, defined relative to the centreline of the hull. The aim of this rule is to prevent a hull which is so narrow as to be deemed unseamanlike, as the narrower a boat is on the waterline, the less stable it becomes. Experience has shown that the hulls that are designed to the limit of this rule, i.e. are as narrow as possible, are the fastest in the class. Some are also the tippiest, though this factor is also dependent upon the shape of the bow and stern.

Prismatic Coefficient. The prismatic coefficient is a measure of the fullness of a boat's underwater sections. Taking a hull's maximum waterline beam, maximum waterline length and maximum draught, a box constructed from these three values would have a prismatic coefficient of 1.0. The boat's coefficient is the percentage of the volume of water that it displaces out of this "box," and is also a measure of how the buoyancy is distributed in the boat, as a high prismatic coefficient means the boat has full, and therefore buoyant, ends.

Garboard Plank. The garboard plank is the bottom plank on either side of the keel.

Ian Proctor 1952-1971

From the time when the Merlin and the Rocket classes came together, right up until the sudden demand for wide-beamed hulls, Ian Proctor had a near monopoly on the class, designing some 18 Merlin Rocket variations.

Of Ian Proctor's designs, the most famous was the "Mark IX". In its early days it gained a reputation for being difficult to handle, a statement some people believe to be justified although others believe to have been popularised to deter others from ordering this design. The "Mark IX" was designed with a long slicing bow, a flat run aft and firm bilges. Moderately low wetted surface area for light weather performance coupled with characteristics of lift and a low-drag run to achieve high planing performance, gave a good all-rounder.

The "Mark IXB" was a direct development of the "IX" with increased flare above the waterline to increase the sitting-out power and dryness of the hull. The turn of the bilge in the stern section was rounded so that the stern would spin more easily when short-tacking. It also had the effect of reducing the emphatic stern wave when planing at high speed. Wetted surface was still the minimum compatible with a hull to provide dynamic lift for planing, with more power than the "IX". The "Mark IXC" was similar to the "IXB" with more flare to increase the sitting-out power. The "Mark XI" which won the 1959 Championships was based upon the "IX", but was not as successful as the "IXB". It was supposed to be a "IX" with easier handling characteristics, designed in expectation of some traditionally heavy weather championship sailing at Whitstable the following year. The lesson learned was that if you wanted to win, be brave and sail a "IX" – they won 5 of the next 6 championships.

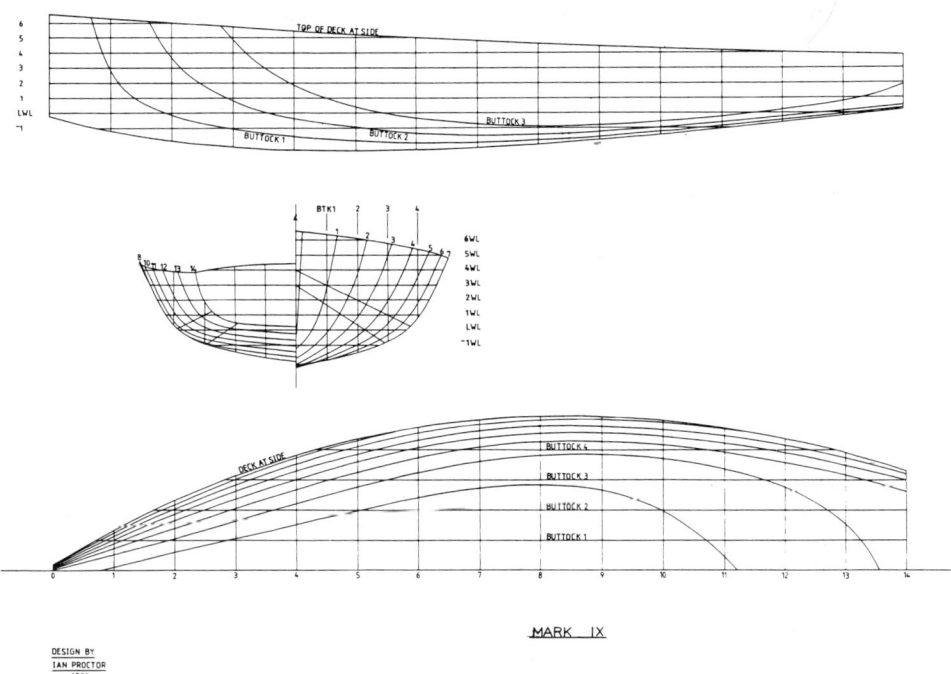

MARK IX

DESIGN BY
IAN PROCTOR
1955

The "Mark XII" was designed primarily as an inland water performer and was not as powerful as the "IXs". Each plank was treated separately rather than collectively as a planing section. The roundness of the sections gave a low wetted surface even when heeled and this was incorporated without spoiling the off-the-wind performance in a blow. With a long slim bow to slice through waves when sailing to windward, the design gave quick tacking and good acceleration in intermittent winds. This design won the light weather 1964 championships and 3 Silver Tiller series and was extremely popular with the new reservoir clubs which sprang up in the 1960s.

Martin Jones 1966-1972

The "Xpectant" design of Martin Jones was derived from the successful National 12, *Lucky Number*, and had a fine "V'd" bow, round midship section and firm flat run aft. The "V'd" bow gave an easy motion through waves and a good performance to windward while the rounded midship section gave maximum buoyancy and therefore reduced wetted surface. The flat run aft made for a stable boat downwind, while to help sitting-out power the hull was well-flared, but because the flair was all above the waterline, there was no drag penalty.

The "Xpectant" was the first Merlin to be designed with the planks drawn out by the designer. Previously, the boatbuilder had to interpret a set of smooth transverse sections and space the lands as he saw fit.

The most successful "Xpectant" at the championships in 1967 was *Krakatoa*, sailed by Alan Warren. The boat had originally been started for an owner in Bristol, who had run out of money. So the shell had been left in the shed, hung up in the loft. One day Alan and his father arrived at Rowsell's yard, saw he shell, and offered £70 for it. Alan's father finished the shell himself and many argue that boat should have won that year at Poole. In fact, Alan won the first two races and then came 2nd. David Potter in a Proctor "IXB" equalled this score and all depended on the last race. Potter won this to take the championship, but many thought he was over the line at the start and that *Krakatoa* should have been the champion boat.

Furious, a highly successful "Xpectant," designed by Martin Jones.

Photograph by Guy Gurney

"Xpectation" was a development of this design with even more beam for greater sitting-out power together with a slight slackening of the bilge aft, otherwise the underwater shape was substantially the same in both boats. The slacker bilge aft was intended to reduce drag when sailing slightly heeled, particularly advantageous to windward; there was also a slight reduction in wetted area and downwind performance was unaffected. However, the "Xpectation" was not a popular design.

Tom Booth 1965-1972

Tom Booth was a Navy boffin, involved with underwater warfare. He was initially involved with the National 12 class before he moved into Merlins. His Merlin Rocket designs were aimed at a range of crew weights of 150kgs or 22½ stone (to suit himself) to 170kgs or 27 stone (to suit Spud Rowsell) and all were designed to perform well at sea and in the confined waters of the Exe estuary. His first design was "Intrepid," a copy of the Proctor "IX" and was commissioned by Spud Rowsell because Spud couldn't obtain

The remarkable "Outrage" design of Tom Booth. Only six were built, but every one seemed ▶ to go well in any conditions. Here, Chris Rathbone is seen sailing *Gigolo*

Photograph by Pat Blake

a licence to build any of the Proctor designs. "Intrepid" had markedly "V" sections, and performed well, but she convinced Tom that heavy-weights would be better served by lower wetted area and more flare than was then customary. From these observations, Tom designed "Rampage," so named from the dictionary definition "to go about wildly," which performed excellently in the Exe estuary, but was too full forward for the sea, causing excessive slamming upwind.

Her successor, "Rage," built with a slimmer bow, influenced by Michael Jackson's "Sugar Plum," gave Spud his first win in a championship race, and also a considerable order book. "Outrage" was a production version of "Rage," being slightly wider at 6ft, and having a slight hollow in the bow. *Outrage* and her sister ship, *Gigolo*, were superb to windward at sea and achieved the objective of a boat in which heavy-weights could win in light as well as heavy weather.

"Courageous" was again similar but wider still at 6ft 8in, and the displacement was less concentrated in the centre so that she planed more rapidly. Given a lower aspect ratio rig, she could be raced successfully with crew weights as low as 140kgs or 22 stone. The "Courageous" design came 2nd and 9th in the famous Pwllheli Championships in 1970 and the "Outrage" designs were 3rd and 6th.

Tony Watts 1968-1973

For a while, some of the most popular types of Merlin Rocket were the "Wot" series, designed by Tony Watts and built by John Freeman. The design was developed from the original "Wotnot," and progressed to the "Wotbeta," "Wotdelta" and "Wotgamma."

The original "Wotnot" was one of the first of the wide designs intended to be a good all-round boat for medium weight crews, and with its wide beam giving sufficient

Twenty years of progress: the 4' 7" wide *Sealgh*, an early Holt design, alongside the 6' 8" wide *Krakawot*, one of the "Wotnot" designs from Tony Watts, in which Alan Warren won the 1969 Championships. Note the torches on the lighting set!

power for lightweights to be competitive in a breeze, conditions in which the boat excelled. The keel rocker was moderate, giving a long run aft and with its fine entry the boat had good windward performance.

The variations on his original design were aimed to either increase the weight-carrying ability of the boat or to improve its light-weather performance. In fact, these objectives went hand-in-hand and were achieved by minor modifications to the keel rocker and/or the sections amidships. The good heavy-weather performance arose largely because of the smooth shape of the hull which made handling easy and vice-free in these conditions. Based at Shoreham, a part of the coast noted for strong winds and waves, Tony believed that to win you must stay upright!

The "Gamma" development of the basic design (by modifying the original building jig) had reached a point where little advantage could be gained by making further alterations, and so the "Rapidity" appeared as an alternative concept. It had a "V" configuration, but the "V" disappeared in a slight bustle near the transom where the garboard planks were flat. The entry was fairly fine and there was a long clean run aft. The width was not extreme and approximated to 6ft 8ins. The rocker was more of a fair continuous curve throughout the length of the hull and was designed to carry the big chaps.

The verdict of history on the Watts designs is that they proved a powerful, easy-to-sail boat for light-weights and novices, but when narrower waterline beams came in with the Morrison era, they did not have the speed to survive in the 1970s.

Greg Gregory 1970-1979

The "Ghost Rider" was an interesting example of a boat designed to very specific instructions from the owner, in this case David Robinson. David's particular problem was a lightweight helm and a heavy crew. Greg's answer was a total departure from the

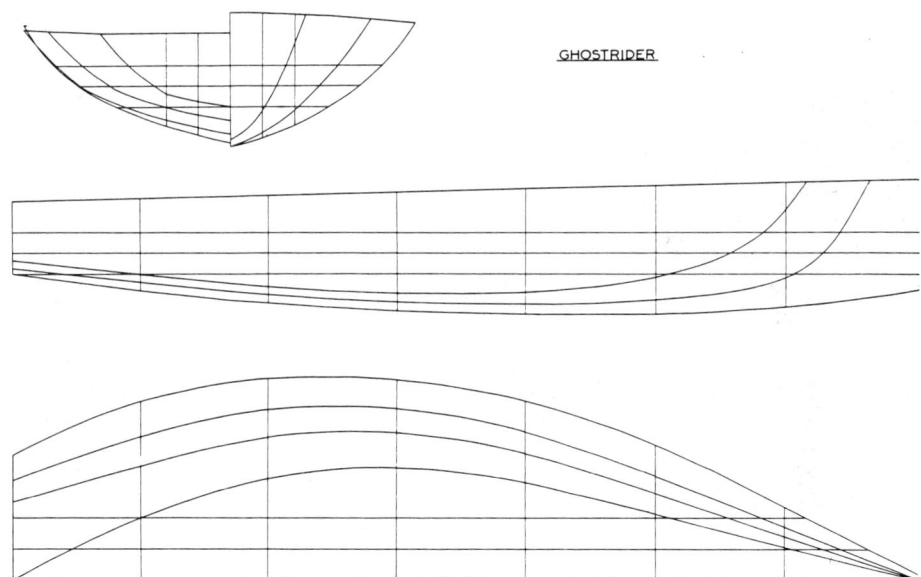

GHOSTRIDER

traditional Merlin Rocket shape, drawing a hull with very V'd cross sections and a tucked in transom, and he gave strict instructions to David Robinson on the rig, weight of fittings and sail plan. Rowsells were given the plans, which had them shaking their heads in disbelief! However, they stuck to the drawings and produced this very strange boat which looked as if it could plane on either side of the hull. History showed that it was extremely successful and order began to pour in. This enabled a few "variations" to be tried, but it was widely believed that any "Ghost Rider" not built exactly to the plans, i.e. with maximum rise of floor, was inferior. Certainly, David Robinson insisted that this was true. Many people still believe that the "Ghost Rider," as originally drawn, is one of the fastest hulls available for lightweights. The original "Ghost Rider" should have won the 1970 championships, but Robinson broke a rudder in one of the races. He sold the boat to obtain enough money for a deposit on a house, then one year later phoned Spud and asked for an identical boat. It was only then that it was realised that the original frames no longer existed as Spud by this time had modified the design to cater for the "heavies" in the class.

Gregory's second design was the "Echo" for the 1973 championships at Poole. Basically, it was a round-sectioned development of the "Ghost Rider" with a full, shallow entry and narrow rounded transom. On smooth water, this design shared the characteristics of the "Ghost Rider" but slammed badly when sailing to windward against a short chop, and therefore quickly earned a reputation as a bad seaboat. A full bow is not usually associated with nose-diving tendencies, but in the case of "Echo," the extra resistance when the bow became immersed made the boat difficult to control in strong winds, especially in waves. The Poole championships effectively killed off this design, as a number of pundits, including local star, Rodney Pattisson, failed to do well using the design. The last "Ghost Rider" to be built was in 1979.

Keith Callaghan 1966-1978

As Pat Blake's crew for four years, Keith's philosophy was that inland you must point to get away from the crowd and at sea you must get to the windward mark first, because a good spinnaker hoist by the crew just then could double your lead.

The "Hornblower" was designed by Keith Callaghan for the 1972 season, and in that year finished 4th in the National Championships and 2nd in both the Silver Tiller and Golden Touch series. The boat had a very long fine entry, with the maximum waterline beam situated at the helmsman's position. The powerful aft sections were very flat at the centreline, with a rounded turn of bilge. The overall effect was that of a very "smooth" hull shape, with no hard edges. The design went well in a blow but stuck in light airs.

"Hexagon" appeared at the beginning of the 1973 season, and proved to be Callaghan's most successful design. In that year, "Hexagons" were 2nd in the National Championships, 4th in the Inland Championships and 1st in the Silver Tiller series. Laurie Smith and Pat Blake scored 2nd and 3rd places overall in the 1974 Pwllheli championships and Blake again won the Silver Tiller. The hull shape was similar to "Hornblower" but had the waterline beam reduced at each section to reduce wetted area, a "bustle" incorporated in the aft run, to aid performance at high sub-planing speeds, and the bow sections made more "U." Finally, the overall beam was increased slightly to 6ft 10ins to counteract the rather less powerful hull shape.

Kevin Haynes sailing the "Ghost Rider" design, *Phantom Rider*. The success of this boat was due in no small way to the skills of Kevin, demonstrated here in this photograph taken at Salcombe. This boat won in its time Salcombe Week, The Silver Tiller and the Inland Championships
Photograph by Robert O'Neill

Keith Callaghan, crewing for Colin Humphreys.

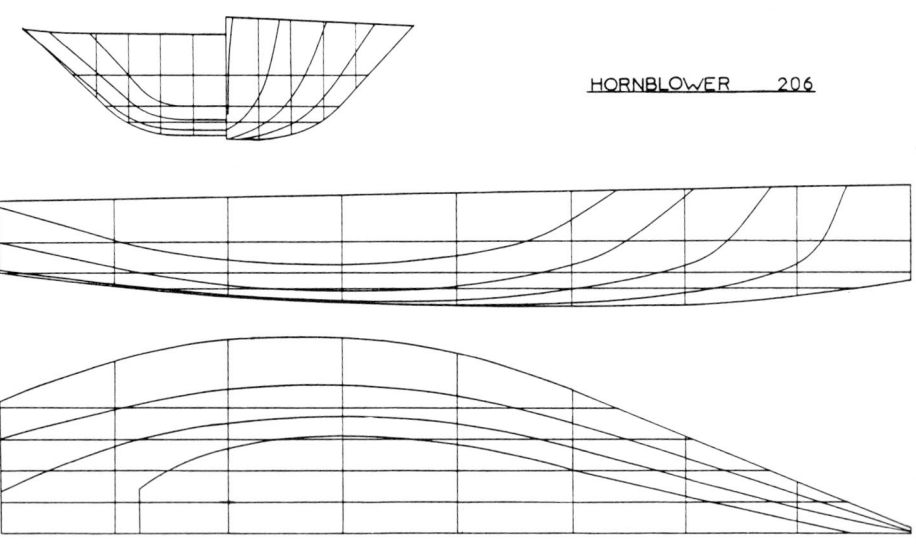

HORNBLOWER 206

15-9-72

72

It was rather difficult to compare the performance of the two designs, as they were so similar, but the "Hexagon" appeared to be marginally faster in winds below Force 3 and as fast as "Hornblower" in stronger winds.

The "Hysteria" design was produced for the 1974 season. It was basically similar to the "Hexagon" but had a narrower waterline, even more "U" sectioned in the bows below the waterline and less bustle aft. These modifications gave less wetted surface area and a slightly more manageable hull form, but resulted in a hull that would not carry quite so much weight, about 2 stones less. Vernon Ralston came 6th in the 1975 and 1976 championships, and another "Hysteria" sailed by Colin Humphreys came 4th in 1976.

For the 1977 championships at Hayling Island, said to be one of the windiest spots on the South Coast, Callaghan produced for Colin Humphreys his last design, the "Hazard." Built by Aln Boatyard (who had taken over Callaghan's designs after the "Hexagon" when Spud Rowsell had decided to keep to Morrison designs), the "Hazard" was a very stable boat. She was designed to keep upright at Hayling Island and, as so often happens in a desire to produce stability, speed suffered.

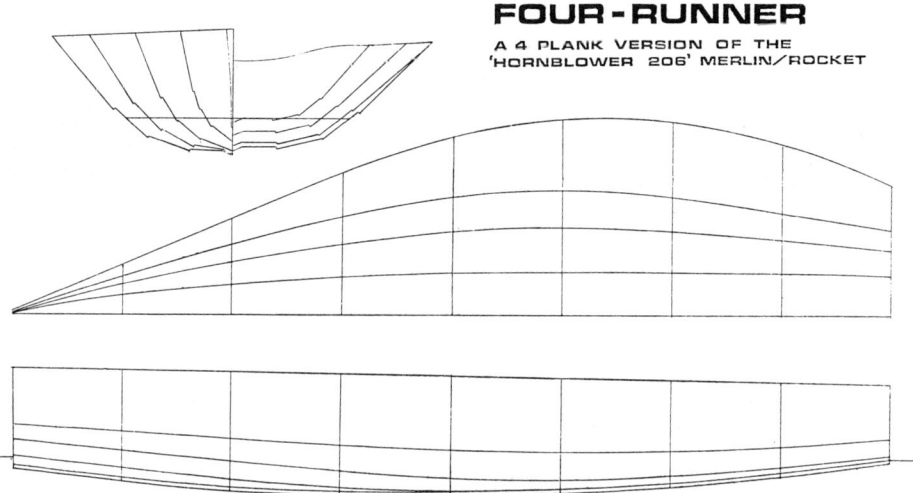

FOUR-RUNNER
A 4 PLANK VERSION OF THE 'HORNBLOWER 206' MERLIN/ROCKET

Disillusioned at the failure of his ideas to build GRP Merlin Rockets based on a four-plank design and eventually to develop smooth skin hulls, Callaghan left the class. His designs however, still succeed, particularly at club level inland.

Stephen Jones 1975

Some Merlin Rockets have been singularly unsuccessful, and one of the most interesting within this category must be *Shaft*. David Robinson, he of "Ghost Rider" fame, had been racing the Stephen Jones designed quarter-tonner *Wings* very successfully in the early 1970's. From this association came an agreement that Stephen would design David a new Merlin Rocket which would be somewhat "different." The most striking feature of the design was the bow section. It was so thin that there was no apparent buoyancy anywhere in the forward sections until the water reached the sections under the mast. With a wide overall beam plus humped decks, a pinched in

The razor sharp bows of *Shaft*, the Stephen Jones design.

Photograph by Robert O'Neill

transom, the hull was a mass of curves in all directions. Stephen was most emphatic that a Merlin Rocket must have U-sections and this was followed through to the extent that after the keel band was fitted to the hull, it was then faired into the hull using plastic padding on either side, so that the bow sections were completely smooth. The stem was incredibly fine by Merlin Rocket standards, with the jib tack in front of the spinnaker chute. The reverse sheer and hollow deckline left everyone wondering where to start comparisons with the rest of the fleet.

As for the sailing, it appeared quite satisfactory in light winds, but was quite dramatic in a breeze. Whilst the boat would plane flat and level, it would furrow into the water, rather than go over the waves. To overcome this problem, an illegal (desperate boats call for desperate measures) wedge made from isopon was laid onto the planks at the stern to "bend" them straighter. Unfortunately, this was a waste of isopon because the performance did not change.

This one boat included so many radical ideas that it was difficult to assess which might have helped performance and which hindered it. David used to complain that he would be planing quite happily, except for the entire fleet sailing away from him, and the next thing he could remember was his head coming to the surface as once again *Shaft* bit the dust. With no "boat" forward of the mast, there was virtually no warning prior to a nose-dive or broach. David's next boat was an "NSM" . . . .

Guy Winder 1973-1983

Guy Winder's first Merlin Rocket, No. 2778 *Wideguy,* was based on the "September Girl," but because of his 19½-20 stone crew weight, he decided to increase the beam to 7 feet. Increasing the flare, yet retaining the same hull depth, would have increased wetted area at planing speeds and would have increased it when heeled in very light winds. Thus, Guy decided to flatten the hull only slightly and increase the freeboard to obtain the increase in beam. He reduced the depth of stem and stern until the area presented to a beam wind was identical to "September Girl." The reverse sheer gave the boat a distinctive (to Keith Callaghan – slug-like) appearance.

The hull was planked with the best light-weight 6mm Brunzeel, the deck layout was designed for great strength in the mast area and the windage kept to a minimum by reducing the gunwale width to a minimum fore and aft of the sitting positions. The shrouds were continued to a remotely controlled winch at the mast-step. Seven pounds of correctors were required.

No. 2887, *Late Night Extra,* differed from the first boat in having a finer entry, less wetted area, the centre of buoyancy 4ins further aft, the chine made more pronounced, and the transom deepened slightly but reduced in width. It was not possible to obtain the light-weight Brunzeel ply, so 6mm solid mahogany was used. Extra struts were incorporated into the hull to increase stiffness, but the finished hull was a little overweight and thought to lack the great stiffness of the first. A similar shroud arrangement was fitted, Guy's belief was that by taking the shrouds to the foot of the mast, the thrust load on the keel is opposed by shroud tension and the possibility of the keel failure is virtually eliminated. The compression stresses across the mast gate must be opposed, however, and once again the hull was built very strongly in this area.

Guy followed these with the "Winder Box" and a few variations, but his most interesting design was the "Stiletto." The hull had an extremely wide flat transom, with a delta-shaped waterline section. The idea was that the boat should be sailed slightly heeled when going to windward with the waterline running from the stem to one corner of the transom. To match this "crabbing" angle of sailing, the centreboard originally fitted in the boat could gybe to line up with the angled waterline. To cut a long story short, this hull didn't work, and the boat underwent some drastic surgery, with the transom taken off twice and the planks pulled in to reduce the width and wetted area of the aft sections. The bow was also made deeper. The results of this boat have been very erratic but its moment of glory came in 1984 when Guy won the last race of the Nationals to round off an otherwise very depressing week.

Hemlock, one of Guy Winder's "Disguys" designs, which came 3rd overall at the 1979 National Championships in the hands of Graham Pike and Tessa Godfrey.

Photograph by David Eberlin

Rob Inglis 1974-1982

During the winter of 1973, Rob Inglis designed a new Merlin Rocket, *Risk*, and launched it in Spring 1974. Its most striking features were the low amount of rocker forward, the very fine and long entry, and the very fine U-shaped bow section. These had the effect of (a) keeping the centre of buoyancy well aft, thus lowering wave making resistance, producing high dynamic lift, which promoted early planing and reduced the tendency of the boat to bury its bow; and (b) keeping stem immersion high, which improved windward performance, slightly reducing wetted area forward.

The fairly full midship sections were tight on the rise of floor limit and flared to an overall beam of 6ft 10in. The slightly V'd run aft did not feature the then currently fashionable bustle, as Rob believed this reduced speed when planing. The transom had fairly slack bilges, which eliminated any tendency for the boat to drag the transom, yet did not adversely affect the planing performance.

View of the narrow transom belonging to the "Bad Company" design.

Following a study at University College, London, the most striking discovery was the large part played by sail drag when beating, an indication that sail shape was more important than hull shape when sailing to windward. Also, a reduction of wetted surface area and hence skin friction generally gave the largest improvement on the run.

The second phase of the project entailed representing the hull of a Merlin Rocket on computer. This enabled a much larger range of hull shapes to be examined before making the final choice. It was possible, using this facility, to change a single point on the hull and to have not only a visual image of the boat but also immediate information on

The famous duo of Spud Rowsell and Jon Turner powering down a reach at Salcombe.
Photograph by P. Blake

Paul Seddon and Stuart Aston keeping their boat perfectly upright at a recent open meeting at Upper Thames SC.

Photograph by Ian Holt

draught, trim, displacement, wetted surface area, prismatic coefficient, longitudinal centre of buoyancy and initial stability for a range of crew weights. If one wanted more information the boat could be heeled or the crew moved fore or aft to see what happened to wetted surface area and trim. Wave making resistance was catered for by keeing the entry fine and choosing what was considered to be an optimum prismatic coefficient.

The outcome of this work was "Bad Company," which at the end of the 1970's was winning more Silver Tiller meetings than any other design. However, these boats have never been prominent at championships.

Phil Morrison 1968-Present

If Ian Proctor stood out in the past as the primary designer within the class, his place in the present has been emphatically taken over by Phil Morrison.

In September 1968, Phil designed a Merlin Rocket called *September*. Having previously designed a famous National 12, "China Doll," Phil decided to make some changes to this concept which he incorporated in "September" (and a National 12

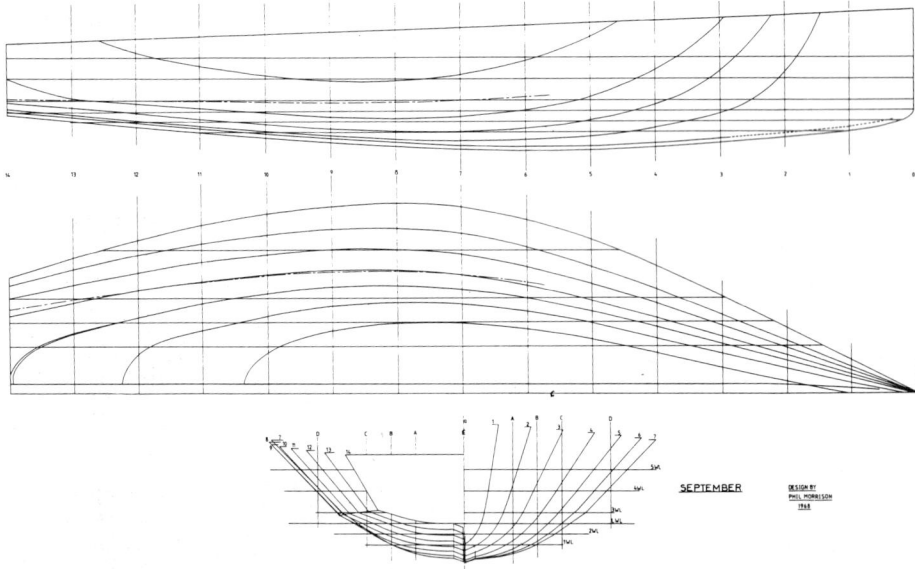

called *5 Star*). These included making the ends very fine and incorporating a slight hollow in the run aft. This second modification had come as a result of spending ages looking at Mike Jackson's National 12 *March Hare* and deciding that the secret of its speed lay in a slight hollow in the aft section.

Pat Jones built another "September," No. 2311, but unfortunately positioned the frames in the wrong place at the aft end, and constructed a bustle instead of a hollow in the run. This boat was affectionately referred to as *Sceptic*. Phil sailed *September* in the 1969 and 1970 championships where he showed promising form, but attention was very much focussed on the Watt's and Jones' designs and the new *Ghost Rider*.

Then, in 1970, Peter Doughty asked Phil to design "September Girl," which Peter wanted to be more precisely based on the National 12 "China Doll." This was called

Moonlight Flit and was built a year before Phil's own *September Girl*. Spud built *Moonlight Flit* and one other, and took one out for sail with Jonathon Turner before the owner arrived to take delivery. So impressed was he that Spud actually phoned up the owner to try to dissuade him from collecting it. Being unsuccessful in this ploy, Spud built himself *Philistine*.

It was not until the Plymouth Championships in 1971 where Spud and Phil came a close second and third overall, in *Philistine* and *September Girl*, that the design became popular. The demand for an even wider version was evident however, if the "Ghost Rider" was to be beaten. Further, David Spiers sailing his Jackson "Superstition" *Will Shakespier*, had struggled against the *Ghost Rider* and *September Girl*, so Morrison designed two boats for the 1972 championships. The first was "Phantom Kipper," simply a flared out "September Girl" with an extra "kipper" plank. The concept for these designs was simple; the waterlines were kept as slim as possible without any hollows in the bow, flat garboards under the mast for a good planing performance, and sufficient buoyancy in the sections to keep the wetted area respectable.

The weak points in the design were probably windward work in a seaway as the full bow section tended to slam unless sat on firmly, at which point the waves started to enter the boat via the spinnaker chute and foredeck. The other problem area was close reaching where "Ghost Riders" definitely had an edge. Fortunately, this didn't often occur at a championship, where the reaches were normally broader.

His second design for 1972 was "Satisfaction," designed for the likes of Spud Rowsell and other well proportioned gentlemen in the class who required a good weight carrier. Basically, a bit more rounded at the back with the corners knocked off, it proved extremely successful but resulted in the heavyweights actually having to sit out quite

A view from above of a "Smokers Satisfaction," giving an impression of the fine bows and generally curved lines of the design.

Photograph by Robert O'Neill

hard in a breeze, so they all went back to Phil asking for a bit more beam. The result of this was the "Smokers Satisfaction" design for the 1974 season. This design could be summed up as an extremely good all-rounder but couldn't excell in any particular condition.

At the same time, Phil designed "Infidel" for himself. This was actually his first pure Merlin Rocket design, as opposed to being derived from any of his National 12 developments. Strictly for lightweights, 22 stone was the maximum that it could carry. As lightweights tended to get knocked about in a sea, Phil indulged a little hollow in the bow waterlines to keep the bows immersed and generally reduced the buoyancy to maintain the sailing length. This hull proved very much a "horses for courses" boat, and was rather slow in light winds. Although the "Hooligan" was a refined version of the "Infidel," Phil eventually dropped this design philosophy as it appeared to have come up against a brick wall.

His next idea was the "Mustard Seed" and "Super Seed" hull. The idea behind these was to have a "gull-winged" midship section, i.e. the keel line was tucked up above the

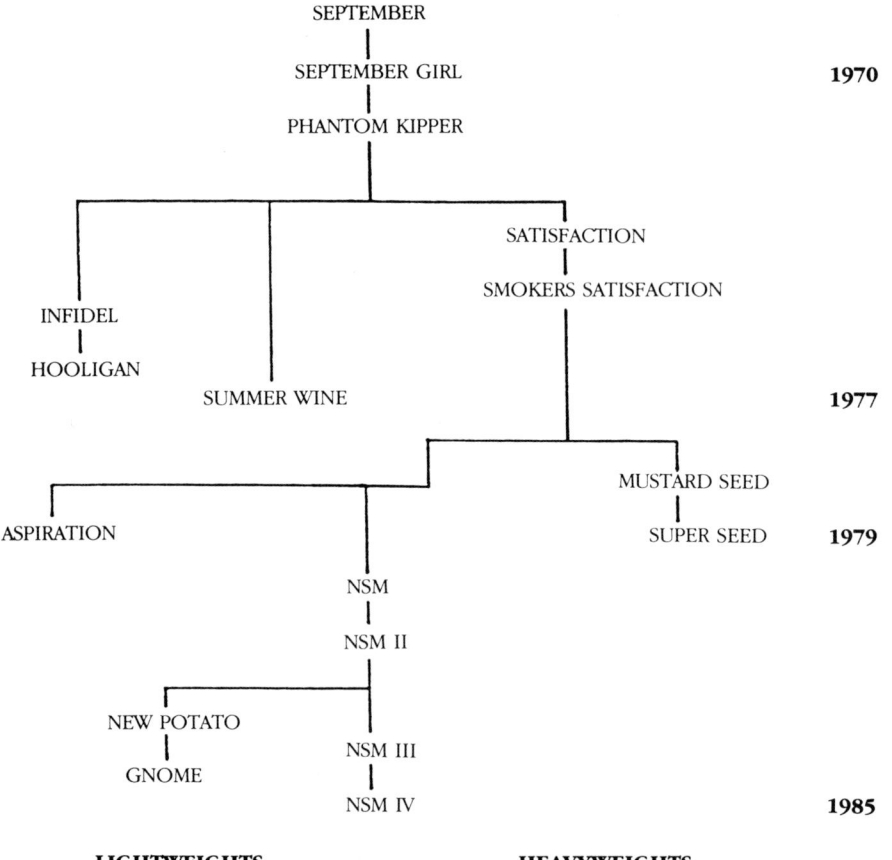

The Morrison Design Tree

82

outboard edge of the garboard plank. This in effect was a slight rule dodge as it raised the rise of floor measurement point on the skin. It also produced a small cavity under the hull, similar to some power boat hulls. Spud Rowsell won two races at the 1975 championships in a "Mustard Seed," but the feeling was that the design had a bit of speed hump. It was one of the few Merlin Rocket designs where there was a very noticeable difference between planing and not planing. It should be mentioned, however, that the two "Mustard Seeds" built by Bill Twine to this design, *Oberon* and *Quince*, both had good records, proving very fast on two-sail reaches.

After the 1975 championships, Phil introduced a new version, the "Super Seed," which he described as having a "Super Big Prismatic." The story of this boat could best be summed up by recalling that Spud abandoned it after Salcome Week in 1976, and borrowed Chris Andrews' *Fantasia*, a "Smokers Satisfaction" for the championships that year. Another brick wall had appeared!

Phil's rethink produced the "Summer Wine," which proved to be very much the shape of things to come. The hull was about as extreme as it was possible to go, with a very fine U-shaped bow and moderate to full stern. Phil confessed that it "can be a pig in strong winds," but the design revolutionised the Merlin's marginal planing performance.

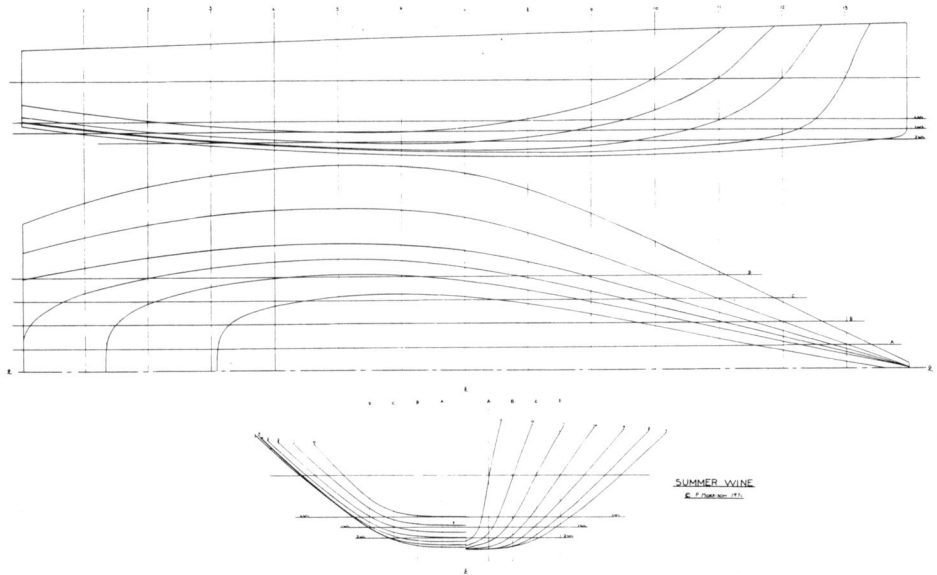

Arriving with this boat at the 1977 championships, Phil was perhaps unlucky to come up against Pat Blake in his extremely fast *After Myth*, which was superior to the "Wine" (and anything else) upwind in a breeze. Part of this problem could be attributed to the rig, which is discussed elsewhere in this book. Phil was renowned for not starting too well and usually spent most of his championship races overtaking everybody, though as Jon Turner recalled having crewed for him in two championships, Phil used to claim that the only way to advertise a boat was to start badly and then go past all your potential customers. Just for the record, the only time that Phil did manage to be on the start line at the gun he sank Gavin Willis, having put a large hole in his boat!

As a result of Phil's success with the "Wine," requests came in for a boat that would carry the heavy-weights through the water just as quickly. The result was a boat between the "Smokers Satisfaction" and the "Summer Wine," called "NSM" (New Smoking Material). Basically a flattened out hull with less rocker than the "Smokers Satisfaction"

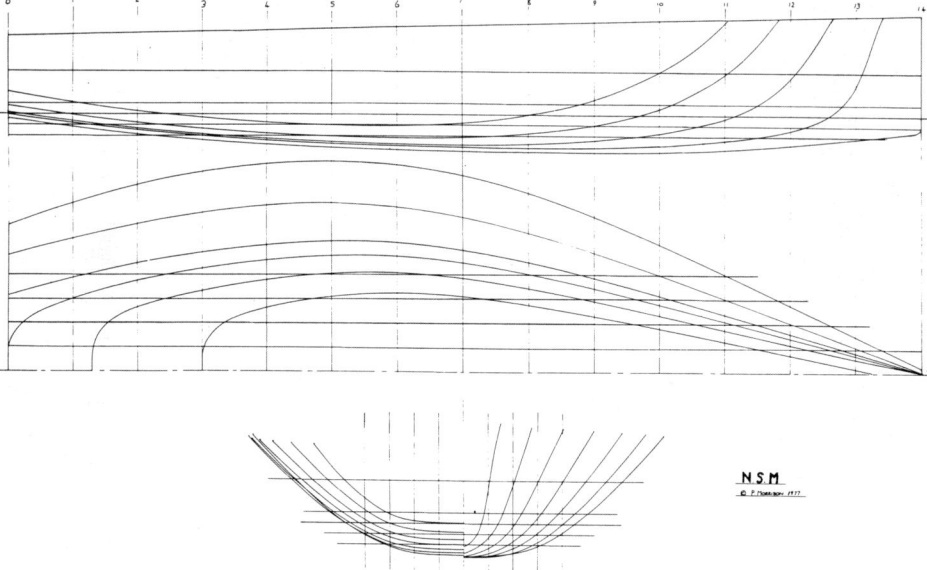

it was less of a compromise shape, aimed at keeping up with the "Summer Wine" in a breeze. With three out of the first six at the championships in 1978 to this design, it was immediately a success although it was admitted by Spud Rowsell, who won those championships in *Foot Loose,* that he wasn't sailing any faster than John Patterson in his "Winder Box." This design also temporarily brought about the premature, though only temporary, demise of the "Summer Wine" design.

The second owners of the original *Summer Wine* were Paddy Atkinson and Bob Kyle. Following two very promising championships with the boat in 1978 and 1979, they went to Phil and requested the ultimate planing Merlin Rocket. Phil's answer was "Aspiration," a genuine experiment in ignoring the rise of floor rule, basing his train of thoughts purely on a planing hull for lightweight crews. A huge hull, more commonly known as the *Iron Lung,* quickly became lost in obscurity for the simple reason that it really did not work.

The next design was a development of the "NSM," with slightly fuller sections, named the "NSM II." These two designs between them almost standardised the class for a couple of years in spite of the fact that Phil himself came second overall in 1982 with another new design, the "New Potato." This achievement was apparently completely ignored by the entire class, and still further ignored when Phil King won the Silver Tiller in 1984 with this boat, now three years old. For some strange reason no-one else was interested in the design, but instead the boat that came into vogue again in the early 1980's was the "Summer Wine." Phil personally put this down to desperation within the class, because they were all looking for something with which to beat the "NSM"

The bow of the "NSM" design, showing the fine conical bow sections, with V'd sections flattening out under the mast.
Photograph by David Eberlin

◀ Phil Morrison and the "NSM" *Second Chance.*
Photograph by David Eberlin

stranglehold, but weren't prepared to risk the "Potato" which appeared to be a bit extreme to their "NSM" minds. *Penelope*, a "Summer Wine" owned by Chris Haworth, won the Silver Tiller in 1983.

Phil and Jenny King sailing the Morrison design "New Potato," in which Phil won the Silver Tiller in 1984.

Photograph by Roger Lean-Vercoe

Two further designs have developed from the "Potato," the "Gnome," and the "NSM IV." The "Gnome" was built for the 1984 championships at Exmouth where Phil came second overall (again) and it then won the 1985 championship at Shoreham in the hands of David Robinson (each time with Nigel Appleton crewing). The "IV" was a further progression towards a still flatter general purpose hull shape, but again the changes were so small that the hull sections for the "I," "II" and "IV" are all on the same drawing, and in underwater sections very difficult to distinguish. The "IV" was given an increased overall beam which Phil thought the class was ready for, because the average all up crew weight continued to fall.

The "NSM III" appears to have never really existed apart from on some of Spud Rowsell's frames where a cosmetic change to the transom shape produced the *Black Adder*.

A good idea of the state of the class can be gained by examining Phil Morrison's current design philosophy. The changes that he is making to his "NSM" concept are very small and to generalise he has developed this design by only about half an inch (here and there) over seven years. That is very little by previous standards. The lightweights' alternative, the "Gnome," is a "New Potato" hull on a "Summer Wine" rocker line. Again, no big changes. More importantly, however, the two options on hull shape offered by Phil are very slowly coming towards each other. The changes being made to the "NSM" are all one way, making the hull a little bit fuller and flatter each time, which is making small steps towards the lightweights' hull. Clearly, Phil believes that this is the way to go, or if it isn't, he will succeed with this approach if everyone follows suit. If we all sail flatties then we will all go slowly in light winds, but very fast in a breeze. It appears that the very obvious speed advantages of the flat hulls are too great to ignore. The feeling in the class at present is that this is the type of hull required to win the Nationals which is what those who have any influence in design are interested in winning. It is interesting to note that these "NSM" changes are being categorised as new designs, whereas before, in the days of the "Smokers Satisfaction," larger variations were being tried out by the builders which were not designated as new hull designs. This could suggest that the Class is possibly approaching the "perfect" Merlin Rocket hull. Or are we?

Ian Holt 1983-Present

Since 1984, the only Merlins built that were not to one of Phil Morrison's designs have been those designed by Ian Holt. His first design, "Nice Legs," No. 3330, was very much a shot in the dark and the resultant appearance of the boat was somewhat unconventional. Nevertheless, the boat achieved some respectable results in the 1984 Silver Tiller series and was followed by "Once Bitten," No. 3355, with the changes to the design aimed at improving straight line speed. This aim was achieved at the expense of the hull's weight-carrying ability but in the hands of Alan and Martin Warren during the 1985 season it showed tremendous boat speed in a breeze – so long as it remained upright, a recurring fault which was diagnosed as a rudder problem.

Ian's third design was "Diamond Smiles," No. 3372, which was almost identical to "Once Bitten," but with a fraction more rocker at both ends of the hull. In the hands of Mark Littlejohn this boat finished 6th overall at the 1985 Championships, proving the boat's potential. However, it was not until 1986 that anyone placed an order for one of Ian's designs, possibly because of their previous lack of good results in big races.

Ian's first commission was for Nick Aubrey, who requested "something different from anything else" and received in response a modified "Diamond Smiles" with the emphasis on weight carrying ability, known as "ROTS." The fifth design was for the boatbuilder Alan Jackson, who wanted a boat essentially for inland sailing (doing well at Salcombe Week was high on his list of priorities) which would still be competitive at the Nationals.

It had become apparent that "Diamond Smiles" was a satisfactory championship design, but not versatile enough for inland sailing on restricted waters. This was caused by having a transom which was very flat for the first two planks on either side of the hull's centreline, and a large overall beam at the transom which resulted in too much wetted surface area and the gunwales becoming submerged at relatively small angles of heel. These characteristics were therefore reduced and the rocker increased at the aft end (by ½ inch) to help raise the transom in light conditions. The overall design philosophy of having a very flat forefoot (almost a hard chine forward of the mast) was maintained in all these designs, as Ian believed that this enhances the boat's reaching performance in strong winds.

Once Bitten, showing the very flat underwater sections in the bow.
Photograph by Ian Holt

Three photographs taken at the same part of a course during an Open Meeting at Queen Mary SC, showing the planing attitudes that different designs adopt at high speed. 3355 is *Once Bitten*, 3338 is *Uptown Girl*, a modified "NSM II" and 3297 is *"New Potato."*
Photograph by Ian Holt

CHAPTER 6

The Rig

So many features which are now regarded as commonplace in rigs started in the restricted classes, in particular the Merlin Rockets and National 12s. Looking back over the years to 1952, this is certainly true of metal masts and sail cloth development. When the Merlin Class was first conceived, the intention was for it to represent the absolute latest in technology. Its advanced features included very high aspect ratio rigs (considered an all important feature for catching the wind over the river banks, buildings and trees when sailing inland – particularly at Ranelagh) and rotating masts. A national daily newspaper stated at the time that with the aid of its revolutionary rig the Merlin could sail directly into the wind without tacking!

In the beginning, masts were made of wood and the sails were made of cotton. The masts were beautiful, delicate, inconsistent and an absolute bore at fitting out time. They would not bend in any reasonable way, so there was no thought of cutting sails to take advantage of the characteristics of the mast. The 25 feet tall mast was deck stepped, rotating on a ball and socket joint and it usually had three sets of diamond stays. It was a masterpiece of craftsmanship in wood, very deep in section and aerofoil shaped, designed so as to behave like a wing mast with particular emphasis on improving the efficiency of the mainsail above the jib overlap area, or slot.

In retrospect, the punishment these tall spruce masts would take before they broke seems amazing. During this era, getting a good mast for a racing dinghy was a real problem as good spruce was scarce and variable in quality. Masts often warped if left badly supported, or even standing in the boat on a sunny day. The cotton sails used on these masts would not withstand anything like the leech tensions that are applied today and the kicking strap was a modest affair, designed primarily to prevent a chinese gybe.

In 1949 lower rig heights were allowed, although the high aspect ratio rig was considered so efficient that the rules were worded to give a bonus of extra area to shorter masts. Most boats were rigged to take some advantage of the extra sail area, causing the gradual disappearance of the tall rotating masts. The current-day formulae for determining mast height and sail area were the result of a set of very effective trials commissioned by the Association and undertaken at Hayling Island by Beecher Moore and Jack Holt. One of the early boats to exploit this bonus was *Joy*, No. 68, owned by the brothers Geoffrey and Brian Saffrey Cooper. The section of mast chopped off has been retained for posterity as the trophy for the Class team racing championships.

Metal Masts

By 1952, there were indications to suggest that aluminium masts might be the thing of the future. The Firefly class, introduced by the YRA in 1946 and made by Fairey Aviation, had a metal mast. It also had an aluminium boom and a hot moulded plywood hull. The mast was made by Reynolds Aluminium, folded from a round tube. The maximum length of section which could be made in this way was around 16 feet, so the masts were in two sections, joined at the hounds. The tubes could not be tapered, and looked crude because they were in one straight length, so after a few years a tapered wooden topmast was introduced. The Firefly's mast was made of metal primarily for economy of production rather than for a performance advantage, as was the whole boat. The idea was to up-date the boatbuilding industry by utilising the production equipment and expertise developed in aircraft manufacture during the war.

In 1952 Ian Proctor was put in touch with Reynolds Aluminium by Alan Vines, a director of Fairey Aviation, to work with them on mast design. Together they developed a mast made from round tube which was taper drawn at the Redditch plant, now part of British Alcan. To this round tube was riveted an aluminium sail track. They made two masts, one for Ian's new Merlin *Cirrus*, No. 290, and one for Cliff Norbury's National 12, *Sheherazade*. These two boats were Ian's first foray into dinghy racing design, so new hull designs and new rigs were being tried out at the same time.

Ian and Cliff sailed *Cirrus* seriously for the first time at the National Championships at Poole that year, and discovered that the mast was initially a little too flexible sideways. The Class rules allowed only one set of diamond spreaders, so they fitted two sets of wires over the spreaders, one short pair covering about half the span, and one longer pair spanning the hounds to the gooseneck. They won the first race quite easily, although one of the diamond wires broke where it joined the rigging screw. After the race, the mast was taken out of the boat and carried to a shed to make a proper repair, a task performed before the rest of the fleet had come ashore. The mast was not re-stepped until the next day, by which time all the other competitors had been searching for the magic mast. Ian did the same thing the next day, just to keep everyone guessing.

Cirrus won the Championships and Cliff Norbury would have almost certainly won Burton Week in *Sheherazade* had he not had to miss the last race to sit an examination. Brian Rowsell sailed the boat in that race, finishing 3rd. This gave the boat enough points to win but as it had been sailed by two different helmsmen it instead finished 2nd overall. The success of these two boats obviously created a great deal of interest in masts and rigs, and considerable discussion as to the reasons for their speed.

Actually, the performance advantage resulted from two factors. Firstly, the metal masts were smaller in section than their wooden predecessors, producing less turbulence over the sail, and secondly they were lighter, the real importance of which was not appreciated until much later. However, by far the most important performance advantage came from the ability to control sail shape by bending the mast forward in the middle. For the first time it was possible to use the same mainsail over a wide variety of conditions, flattening it by bending the mast more as the wind increased. The sails designed for these new masts were cut with more round in the luff than usual, making them fuller for light winds but capable of being flattened in stronger winds. Some people suggested that the extra sail area gained by this added luff curvature was the main reason for the rig's success, and there were calls for the sail measurement rules to be changed to restrict the width at half height. However, this did not come until much later, when Terylene sails capable of supporting larger roaches were introduced.

Sail Development and Control

As with every class except the National 12s and International 14s, the Merlin Rocket Class's venture into Terylene was slow and cautious. The other two had the advantage of being pre-war classes, who did not have any restriction on materials as there had been no alternatives at the time of their evolvement. The first Terylene sails of any merit were those imported from the United States and which were used quite extensively in the National 12 class. This caused mixed feelings and a certain amount of resentment because the sails were extremely expensive. Ian Proctor, commenting on it in the 1956

Soo Mee, the Proctor "VI," in which John Oakley won the Championships in 1956. The photograph ▶ is a good illustration of the cotton sails that were used n those days, with the colour change in the lower half of the sails showing where they have become wet.
Photograph courtesy of J. Chippendale

Yachting World Annual, drew attention to the absurdity of paying more than £60 for a suit of sails in a class where the all up price for the boat was restricted to £140 by the class rules.

The price conscious members of the Merlin Rocket Class initially outlawed these Terylene sails, and some of the more enterprising owners tried to circumvent this by using sails of plasticised cotton made by Van Reeken of Holland. Sails from this cloth were of dubious technical merit and not without their own premium on price. Possibly, however, the reason for the change of policy within the Class came about following one wet and windy open meeting in the West Country, where Merlin Rockets and National 12s were racing together. At lunchtime, all the National 12 helmsmen, with their large-roached, drip-dry creations, were in the bar whilst the Merlin Rocket owners were panicking as to how they could get their sodden masses of cotton dry for the next race.

The introduction of synthetic fibres created quite a revolution in sailmaking. Some of the early sails were a total disaster because sailmakers failed to realise that they had to use a new technique of building up the shape. Bruce Banks, who was still a civil engineer at the time, took a particular interest in this. Sailmaker Colin Lucas was having some difficulty in adapting to the new material and he took Bruce into partnership with the main objective of building up Terylene sail technology.

Developments now occurred in the Merlin Rocket Class that transformed the rig which had remained largely unchanged for the previous ten years. Initially, the roach of the mainsail was increased by pushing out the bottom batten, as everyone felt that the

An early suit of Mountifield sails, showing how extra sail area was gained by pushing out the bottom batten.

Photograph courtesy of Ranelagh SC

top batten had to go from the luff to the leech (pushing out the bottom batten was first thought of in the 5-O-5 class). As all the battens were restricted to 3 feet in length, there didn't appear to be any changes that could possibly be made to the top section of the sail. Such sails were made by Banks, Ratsey, Leech, Mountifield, and the Dutch sail loft, Jongkind, who became involved in the Class having gained a good reputation for sails in this country through the Flying Dutchman class, where Keith Musto was using them. One of the first Merlin sailors to use the loft was Lionel Mendoza, from Wembley Sailing Club. Having regular business trips to Holland, he called in at the loft with details of the Merlin rig, and was made one of the first suits of sails to have the extra sail around the bottom batten. These sails were also, interestingly enough, cheaper than the equivalent suit of sails from an English sail loft, which helped to explain the popularity of a foreign sailmaker within the Class.

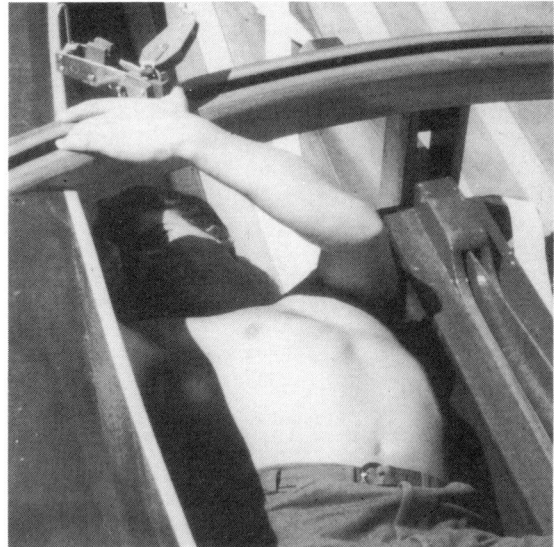

Ken Rose, fitting his mainsheet traveller to *Cha Cha*. The assembly consisted of a modified roller skate mounted in a tufnol traveller.

Photograph courtesy of Ken Rose

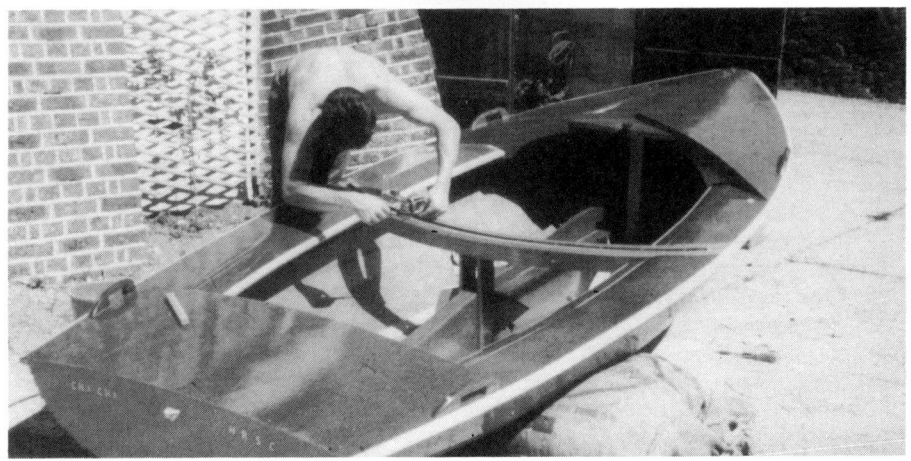

One of the most interesting rigs of that era was the one created by Ken Rose for *Cha Cha*, No. 1001. Ken (later to become firmly involved with sailmaking and to join Bruce Banks) had given a great deal of thought towards improved methods of control over the larger mainsails and decided that the best arrangement would be to use a curved mainsheet traveller at a radius of 4 feet from the mast. The traveller track came into the side decks approximately one foot aft of the chain plate, making the use of a kicking strap unnecessary. The traveller itself consisted of a laminated assembly of mahogany and tufnol which enclosed a roller skate with four little wheels. Unknown to Ken, Brian Saffrey Cooper's *Racketeer,* No. 863, which he and Alan Warren used to sail to and from open meetings, as they did not have a road trailer, had used a central mainsheet traveller the previous year. Brian's had not been radiused horizontally but vertically, with the result that the movement of the traveller altered leech tension rather than maintaining it constant. However, Alan Warren removed the centre traveller as it always succeeded in catching him around the ears, and they seemed to sail faster without it. About two years later, Alan copied and modified the centre post "invented" by Tom Lance at Sussex Motor YC. In Alan's opinion, if he had only made this post then as high as the current-day hoops, he would have saved much effort and trouble trying to make the early travellers work. It was not long after these early efforts appeared that Proctors designed a standard roller bearing traveller for dinghies.

Another innovation which was tried on *Cha Cha* was to use a tall, narrow jib made to the minimum proportion of the total sail area (20%). The tack of the jib could be attached to the deck in different positions over a total fore and aft range of about 18 inches. The idea was to vary slot widths to suit different wind strengths to a far greater degree than was possible by changing the sheeting position alone. In very light winds the jib would be tacked as far aft as possible for the narrowest slot, with the added effect of giving the helm a bit more feel by moving the centre of effort further aft.

Perhaps *Cha Cha's* most important and historic contribution to the Class was her spinnaker. Before 1959, the Class rules only allowed the spinnaker to be set with both sheets and halyard on the same side of the forestay. Thus it could be used for running only and little attempt had been made to improve its efficiency of shape. When the rule was changed to allow the spinnaker to be flown around the forestay, there seemed an obvious potential to develop something entirely new. In spite of this, spinnaker shapes went through no immediate or dramatic change, leaving Ken Rose bewildered at the lack of any imaginative development. He felt the best solution would be to rationalise the spinnaker shape by analytical geometry so that he could give the sailmaker the mathematical curve form he required for every seam and hope that it would work. The sailmakers, however, looked at his mathematical expressions in bedwilderment and said that they were sorry, but they did not (could not?) make sails that way. The only one who showed any genuine interest was Bruce Banks, who gave Ken every encouragement, supplied some cloth, but advised him to build the sail himself. One or two others in the Class were very interested in the project and anxiously awaited the appearance of the first ultra flat reaching spinnaker. The week after its first race Ken had a request to build nine such spinnakers and was forced to buy a sewing machine! Bruce Banks showed immense interest in Ken's sail and they reached an agreement that Bruce would pay a manufacturing royalty for any of Ken's spinnaker designs. In those days, Bruce was still working for Colin Lucas and living at Southsea. They spent considerable time together with a mast rigged up on a trailer on Southsea Common, pulling up spinnakers of all sorts of shapes and sizes. The first tri-radial and starcut spinnakers appeared in this way for International 14s and 5-O-5s in the early 1960s, some 25 years ago.

By now, a few more metal masts had appeared, but Reynolds had decided that there was no commercial future in metal masts. Ian Proctor felt differently and therefore looked for an alternative source of supply, whilst at the same time tried to improve the design by extruding the sail luff groove as an integral part of the section. This required the development of new extrusion techniques and a new way of tapering the masts. Ian solved his problems when he came upon Northern Aluminium in Banbury, now part of British Alcan and still Proctor's main supplier of sections, who were able to supply the extrusion and provide the technical assistance with the welding. Ian worked with a small sheet metal company in Swanwick to produce the masts, subsequently buying out the mast division to form Ian Proctor Metal Masts Ltd. From this time onwards, the research in masts has been for thinner walls without compromising the compression strength or increasing the overall size of the section out of proportion to the weight.

An interesting comparison in approach appeared at the end of the 1960s, when David Hunt formed Needlespars. Proctors had always believed that masts should be as light as the class rules allowed, particularly for boats with tall rigs such as the Merlin Rocket. Needlespars, however, choose to develop masts which were smaller in section, causing less turbulence around the leading edge of the mainsail, but heavier for the corresponding stiffness.

Meanwhile, the sails were still developing. In 1964, after the America's Cup, Bruce Banks and Ken Rose stayed in America to investigate thoroughly both the quality and construction of sail cloths from all over the world. They were convinced that the British had not had the opportunity to make their Twelve Metre sails as good as those of the Americans because the quality of cloth was not available. This applied all the way down the scale of sailing, dinghies included. From these studies they managed to piece together what were the salient features required by different cloths for different purposes. It was also as a result of this study that some of the very first "yarn tempered" Dacron was brought to Britain. Now there was a completely new scope for improving the shape of really large roached mainsails.

It was in the Merlin Rocket Class that the most fun was to be had, because the only restriction on the girth of the mainsails was at half height (there were no quarter or three-quarter height limits) leaving tempting scope for the ambitious to exploit unmeasured area. At the time the mainsails were measured with four battens not to exceed 3 feet in length. The amount of area that could be built into the top of the mainsail depended therefore on how clever the sailmaker was in locating the top batten within the limits of the rule. It was Michael Jackson from Ranelagh who took the first big leap into the dark, by moving the inboard edge (known to sailmakers as the "toe") of the top batten well back from the aft face of the mast. Mike sailed at Ranelagh in his own design, *March Hare,* No. 1723, and was convinced of the necessity for as much sail area at the top of the rig as possible for river sailing. His first such mainsail (Mike made sails only for himself, never for other people) had the toe of the top batten some 10 inches out from the luff. The sail was made from a polyester cloth supplied by Lewis Clark, now called Windmaster, which was really a very soft cloth. One advantage of the top batten idea was that it enabled some camber to be induced into the top section of the sail as the wooden full length top battens were too stiff to bend and help the top section of the sail flat. Bruce Banks Sails were able to adapt the same idea but used their knowledge of available sailcloth and produced sails with firmer leeches in CYT, which proved far more successful. At the end of the 1960s, Bruce Banks Sails enjoyed a virtual monopoly on sails in the Class.

New Ideas

Whilst these developments were occurring, another character was appearing on the scene. In 1967 Michael McNamara, then a schoolteacher, was sailing a Mike Jackson designed National 12 at Ranelagh. Deciding to move into the Merlin class, he ordered a Jackson "Superstition," *Emotion,* No. 2138, for the 1969 Championships. He also made his own sails, which were basically a copy of Mike Jackson's rig and methods (sewn together at Ranelagh Sailing Club) which proved very fast though somewhat lacking in durability – the mainsail clew pulled out sailing up the last beat whilst leading the race. That same summer Mike McNamara joined Jack Holt's, working in the export office and sailing Enterprises and other Holt designs, whilst still trying to sail National 12s and Merlins. By 1970, Mike had moved and was working with Stuart Westaway to form Ace of Club Sails and was starting to attract a steadily increasing number of Merlin customers, led by David Robinson in his typical search for "something different." Having a suit of his sails on *Ghost Rider* probably helped Mike considerably, as it was one of the most talked about Merlins of 1970.

The masts which were proving the most popular during this period were almost exclusively made by Proctors. The D, unsupported by either spreaders or diamonds, was the most common, with the alternatives being the larger B section, which tended to produce a rig which was very fast downwind but not so successful upwind, favoured in those days by a very young Graham Pike, or the more flexible C section which David Robinson had on *Ghost Rider.* In 1969 the National 12 champions, Hugh Welbourne and Martin Challis, turned up at the Championships with a very small section mast from Stainless Steel Spars Ltd. This mast was only 1¾ inches in diameter and noticeably more flexible than anything else used by the fleet at that time. It survived the windy Championships but the impression was that the section was too soft for medium wind strengths when more power was required. The amount of mast bend and jib luff sag in those rigs was, by present day standards, quite astonishing but was primarily caused by a lack of understanding of how to stiffen up a mast. Set up without any spreaders these rigs would "pant" as the boat sailed through waves, creating a tremendous bellows effect on the sails as the mast flexed, resulting in very open leeches which were always falling to leeward at the top. The luff sag in the jib did not appear to matter as the jib was still sheeted out onto the side decks, similar to Enterprises, and this matched up to the twisted mainsail leech, so the rig seemed quite balanced even though unable to point high!

1970 saw this rig start to change somewhat. Banks were fighting Ace of Clubs sails for dominance in the Merlin Rocket class, Needlespars appeared on the scene to give Proctors some temporary competition, and suddenly the jib sheeting position started to move inboard, causing some rethink in the rig set-up. Aluminium "tripods" started to spout in some boats in the Midlands, which located the jib fairlead "in space" with the aid of a strut extending back off the aft edge of the foredeck, a second strut coming inboard from the gunwale to be all connected together with a third strut coming up from the hull floor. Combined with the use of spreaders, the rig suddenly became potentially more efficient but at the same time required more thought on the part of the helmsman. Gradually, everybody started to play with the position of the hounds,

◀ *Flamin' Go,* a Hoare built Proctor "IX." Owned by Tim Hockin but sailed here by David Robinson and Patrick King, the photograph illustrates the excessive mast bend and jib luff sag that was commonplace in the fleet towards the late 1960's. Tim Hockin came second overall in the 1966 Championships with this boat.

spreader heights and angle, and then mast rams appeared, giving real food for thought. It was the Hamble crowd who led this development, helped by having Proctors and Banks on their doorstep. Sailors such as David Robinson, Tim Hockin, Patrick King and David Potter all kept the pressure on each other with a number of them working within the marine industry, giving that much more incentive and the ability to be the first to try out any new ideas.

That is, until Mike McNamara really took over the sailmaking dominance. Forming his X Sail Loft in 1972, he had an immensely successful first year, producing 160 suits of Merlin sails. Using a stiff cloth similar to that which Banks were using (it was not CYT, but was made by Aquaflite in Holland), he adapted the idea of producing fuller sails, primarily to the requirements of the heavyweights and, in particular, Spud Rowsell, whose yard was approximately 100 yards from Mike's sail loft. These sails were not cut for bendier masts – the idea was still to keep the mast as stiff as possible, but to generate more power from the rig since there was now the means available to control and restrict mast bend. Astonishingly, however, the sails Mike made in his first year were all from just two patterns – a 21ft 6in rig or a 21ft rig. The shaping was identical and Mike was of the opinion that there was more rig development being done in one-design classes such as the Enterprise than in Merlins. Whilst in one-design classes there were accepted "fast boats" and "slow boats," the Merlin Class was somewhat mistakenly under the impression that they had either "fast designs" or "slow designs." No one thought of really playing with the centreboard position, mast rake or position, or to request different sail profiles. Whatever came from the boatbuilder was the finished article and by 1974 it was becoming increasingly common for Rowsells to supply a finished boat ready to sail. With a mast supplied (by now the Beta Minus had appeared), the shrouds cut to length, and the hounds and spreaders already positioned, there was nothing left for the owner to do except take the boat for a sail.

To go back just a few years to 1972 again, although this was McNamara's year of dominance, it was also the beginning for another sailmaker, Neil Thornton of Number 1 Sails. Selling to the sailors in the Midlands, he had no real rival in that area, and was able to expand his market largely unopposed. In 1973 Neil was finding his way through the problems of making Merlin mainsails and, in particular, of how to achieve maximum half height, three-quarter height and foot length measurements and not have a hollow leech. By 1974 he too had a fair share of the market and was developing sails for a different type of rig which came to its peak in 1977. However, of greater importance in 1972 was the introduction of the longer full-length top batten.

Mike McNamara had been making his sails comparatively full by previous standards, achieved by a combination of luff curve (to accommodate for any mast bend) and seam shaping. With the outboard end of the top batten some 2ft 3ins outside the straight line from head to clew, the back edge of the sail must have a load applied to it to prevent the roach falling away and losing power.

The problem with loading the back edge, done with the use of the kicker, was that it was forced forwards, and without any means to prevent this the sail folded in on itself. Mike received an awful amount of criticism that year from the Larks, National 12s and Merlin classes, who all had similar sail plans and restriction on top batten length and whose sails were being made fuller as the cloth available became more stable. So Mike

◀ Ken Ellis sailing a Tom Booth design, showing a Banks Sunray cut mainsail, a sail that went repeatedly in and out of fashion in the 1960s and early 1970s.

Photograph by Guy Gurney

suggested at the 1972 AGM that the Class try out a full length top batten, and this was experimented with at the Draycote open meeting that year by Mike, adapting an existing mainsail on his "Ghost Rider" *Trespassers W.* The experiment was an overwhelming success, but now there was another problem – the sail would not tack! Previously, the problem had been to try and prevent the leech from falling away, but now with the support of the full length top batten the leech was so well supported that it hooked badly. The solution was to go back a few steps and open out the leech seams again in the top section of the sail. So the sails now went through a period where they were made flatter and at the same time the sailmaker had to learn all about long top battens which were really very rudimentary in construction. Fibreglass battens (Aquabattens) only arrived in 1976 and initially the top battens were still wooden. The angle of this batten was also important.

Generally speaking, mainsails were made with the seams perpendicular to the roach. On more conventional sails, this fitted in nicely, as the roach was usually a fair curve all the way down the leech. On a Merlin mainsail, however, the seams ran almost horizontally up to the top batten area, then changed direction sharply. The top batten was typically placed in line with the lower seams rather than the top few seams. This made tacking the batten very difficult, as to flick it across, the batten must first be straightened out before it could compress again – unless it was soft enough to change shape gradually along its length in the form of an "S" bend. However, the more vertical the top batten was fitted in to ther sail, the easier it was to tack, and it was interesting to see how each sailmaker tried to overcome this problem. The problem is still with us today and each sailmaker has different ideas on the correct angle for the top batten. Neil Thornton makes his top battens closer to the vertical than anyone else at present in an attempt to reduce the compression loads, and this always results in a much easier sail to handle in light airs. Conversely, however, this tends to produce the sail with the least powerful top section as it is the sail with the most open leech.

Jibs had changed over this period as well. In the 1960s the normal size for a Merlin jib was 30 square feet (2.79 square metres), as much because it was a nice round number as for any other reason. On the south coast, however, there was a belief that a larger jib, and hence a smaller mainsail, would be more beneficial on the sea, as a large jib would help to pull a boat through the seas, when in strong winds the helmsman was forever trying to spill wind from the mainsail. Tim Hockin started the trend by changing to a jib of 32 square feet, but was surpassed by David Robinson in *Tantrum*, his Bob Hoare "Mark IX," with a jib 2 square feet larger, before taking the advice of Greg Gregory in 1970 and changing to 36 square feet (3.3 square metres) on his new *Ghost Rider*. The logic behind this decision was that as David was a lightweight in the Class he would not need as much sail area in the mainsail as was then normal to be competitive downwind. As already mentioned, the jib sheeting angle moved inboard at the same time as the jib size was increasing, and people were now beginning to give the jib far more thought.

The "tripods" for the jib fairleads were quickly discarded for fore and aft sheeting tracks glued onto the hull planks, typically on the fourth "land" (join between two planks) out from the centreline. Up until this time, the jibs had been long-leeched, with the clew situated close to the fairlead. Now with the fairlead down inside the hull, new ieas were tried. It was realised that any extra area in the jib added by rounding the foot would be unmeasured and the Class went through a short spell of seeing some very weird jibs with huge droopy foots, with the foot flapping about below the deck edge, hoping that it would increase the sail area on a reach. Instead, all that this achieved was a severe flapping of the bottom section of the sail which disturbed the air flow across the entire jib. However, out of all this came an overall improvement in jib bottom panels. Anderson Aerosails developed an oval bottom panel which compromised between a small amount of extra area and improved shaping of the sail. Both Banks and Aerosails had an adjustable shockcord sewn into the "skirt" hem of the foot. The difference in lengths between the luff and leech was typically around 9 inches, but it was then realised that by raising the clew and adopting the fuller bottom panels, a more efficient reaching jib could be made which did incorporate some extra, effective sail area. This move was led by Pat Blake and his crew/designer, Keith Callaghan, who had differences in their luff and leech lengths of some 1 ft 6 ins, and in addition changed the jib to a taller aspect ratio. They also sheeted correspondingly further back in the boat, with the jib fairlead being situated near to the thwart, and adopted the idea of having two jib tracks on the hull for conventional or closer sheeting angles as desired.

By the mid 1970s the "gadget" brigade had standardised the required controls necessary to operate the rig. Kicker, cunningham and clew controls were standard for the mainsail, a mast ram with an 8 : 1 purchase led back to the helmsman was also essential for keeping the mast straight, and "quadrant" levers were used to tension the shrouds as the jib halyard was usually still hooked on to a rack on the side of the mast. The mainsheet was set on a straight, nearly full-width traveller, with great emphasis being made to the necessity of constantly playing the traveller to control the twist of the mainsail leech. With the advent of "muscle boxes" on the jib halyard, some of the more successful helmsmen were taking the mast aft when sailing upwind, by easing off on the jib halyard and applying more load on the mainsheet to keep the luff of the jib tight. One of the interesting side effects of this sail control was that when the mainsheet was sheeted in hard and the traveller was eased out, the mast would be pushed to windward, opening the slot between the jib and mainsail, which could be beneficial in strong winds but again depended on accurate use and understanding of the traveller. It was apparent that the use of the traveller as a sail control had an influence on more than one characteristic of the rig but was rarely used correctly.

The hounds were by now very high up on the mast with correspondingly high, short spreaders, all aimed at stiffening up the top section of the mast for the benefit of the heavyweights, who were dominating the Class. Lightweights were also being sold this rig, mistakenly under the impression that it was the "only" successful way to set up a Merlin. The fact that they were not winning races only served to highlight the Merlin Rocket as one of the Classes suitable mainly for beer-drinkers and heavyweights. The situation was developing where there was a clear domination of the Class by the heavyweights who were consistently at the top of the Championship results. It was time for a change.

The Rethink

In 1976 the order at the top of the sailmakers league changed quite dramatically, literally overnight after the Championships that year. They were won by Lawrie Smith in the old *Satisfaction* using McNamara's sails. However, shortly afterwards Mike found himself out of favour with almost the entire Class. The problem was in the rig, where he had now apparently developed a design fault. Mike had been trying to shape the sail so that it had a dead straight luff. This performed very well in light winds and seemed to suit the heavyweights but was very inflexible. It was a copy of the contemporary Fireball rig as used at that time in America, using struts to develop as much power as possible. In the Merlin Class, where the hulls did not have a particularly powerful underwater shape but where rigs were highly loaded, all the power was transmitted straight to the hull; this approach quickly proved unpopular. So people now started to look elsewhere for their speed.

That elsewhere was with Neil Thornton and Phil Morrison. Neil had already had a very good year in 1974 when he crewed for a very young Lawrie Smith in a "Hexagon," and they had come 2nd overall at the Championships using Neil's sails. By 1977, he had developed a rig with Pat Blake for *After Myth*, No. 3054, which made use of the standard

Pat Blake and Dave Webster sailing *After Myth*, National Champions in 1977.

Photograph by Chapman

rig and controls, but resulted in a very different concept. A smaller section Proctor Alpha Plus mast was used, which bent more in a breeze than the alternatives, the larger Beta Minus or the D. Neil was also using "droopy booms," giving some extra unmeasured sail area low down. The bendier mast resulted in a rig that was far more tolerant and easier to handle in a breeze compared to the then current favourite of Rowsell and McNamara. The only problem was that it needed a bit of a breeze to get the mast to adopt the correct bend characteristics the sail was designed for, but once it had these conditions, the rig was unbeatable. To help with this light airs problem the leech was cut very open so that the kicker could be applied slightly sooner than normal as the wind increased. Once the wind was sufficient to warrant a lot of kicker and mainsheet tension, bending the mast to the correct shape, the natural flexibility of the mast did the rest, depowering automatically whilst everyone else had to work the traveller or kicker.

Phil Morrison sailing *Summer Wine* in 1977. This was the boat that really started the trends ▶ towards the modern-day rig currently in use

Photograph by Alistair Black

After Myth did not point particularly high when sailing to windward, but had tremendous boat speed and as the Championships that year were held in winds which steadily increased throughout the day, Pat Blake and his crew, Dave Webster, were invincible.

This was very unfortunate for Phil Morrison because he had developed a new rig for his *Summer Wine*, No. 3090, which was to a degree the opposite of that on *After Myth*. Whilst Pat's rig was perhaps the ultimate of the "old establishment" style of rig, Phil was bringing in the first of the "new order." His idea was for a similar rig which would work in light winds as well as in a breeze, enabling the lightweights to be more competitive, but employed totally different ideas in the attempt to achieve his aims. First of all, he discarded the mainsheet traveller, arguing that it controlled too many variables, affecting jib luff tension, mainsail leech tension as well as boom angle, all simultaneously. The mainsheet should only be used to control the boom angle as the boat had a hoop, whilst the kicker's job was to control the mainsail leech tension. However, applying the kicker also had the effect of bending the mast because it transmitted a horizontal force on the mast at the gooseneck via the boom. To prevent this, Phil fitted two non-adjustable struts coming up from the foredeck to the front of the mast at boom height to lock the mast solid. Two struts were thought necessary as when the boat was sailed upwind in strong winds the boom was usually out over the corner of the transom, meaning that the bend force was not forwards but about 15 to 20 degrees off the centreline. The jib was made much smaller, so that there was no overlap between jib leech and mainsail luff. This enabled the boom to be eased out far more when sailing upwind and overpowered, thus depowering the rig without chocking up the "slot" around the leeward side of the mast and mainsail. Curiously enough, the jib was again around 2.8 square metres, which was virtually the old 30 square feet configuration. Now, however, the jib was sheeted well inboard on a transverse track on the after edge of the foredeck, with the jib halyard tension being controlled initially on a drum at the foot of the mast. The mainsail was cut fairly full, with more luff round than was then customary. The mast was matched to this curve by a combination of strut position and jib halyard tension. The struts were set up so that in light winds, with the jib halyard slightly eased, the struts were pulling the mast forwards at the gooseneck height, inducing a bend all the way up to the hounds. The mast was the Alpha Plus section, but it had jumpers above the hounds which could be adjusted whilst sailing. The idea here was that in light to medium conditions the jumper wires would be tightened to stiffen up the mast, but in a breeze they would be slackened to let the top section bend and depower the rig.

Well, it did not quite work out as planned. Firstly, the struts acted low down on the mast and the prebend induced by them gave a different mast bend to that caused by wind loading and mainsail leech tension in a breeze, so the mainsail luff round did not quite match that of the induced mast curve in light winds. Second, and more important, however, was the problem found in strong winds. To maintain a straight jib luff, the jib halyard tension had to be increased, there being no mainsheet load to maintain the jib luff tension. This had the result of pulling the top of the mast forwards, against both the struts and the spreaders, so actually straightening out the mast just when this was least wanted. Another effect was that it also tensioned the jib leech as the head of the sail moved forward very slightly, which as there was no "give" in the sheeting system on the deck, led to an immediate change of relative sheeting angle, although the jib fairleads could be moved outboard and aft to compensate. It is an inherent problem of transverse deck sheeting that it is very susceptible to slight changes in mast rake or even mast bend, which is discussed later on. The result of all this was that Phil was always the fastest boat on the way out to the starts of the races in the 1977 Championships, in the lighter winds, but as the breeze came in he was gradually overhauled by Pat Blake during the races, often on the last beat.

Prebend

Phil's answer to the rig problems was to fit adjustable quadrant levers for the shrouds. Now when the wind increased the shrouds were tensioned up to pull the rig aft, and Phil was rewarded with a much improved windward performance at the windy Inland Championships later the same year. However, it was clearly not the final solution, so they went "back to the drawing board." It was one of his employees, Nick Lightbody, who jokingly came up with the next idea. Remarking on Phil's prolific amount of rigging on *Summer Wine* he suggested hanging some wires off the spreaders as well – just to balance it out a bit. Having then sat down and thought about this, Phil realised that it could actually be rather a useful idea, so developed the "Morrison Wires." These were thin, single strand wires which were attached by talurits to the shrouds immediately above the spreaders, passed through the spreader tip then down to the front of the mast at gooseneck height, where they were attached using bottlescrews (on some boats they were led through the spinnaker eye on the mast to prevent them from fouling twin pole systems, where the spinnaker poles were stowed along the boom). These wires created a "bow and arrow" effect on the mast, with the mast as the bow and the spreaders as the arrow. Tensioning up the bottlescrews also tensioned up the top section of the shrouds against the spreaders. The greater the tension, the more the spreader tips were pushed forwards, so bending the mast. With the spreaders five-eighths of the distance up from the deck height to hounds position, a fair curve was developed in the mast between these two points. However, it had no effect on the top, unsupported section of the mast which in strong winds was heavily loaded by the kicker. The resultant mast bend in such conditions was therefore influenced by this topmast bend and resulted in a maximum bend position at a point somewhere above the spreader position. This could be countered by bending the mast below the gooseneck to even out the loading somewhat, but this required adjustable struts. The mechanics of adjusting two such struts was thought to be prohibitive, so a compromise was arranged whereby one central strut was attached to the foredeck via a large under-deck lever giving a large mechanical advantage, which was relatively frictionless. The 21 feet 4 inch Alpha Minus mast section was replaced by a 21 feet Alpha Plus on *Summer Wine* by Paddy Atkinson and Bob Kyle. There were then further experiments over the next few seasons with D's and C's until the D once again gained ascendancy, with the benefit that it could survive without the lateral support of two struts.

The single-strutted, Morrison-wired prebent rig, complete with Morrison sails, had an immensely successful 1978 Championships, having 4 of the first 6 boats rigged this way, and also overcoming the might of *After Myth* in its own wind strength (though this was helped in one race by Dave Webster pulling one of *After Myth's* jib fairleads out of the boat). Spud Rowsell, the overall winner of the week and sailing with such a rig, was not actually sailing any faster than John Patterson that year, and John was also using Neil Thornton's sails, so it is probably fair to say that Phil had now developed a rig that would work at the Championships in either light or strong conditions, whilst Neil had a proven heavy weather rig that was slightly off the pace in medium wind strengths because of its more open leech. However, Neil's rig was still very popular inland, probably largely due to the easier-to-use top batten configuration, as previously explained.

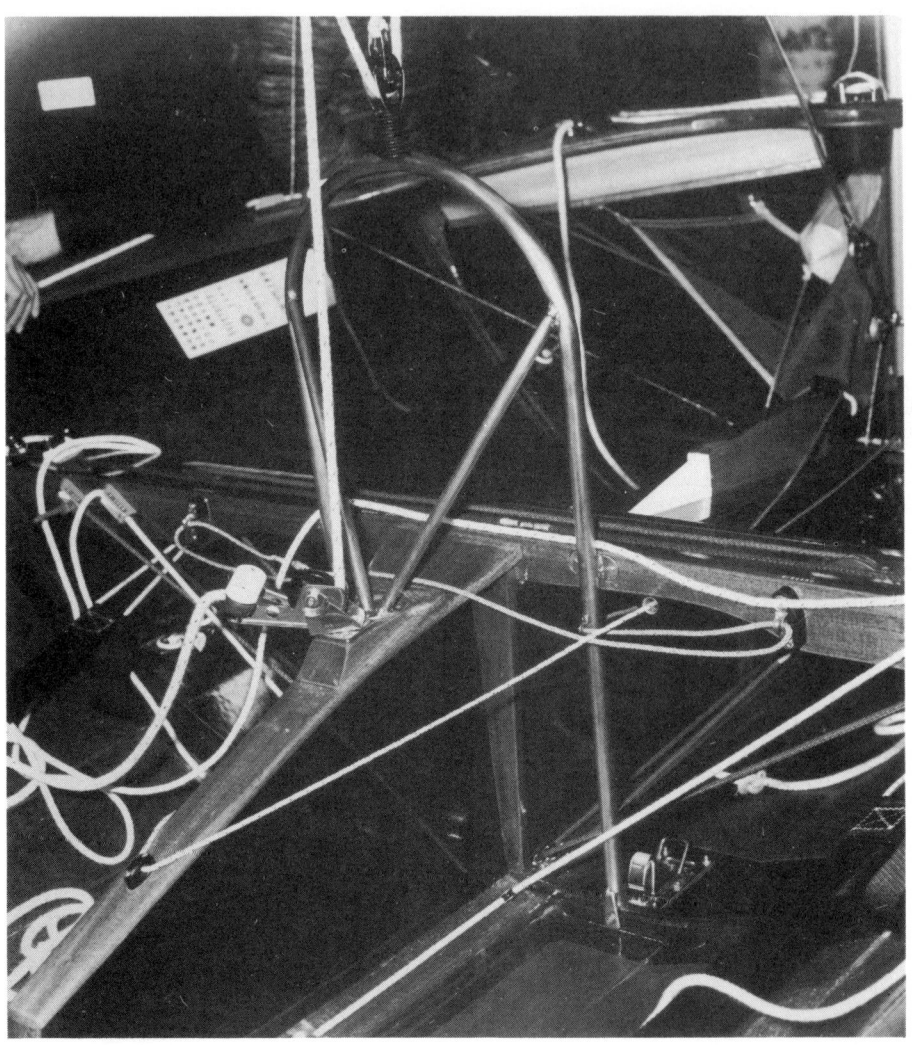

One of the first mainsheet hoops to appear in the class was that on Neil Thornton's *Stripes*.
Photograph by Robert O'Neill

1977 had seen the introduction of the mainsheet hoop, by Neil and Phil simultaneously on their own boats. By the following year it had quickly found acceptance throughout the fleet and very few new Merlins have been built subsequently that use any other system. About the only helmsmen who still preferred the traveller was Pat Blake, but this was largely because he spent a considerable amount of his time in Flying Dutchmen, where such a system was essential and Pat was well used to controlling the system. The ability to pull almost horizontally at the boom rather than vertically, as with the traveller, led to much more rapid adjustment of the boom angle in gusts. In many cases this allowed a reduction from a 4 : 1 to 3 : 1 purchase on the mainsheet requiring less rope having to be pulled in or let out.

Three photographs showing variations in the sail plan. *Flamin' Go,* No. 1793, is typical of late 1960s, whilst *New Potato,* No. 3297, shows the more modern fashion for jibs that do not overlap the mast. *Still Crazy,* No. 3322, shows a more extreme approach, using a very small jib of extremely tall ratio, with the mast positioned well forward. Such a rig is more common in the National 12 class.

Jib sheeting was being experimented with. Following Phil's adoption of deck sheeting the previous year, some boats were seen modified with aluminium bars running transversely across the hull at deck level, or just below, onto which was sheeted the jib to allow variations in transverse sheeting angles. This eliminated some of the "give" in the system caused by not having the jib clew rigidly fixed in the transverse plane which was felt to lose some of the power developed from the jib.

At around this time one or two people were playing with alternative kicking strap arrangements, and fully curved mainsheet tracks. The kickers were being altered so that there was no horizontal force at the gooseneck and therefore no mast bend induced when the kicker was applied (in effect, an alternative to the conventional kicker plus strut configuration). This was achieved by attaching a horizontal strut which would pivot about the aft face of the mast at deck height, in line with the mast ram. This strut would be prevented from moving up at the outboard end by means of a wire strop from the strut down to the mast heel. The kicker was then a wire which came off the boom and went vertically onto the aft end of the strut. The tension could then be adjusted by running this wire round a pulley and then forward to a muscle box fixed on to the strut. By sliding the attachment point of the kicker forwards or backwards along the boom, mast bend could be induced or eliminated depending on whether the kicker wire was angled forwards or backwards as it came off the boom (if it was angled backwards, then the boom had to be bolted onto the gooseneck, otherwise the boom would be pulled off the mast). There was, of course, a horizontal component in the system, but this was transmitted into the mast at deck height where it was countered by a conventional mast ram.

The very brief resurgence of the fully radiused mainsheet track was an attempt to eliminate the kicker and strut altogether. Instead, there was a wire strop that came off the boom and went directly onto the mainsheet track. The track was radiused such that it met the sides of the hull at the shrouds and so was effective even on a dead run, thus eliminating the basic requirement for a kicker. The wire strop was led forward along the boom and down to a muscle box or drum so that the leech tension could be adjusted. The traveller control was a conventional 2 : 1 purchase which had a direct control over the boom angle. There were, however, three main problems with this system. Firstly, it was difficult to install within the boat and costly to have the track made up to suit; secondly, in the boats that tried the system there was still a great deal of friction on the traveller and it was a common sight to see the crew desperately trying to shift the car around the track by brute force –travellers have improved again since then, and this problem would not arise today; and thirdly, the crews objected to having their already cramped quarters further subdivided by the track and were forever trying to step over the track whilst at the same time not having a hand disected by the car during a gybe. These problems added up to an extremely unpopular system which could not match the combination of an efficient kicker plus mainsheet hoop.

The 1980's Rig

The Merlin Rocket rig of the 80's has developed from the ideas introduced by Phil Morrison and Co. in the late 1970s, and largely uses more efficient means to produce the same effect. The first change to be made was to eliminate the Morrison Wires. This happened more by accident than design. When some of the rigs were modified by removing the wires the helmsmen found that the rig was still generating the required prebend. This apparently had come about through a combination of angling the spreaders further aft to make the Morrison Wires more effective and simultaneously increasing the rig tension, made possible by the new generation of stiffer hulls. These had originated together with the "NSM" hull layout and the revised bow tank construction.

One of the alternatives to situating all the rig controls on the thwart is to let the crew do all the work. This is Nick Aubrey's solution, seen on the Guy Winder built *Uptown Girl*.

Photograph by Ian Holt

Now everyone was trying out the flexible rig with varying degrees of success. The most extreme was Andy Street who in 1981 destroyed a number of Proctor C section masts, which were really considered too soft for the Class, but succeeded none the less in winning the Championships. This convinced people that this concept was the right approach and they looked around for a more suitable mast to perform the task. They found it in the form of the Super Spar M1, supplied and developed by Ken Brackwell, who had previously been responsible for Proctor's dinghy mast division in the 1970s. Ironically, Ken considered this mast to be unsuitable for the Merlin Class, designed for smaller classes such as the National 12. However, once again an "unsuitable" mast won the Championships, this time in 1983 at Whitstable in the hands of Jon Turner with *Passion*, No. 3314. Jon, in conjunction with Phil Morrison who had made the sails, stiffened up the mast by using Phil's idea of two struts, but this time they were both simultaneously adjustable, giving a more controllable rig. Phil himself was using the same section at the Championships which was proof enough in the eyes of the fleet that this must be the correct mast to have. With the market temporarily distracted, Proctors decided that a new mast section was required to win back their market and developed the Kappa section for 1984.

Twin adjustable struts on *Passion* to give lateral, as well as fore and aft support to the mast at gooseneck height.

Photograph by Ian Holt

Ken, meanwhile, was already working on a new section designed to stand up to the stronger forces imposed by the high rig loads and yet be flexible enough to be used for the present concept. The M3 section was tried at the 1985 Championships where the first boat using the mast was 2nd overall. In fact, the top six boats showed an interesting cross-section of the masts in use by the Class, consisting of two M1s, two M3s, a D and a Kappa. However, it would be wrong to assume that the lightweight bendy sections were dominating the Class. The Championships at Shoreham that year were predominantly force 4 to 5 with fair sized waves, requiring a rig that was going to depower itself upwind, no matter how heavy the crew was. In even windier conditions (but smooth water) at the Inlands a month later, Nick Aubrey and Chris Rutter, who were one of the most successful heavyweight teams in the Class, won using the much stiffer M2 section which provided an immensely powerful rig with very little fall-off in the topmast section. Such a rig was in some ways a refined version of the rig used to such good effect by Spud Rowsell in the mid 1970s but it gave a superior sail shape due to an initial small degree of prebend which did not seem to alter, no matter how strong the wind was. The advances made in the rig development within the class have been to bring the lightweight crews up to the same level of competitiveness when sailing upwind as the once-dominating heavyweights, whilst refining the efficiency of the rig in general. Both rig options have their advantages and disadvantages.

As Phil Morrison had discovered earlier, adjusting the shrouds rather than jib halyard was actually the better way to induce or remove mast bend, making the conventional rig layout of the 1970s (a muscle box for the jib halyard and quadrant levers for the shrouds) no longer the correct way to go. The recent years have seen a trend towards fixed forestay lengths with the shrouds being tensioned up either using a system of multi-purchases, levers, or hydraulics, all of which can be adjusted downwind by the helmsman. It is obvious that to adjust two shrouds simultaneously from either side of the boat is far more difficult to achieve than to control a single jib halyard. The resultant systems so far devised are necessarily more complex and indeed usually harder to operate. However, it has been found that they can help to increase downwind speed significantly and seem to be here to stay, for the next few years at least.

Hydraulics made their appearance within the class in 1985, as a means of adjusting the shroud tension. The system shown here is on Martin Warren's *Gnome*, where the master cylinder was located under the centreboard case.　　Photograph by Ian Holt

Whilst the idea of hydraulics in a small dinghy must initially have appeared to be absurd, they do have two very useful advantages. Firstly, they have a power ratio approaching 6 : 1 which is virtually frictionless, and secondly the master cylinder from which the multi-purchase control is taken, can be positioned anywhere in the boat, and connected to the slave cylinder by means of a flexible tube. This system eliminates the compression forces generated within the hull by any system which brings the shrouds together somewhere on the centreline of the boat. A few people have attempted to use these systems to actually swing the rig forward when sailing downwind which would certainly improve the boat's speed in light winds. The actual prebend is applied by compressing the mast until it bends out of column, achieved using the rig tension. This can be further aided by the position of the hounds and the length and angle of the spreaders. The higher the shrouds are attached to the mast above the forestay, the easier it is to bend the mast, as this distance acts as a lever for the force applied to the shrouds. Long spreaders will stiffen up a mast sideways, and this is often beneficial to heavier crews, but it is very easy to get this wrong. If the mast is rigged with high hounds and spreaders which deflect the shrouds outboard it is very easy to push the mast to leeward at the spreader bracket height which, in strong winds, is undesirable as it closes up the slot between the mainsail and the jib. One solution to such a problem is to reduce the rig tension which correspondingly reduces the effect of the spreader deflection. With reduced rig tension it is still possible to achieve the desired prebend by using the longer spreaders, but now angled further aft than for the shorter spreaders. The angle of the spreaders is determined by the combination of mast stiffness and mainsail fullness required, with the modern trend being to have the spreaders angled noticeably further aft than was seen in the 1970s. Tuning the rig of the modern Merlin is a finely balanced operation of developing the maximum power in medium winds from a fundamentally under-canvassed rig and yet be able to lose some of the heeling force when the boat becomes suddenly overpowered in the gusts.

The idea of eliminating the jib halyard has also been given considerable thought and an effective solution has been developed by re-introducing the old idea of using a forestay. This time, however, the forestay is made out of rod rather than wire. Rod rigging has seen favour in some classes after its value had been proven in offshore boats as a means of reducing stretch in the rigging. The rod is threaded through a pocket on the jib luff and takes all the rigging loads, whilst the luff of the jib merely has to be tensioned to eliminate horizontal creases. Phil Morrison was again the first person to try this idea in the Class, initially using small strips of tape along the jib luff rather than a continuous pocket. This has the questionable advantage of being able to lower the jib whilst waiting for the start. It does, however, concentrate the horizontal loads in the sail and unless very careful it can lead to creases and uneven shaping in the profile. The choice now is whether or not the owner wants to have the added problems of such a means of hoisting the jib, which is undoubtedly more complicated. At present, most club sailors are happy with the conventional jib system, whilst those who regularly travel to open meetings and are thus rigging their masts nearly every weekend are more prepared to instal the more complex arrangements, known as a "stuff luff." It has now become increasingly common for the shrouds also to be of rod rigging for the same low stretch advantages.

There have been boats built recently without any form of mast gate to support the mast at deck height. This was another of Phil's ideas and was based upon observing how the lighter section masts were being rigged. Those using "M1" sections were stiffening the mast sideways, either by fitting a short section of tubing up inside the mast to act as a sleeve at the mast gate and gooseneck area, or by fitting lower shrouds which went out from the mast transversely and were in addition to a strut. It became apparent that with the latter system, the mast gate had now become superfluous as the combination of strut and lowers was doing the job of mast ram and sideways mast gate support. Some boats built this way have tried controlling the mast just with conventional lowers connecting into the deck at the shroud position, but this can result in damaged masts caused by the mast bending inside out, usually when planing, or rather not planing, with the spinnaker up in strong winds. The advantage of the strut is that it is a positive restraint on the mast, both forwards and backwards. The disadvantage of a strut is that it is only effective fore and aft, whereas lowers apply tension together to give lateral and forward support.

Amongst the most active sailmakers within the Class in the 1980s has been Dick Batt who first made Merlin sails whilst working for Mike McNamara in the mid 1970s, where he was primarily responsible for the spinnaker and mainsail development. After a period of sailmaking in New Zealand, Dick started up a sail loft on his own in Maidenhead. Based at Cookham Reach SC, Dick's first Merlin was an Omega "NSM" on

Sailmaker Dick Batt and his wife, Gill, sailing their "Summer Wine" *Die Fledermaus* ▶
Photograph by Malcolm Willison   The mast is the small Proctor Kappa section

which he tried out one or two rather interesting ideas. He introduced the idea of twin spinnaker poles which could be raised and lowered by the crew pulling or releasing a line connected to the inboard end of each pole. This line passed through a pulley located on the mast where the conventional eye was normally positioned, before passing down to the deck and to a cleat. The advantage of this system is primarily for lightweight crews in strong winds, when they can set and retrieve the poles without having to come in off the side deck. Spinnaker pole arrangements are a source of constant discussion within the crews' union, with no one system being perfect, but Dick's system – when correctly set up in the boat – was very efficient and fast. Dick's other idea was to try out the use of a flattener on the mainsail, similar to that used on offshore yachts. Simply a cringle located approximately 6 inches above the clew, it has been found to have a far greater effect on the fullness of the sail than to adjust the clew outhaul. Whereas the clew outhaul mostly affects the fullness in the bottom quarter of the sail, the flattener can influence nearly twice this area. Dick took this idea one step further by eliminating the adjustable kicking strap and replacing it instead with a simple wire strop that was not adjusted whilst racing. The leech tension was controlled by the flattener which would tighten the leech and flatten the sail simultaneously. From a practical viewpoint, this system gave the helmsman more headroom when tacking as instead of pulling the boom lower to tension the leech, the boom remained at a fixed height and the leech was shortened. This also meant that the hoop could be higher, and thus more efficient in lighter winds. With all these potentially good points about this system, it is strange that only two boats have so far tried the idea.

Once Bitten showing Guy Winger's solution to positioning control lines in a Merlin Rocket. Instead of having each control duplicated to either side of the hull, the lines were led along the centreboard case and onto a rotating consol (known as the "Coffee Table"), with the cleats some 16 inches away from the centre of rotation. The position of the consol was controlled by the pull of the mainsheet, which was situated on the top of it.

Photograph by Malcolm Willison

Dick's ideas on mainsail shape are very distinctive. As already mentioned, considerable thought is necessary prior to producing a sail with a leech that will both tack easily and open out when overpowered, yet generate adequate power on the reaches. His interpretations of the requirements led to grouping the battens more towards the head, thus meaning that the shaping which supports the leech need not be concentrated solely at the topmost batten. The reduced shaping caused less compression at that batten resulting in fewer tacking problems. At the same time this helped to create more controllable twist characteristics in the sail.

Spinnakers' have not changed a great deal during this period and it has been found that the best compromise size is somewhat smaller than the maximum permissible, caused by the fact that the pole is not thought to be long enough to keep a maximum sized spinnaker away from the mainsail on a reach. To do this would require the foot to be shortened, creating a more spherical sail which would therefore be correspondingly fuller and very difficult to control on a close reach. The fashion for tri-radial spinnakers has largely died out, as it has been found that a conventional cross-cut sail has leeches which stretch slightly under load, helping to free the leech somewhat in windy conditions, and keeping the head profiles flat. Perhaps more important, however, is the fact that cross-cut spinnakers are both easier and cheaper to make, as all sailmakers are well aware!

Jib sheeting system on *Nice Legs*. The track proved extremely effective downwind but was later removed in the search for improved upwind performance.

Photograph by Ian Holt

The jib sheeting in Merlins has now developed into perfecting the two very different methods now in use. The Class still cannot decide whether it is better to have the clew rigidly supported in all directions by having the fairlead located on the deck close to the clew, or to be "conventional" and have the fairlead in the bottom of the boat to allow the jib to open out slightly when hit by gusts whilst sailing to windward. The consensus of opinion appears to be that the latter method is best for sailing upwind (and is certainly the least critical) whilst the former is best for reaching as it provides an easier means of preventing the leech twisting as the sheet is eased. The top boats in the fleet at the Championships are usually evenly divided between the two methods and it is interesting to note that the sailmakers also differ on this point.

The Future Merlin Rig

Over the last eight years or so the Class has learnt how to produce more adaptable rigs for various crew weights and sea conditions, and the recent years have been spent refining and perfecting the tools available to match the requirements. The talk in general throughout the sailing world is now for lighter masts and laminated sails, producing a lighter rig which will make the boat easier to sail through seas as the pitching motions will be reduced, coupled with sails that will not stretch and lose their power and shape.

Carbon-fibre masts have been experimented with in the 505s, the International Canoe and Moth fleets, where it was found that initially, although there was a significant weight saving to be made, there were serious structural problems encountered when attaching the shrouds and jib halyard to the mast. The very high local loads could not be spread far enough into the mast and the rigging gradually worked its way down the mast. These problems have now been overcome and some good-looking carbons masts are being used in certain classes but the construction of such a mast is naturally far more labour intensive than the comparable aluminium counterpart, and is not yet seen as a serious method for mast construction for the dinghy market in the near future. It is more likely that superior grades of aluminium will be made available, making possible either smaller sections or lighter masts. The rig heights used by the fleet appear to have stabilised between the "21 feet" and the 21 feet 4 inches" version (the length of the luff plus 0.68 metre), which apparently suits the Class needs. One of the 1985 newsletters had an article discussing the possibility of allowing boats to have more than one rig, to suit different sailing environments, but the thought of trying to tune two complete sets of mast and sails is apparently too much for the Class. The present-day thoughts are that luff length is desirable for efficient windward sailing whilst projected area is better for downwind and "21 feet" or thereabouts is as good a compromise as any.

Wing masts have not been popular for two reasons. Firstly, and by far the most important, they are not commercially available, and secondly they tend to be extremely stiff which as already discussed is not a popular rig for the majority of helmsmen. The ultimate mast for the Class would presumably be a flexible wing mast of maximum permissible size, but at present such a mast is not in sight.

The question of laminated sails was raised at the 1985 AGM and sufficient enthusiasm was shown for the committee to agree to look into ways of trying out suits of laminated sails in races in the 1986 season. Such sails have now become a common sight in the offshore racing scene, where their durability has been proven. It now remains to be seen whether such sails are too inflexible for an easily driven racing dinghy, or whether the material should merely be used to reinforce the leeches of jibs and mainsails to prolong their life.

There are still many ideas for rigging masts that have not been tested fully. Geoff Worsdale was, for a number of years, sailing with some wires dangling from the top of his mast and attached to the spreaders. The idea behind these was rather good, and it is

An idea that could be developed further: upper shrouds from the spreaders up to the top of the mast, used for inducing prebend in the top section of the mast, and to stiffen up the mast downwind. This shows Andy Street's mast at the 1985 Championships.
Photograph by Ian Holt

surprising that only Andy Street was seen experimenting with them at the 1985 Championships. As the top section of the mast must necessarily bend in strong winds, a certain amount of luff round has to be built into the top of the sail to allow for this. In light winds, however, the top of the mast will remain straight, as prebend, Morrison Wires and struts are only effective up to the hounds. The purpose of these wires is just the same as Morrison Wires, but induce prebend in the top section of the mast to match the luff round. It is somewhat harder to develop the correct tension in the wires, as this is, in turn, related to the shroud tension, unlike the Morrison Wires which were unrelated to rig tension. It may be that this idea could be perfected by using a totally independent set of shrouds running from the top of the mast, through the spreaders and down to the deck, which could be tensioned as an individual unit. It may be possible in very light winds to hold the rig up on these shrouds rather than the main shrouds. Shroud tracks on the deck of *Diamond Smiles* in 1985 had originally been intended to enable the mast to be pulled to windward on the reaches, by easing off the

Two photographs of the rig used on *Diamond Smiles* at the 1985 Championships. The first shows the mast pre-bent for windward work, achieved by pulling the shrouds aft along tracks recessed in the deck. The amount of mast bend can be judged by looking at the rope tied between the masthead and gooseneck.

The second photograph shows the rig with the shrouds eased forwards along the tracks. The increase in sail camber can be compared by looking at the fullness of the sail in the area of the sail numbers.

Photographs by Ian Holt

leeward track and pulling back on the windward track. This idea was abandoned as no simple way could be thought of for devising a strut which could move sideways as well as fore and aft. The only alternative would be to have the mast step on a transverse track so that the mast would pivot about the strut when the shrouds were adjusted. This would mean a complete rethink of the hull structure in this area, and would require considerable design work. The principle of pulling the rig to windward, as used by sailboards is, however, perfectly sound and a boat so set up could well have a significant boat speed advantage in a breeze.

How will the rig change in our time? It very much depends on the materials that the Class decides to permit for construction of the hull and rig, the decisions certainly will be very much influenced by costs of some of these "exotic" fibres. At the same time, however, the Merlin Rocket is a development class, and as Spud Rowsell pointed out at the 1985 AGM, it is important for the Class image that if there are any advantageous ideas in rig materials and design worth developing, Merlin Rockets should be leading the way.

CHAPTER 7

The Builders

Introduction

One of the reasons why many people are attracted to the Merlin Rocket Class is because "they are such beautiful boats." Whilst handling qualities are best appreciated on the water, the initial attraction of the Class is the superbly-built boats and their finish. In this respect our best advertisers and recruiting agents are our builders. The result of their skill and cratsmanship leaves one in awe and in these days of mass-produced production line technology can rekindle a belief in the rewards for these traditional skills.

The original Merlin builder was, of course, Jack Holt, more famous now perhaps for his Enterprises and other one-design dinghies. In the early days of the Class, Jack was building and finishing his boats to as high a quality as they are today. The solid planking was so well fitted that no caulking or glueing was used but only layers of varnish were applied to seal the joints.

Shortly before starting to build Merlins, Jack had suffered a major setback when his premises were burnt down, but was able to set up again nearby and at the same time was fortunate to form a partnership with Beecher Moore. This partnership placed Jack's business onto much more of a commercial footing, with Beecher organising the financial side. This left Jack free to concentrate on building and designing.

The traditional method of construction at this time, was to assemble the boats upside down over a series of frames laid on a rigid flat surface. These frames were notched, to accept the hogpiece which was laid over them and fastened with knees to the transom and stem. A centreboard case was curved to the spring of the hog. The midship frame was marked in suitable divisions for the number of planks to be laid and the remaining frames marked off with a fairing batten. The solid mahogany planks were then laid one at a time and the intermediate nailing completed.

The boat, including frames, was then lifted off the flat surface and the steamed Rock Elm timbering was fitted using copper nails. One frame at a time was removed as work progressed. Finally, inner gunwales, breasthooks, quarter-knees, deck framing and decking were fitted. This system of building continued until marine ply became available in sufficient quantities to allow it to be used for the hull planking. Originally, the only ply in existence was that which had been allocated to the aircraft industry and this was just becoming available at the end of the war.

Many of the original and radical ideas used on the early Merlins were first designed and made by Jack. These included the rotating mast, designed to keep a constant angle of attack to the wind and the ingenious centre-board arrangement whereby the slot was kept to a minimum by the use of a roller system on the front edge of the case.

In the beginning Jack designed and made all his own fittings, including modelling in wood the shapes to be used for the metal castings required. These were mostly of brass and were manufactured by the local foundries. He made his own wooden masts and was the first to incorporate an internal luff groove in the section. This design stemmed from his impoverished state at the time and the high cost of the external brass luff track which was the only alternative. When first tried, he discovered to his dismay that none

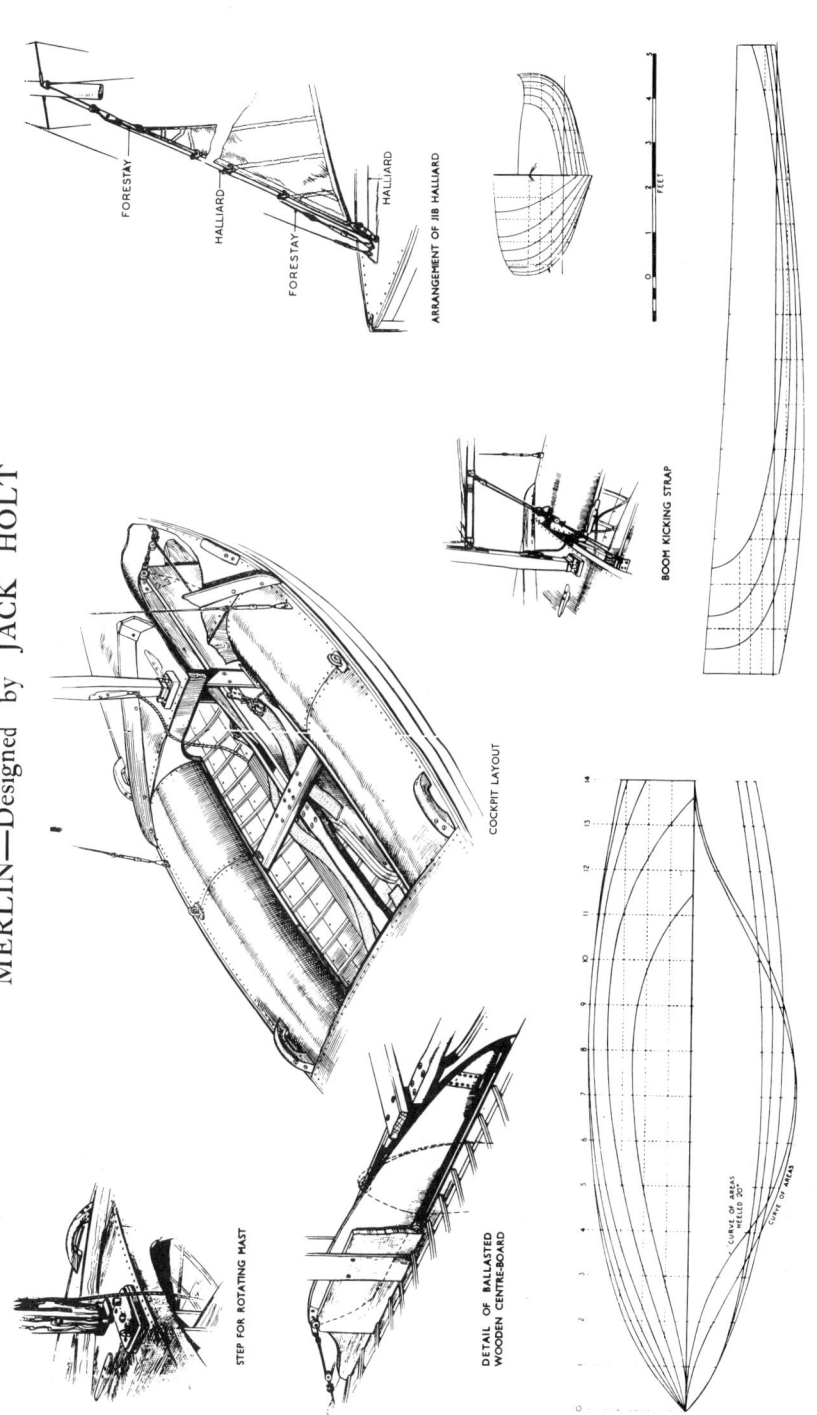

of the sailmakers would supply a sail to fit, saying that it was impractical and could never work. Twelve months later everyone was using internal luff grooves and the sails were readily available!

By 1960, Jack had moved out of the Merlin class and on to building his now famous one-designs. This coincided with the beginning of the almost total dominance of the Ian Proctor designs which were to be built by the firm of Wyche & Coppock.

As early as 1951 the firm of Wyche & Coppock began the development of the Rocket, which they evolved from their experiences of building Jack Holt's Merlin and the International 14s of those days. Initially these boats were constructed to the traditional method mentioned above, but upon moving premises and installing woodworking machinery, they developed the idea that as each new design came along, so an accurate pattern of each plank would be drawn and from this pattern they would cut planks 1" thick, which could be sliced down the centre on a swage saw, to make two equal and opposite planks. These were planed down to the required $5/16"$.

This mechanisation and later the new plywood construction with glued, rather than nailed joints (developed by Wyche & Coppock), reduced the labour factor considerably. A point of interest here was that boats finished with conventional varnish tended to gain weight owing to moisture absorption but when two-part polyurethane appeared on the market moisture absorption was all but eliminated.

The move from the traditional to ply construction represented a major breakthrough in the history of the Merlin Rocket Class. It not only produced far more satisfactory boats which were quicker and easier to build and thus more competitive price-wise than traditionally built boats, but it also helped the Class holds its own against the one-designs, which had started to proliferate during this period. The early traditionally built Merlins were often leaky until "binged up" which, of course, added considerable weight. The nailing and roving was labour intensive and therefore expensive, and the ability to maintain accurate hull design was poor. None of these disadvantages applied to the one-design opposition, but all these problems were quickly eliminated by the use of the ply construction techniques.

Along with Wyche & Coppock, another boatbuilder to become associated with the Class during the early years was Chippendales. This boatyard dominated the new orders in the 1950s and its part played in the Class history is worthy of more than a passing mention.

Jack Chippendale started his boatbuilding apprenticeship in 1938 with the Hampshire firm of R. & A. Hamper on Fareham Creek at the top of Portsmouth harbour. After the war, the yard was fortunate in the private work which it procured, and amongst the first orders was one for a Merlin dinghy for Geoff Budden, a local schoolmaster and friend of Uffa Fox. Jack Chippendale was given the job of building this unusual boat, and Geoff took Jack down to Lymington one Saturday to see some existing examples. The new boat was No. 142, and along with the National 12 that Jack built before the war, became the turning point for his future career. Shortly after building the Merlin, Jack handed in his notice, having decided to start out on his own.

Jack found premises, just above Bursledon Bridge on the Hamble River, and won a conversion job on which to start work. There then followed a stroke of real luck. Into the workshop one day walked a racing journalist who was working for the *"Yachtsman."* He was a racing helm and was also engaged in dinghy design. His name was Ian Proctor, though Jack confesses that he knew nothing about Ian at the time. However, Ian offered to attend to the correspondence for a couple of afternoons a week and also spent many hours talking about racing dinghies.

The three photographs here show different examples of deck layouts, ranging from the 1940's through to the mid 1960's. These boats were built by Chippendales, who were involved with the Class for more than twenty years.

Photographs courtesy of J. Chippendale

The yard's next piece of luck was born of the fact that the Hamble River Sailing Club was at that time spawning some of the best young helmsmen of the day. John Oakley (still at school), Cliff Norbury, Barry Perry, Dick Vine and others. They formed the nucleus of helmsmen who helped promote Chippendale's reputation as responsible builders and helped to established the yard. When Wyche & Coppock introduced the Rocket, orders for this "new boat" were also received by Chippendales. The name of Chippendale was now known throughout the dinghy scene and for this reason they were invited to build a Rocket at the Festival of Britain Exhibition on the South Bank. It was built in what might be described as a "bear pit" with a roof over it, and the public looked down on the boatbuilders as they worked. They spent the entire Exhibition period building the boat, steam bending ribs with the aid of a primus stove.

The amalgamation of the Merlin and the Rocket Classes brought further orders, helped by the association already established with Ian Proctor, whose designs were becoming extremely popular. In May 1954, Chippendales took a Merlin Rocket to the British Industries Fair at Olympia, and seven months later they were back at Olympia again with a Merlin Rocket, this time for the National Boat Show, and for a period of twelve years following that, Chippendales showed a Merlin Rocket at the Boat Show and offered hospitality to the Class Association. It was during this period that the building methods changed, from the traditional ¼" mahogany planking on steam bent Canadian Rock Elm timbers to the glued clinker, pioneered by Wyche & Coppock.

Sadly, Chippendales no longer build dinghies, instead they have become a small but happy concern building Broads cruisers at Wroxham. Similarly, over the forty years since the Class started in the 1940s, many of our builders are sadly no more, or have

Robert Spolton, a part-time boat-builder from the Midlands, has built some very pretty Merlins. Shown here is *Main Aim*, a modified "Bullet."

moved on to build in classes where the profit margin is higher, for nobody becomes wealthy building Merlin Rockets alone. Jack Holt went to Enterprises, Brian Kennedy to building GRP Otters, Roy Rigden went to Hornets, Wyche & Coppock could no longer find the skilled people to build in wood and confined themselves to glassfibre, Adur are no more, Anderson Rigdon & Perkins, after a fire destroyed their Merlin mould, then began building cruisers. Smaller and lesser known builders have found the financial constraints just too much to earn a living building beautiful Merlin Rockets for just a few orders. John Freeman, who built the early "Wot" boats for Tony Watts and Alan Warren, has left boatbuilding altogether.

Luckily, other more flexible and dedicated builders have taken their places, such as those following in this chapter, who are continuing to build some of the most beautiful racing dinghies to be seen anywhere. Unfortunately, not all our builders are given justice here. In recent years, Boatcraft, Peter Diamond, Alan Jackson and Brett Dingwall have all made their input to the Class and should be encouraged to continue with their involvement. Boatcraft, with its base near Mansfield, is actually two school-teachers, Robert and Jean Spolton. Their boatbuilding activities occur in their spare time, often between 5.00 am and 8.00 am in the term time. Although they do not themselves sail in the Class, they have built nine Merlin Rockets, eight of them being "Bad Companys" and one "NSM II." These were based upon one owner making an initial enquiry as to whether Robert would be interested in building a Merlin Rocket and persuading two other potential owners to agree to ordering new boats, thus making the building more economical. The Spoltons have no intention of going full-time into boatbuilding, but they illustrate how a new builder can break into the field, offering diversity in the Class. The builders who are discussed here, however, are those who have had the greatest latter-day influence on the Class and still have boats regularly racing.

Bob Hoare, 1959 to early 1970s

Bob Hoare states that he has probably been sailing a Merlin Rocket just about as long as Queen Elizabeth has been on the throne. Starting by sailing a Jack Holt designed Merlin, No. 97, built by J. P. White & Sons of Bedford in 1953, he then progressed to the celebrated *Buccaneer 2*, No. 597, a Chippendale built Proctor "Mark VI" in which he came 6th in the 1955 Championships, 2nd in 1957 and 5th in 1958. This boat was still sailing competitively at the 1976 Championships. Bob built his first boat in 1959, to the same "Mark VI" design, in time for the Championships in which he came 6th. He improved still further in 1960, building and personally sailing the Championship winner, *Surfboard*.

From 1960 to 1968 inclusive, one or another of Bob's boats won the Championships eight times and whilst it is true that he gradually cornered the market of the best helmsmen, the very obvious point remains that the best helmsmen went to Bob because they knew that they would get a fast boat, at a price which was still under the standard rate for the other builders. Much of the reason why these Hoare boats had a "heart of gold," was that they concentrated on the basics of providing a sound hull and only the minimum gear which was essential to race the boat fast. At this time Bob Hoare had just started building Flying Dutchmen and his personal experience of the much greater loads placed upon the 19ft 10in Olympic boat (he won a European Flying Dutchman Week) had shown him clearly what mattered and what did not in terms of results, for the 1960s undeniably belonged to Bob. Only Rowsell has so far equalled his record of building eight Championship winners in nine years.

With the building of Joan Oakley's Flying Dutchman *Shadow* in 1966, which won the European and then the World Championships, and then the Rodney Pattisson's *Superdocious* series, which won two Olympic Gold medals, one Silver and three or four World Championships in between, Bob became in great demand as a Flying Dutchman builder, in Europe as well as in this country. The Merlin business took a back seat as he not unreasonably put all his resources into establishing himself as the number one Flying Dutchman builder in the world.

However, Olympic classes appeal to very few people and those who sail in them tend to be very fickle in their choice of builders. Bob subsequently turned his attention back to the Merlin Rocket Class with a view to regaining his position, which he felt had gone to other builders whilst he had been concentrating on the Flying Dutchman class. Having first-hand experience of exploiting a large spinnaker in a Flying Dutchman, he had some ideas on how to make the best use of the new Merlin spinnaker and longer pole which had just been allowed. He was now building to the Morrison "Smokers Satisfaction" design and to the Gregory "Ghost Rider" design for which he felt there was more demand than was apparent for those wanting a stable straight-line machine. He, in fact, designed a similar shape in his own design, "Summer Blues," in order to make the "Ghost Rider" shape a little more manoeuvrable in a crowded space. He therefore offered three designs for the different helmsmen of the Class.

Until recently Bob was still actively sailing the Merlin himself in club racing and has kept in touch with the Class this way over a number of years. Bob feels that although all boats are getting expensive, the price of the Merlin has not risen as sharply as that of other classes and providing that one does not spend a large amount of money on quite unnecessary fittings, it is possible to build a basic hull and necessary equipment for very much less than people seem to think. Personally, he believes that there is a great future in the Merlin Class which is why Bob continued to sail it and build it for the Class over so many years.

Arnott Dobson, 1966 to 1981

Precisely because so many builders and sailmakers raced Merlin Rockets keenly, the Class owners not unreasonably tended to favour with their custom the people whom they saw regularly and talked to about their favourite hobby. For all their apparent omniscience at their own clubs, most owners needed reassurance about their ideas, and more new boats and sails were planned in evenings at the Championships or Silver Tiller meetings than many would have admitted. Those who did not appear on the scene tended to lose custom and the Class lost some excellent sailmakers and builders in this way.

However, one builder who rarely appeared at any Merlin meeting was Arnott Dobson, for many years a partner and builder at Aln Boatyard at Alnmouth, Northumberland. Arnott was unquestionably a Merlin man, having even designed his own boat before leaving such matters initially to Martin Jones and Tom Booth, and then to Keith Callaghan and Phil Morrison. His first boat, the home designed *Doodlebug*, No. 1869, was built in 1965 at the time when Ian Proctor designs were still on top but nobody except Chippendale, Bob Hoare and Messrs. Wyche & Coppock were allowed to build them. Ironically, this very refusal made Arnott turn to Martin Jones whose "Xpectant" hit the Merlin Class in 1966 and started a revolution in ideas about the efficiency of wide beamed boats. This design was seized upon by Spud Rowsell in the South and Aln Boatyard in the North and these two led the movement which finally ended the thirteen year domination of the Proctor designs. Aln Boatyard really started being accepted in 1968 at the time when the Lancashire fleets were all suddenly deciding to buy a new boat, and the boatyard's popularity grew until 1970 when David Childs' *Dropout*, one of Arnott's boats, made the first six in the Championships. Later, David Spiers, Vernon Ralston, Colin Humphreys and Paddy Atkinson were also able to repeat this achievement in Aln boats. However, the distance of some 400 miles from the South coast to Alnmouth had discouraged the very people who would have won the Championships for Aln.

Unlike many builders who started building light and then learned how to make the boat stronger, Arnott Dobson, with the surging North Sea breaking on the beach nearby, had always built a strong boat and then learned how to build it lighter. Aln owners swore that their boats lasted much longer than any others and when they were being produced down to weight offered as good a boat as any. The designs over the years were carefully chosen: "Xpectant," "Courageous," "Ghost Rider," the Callaghan series and the Morrison "September Girl," "Kipper," "Smokers" and the "NSM." Aln consistently turned out superb boats and the comparatively few recorded race successes probably led the Aln Boatyard to be the most undeservedly underrated yard of all those which have built Merlins. Some of their orders came about because many helmsmen suddenly found in the spring that they could afford a new boat and went to Aln for no better reason other than the boat could be delivered in time for the Championships, and were almost invariably puzzled as to why more people did not go to this excellent firm.

A few years ago, Arnott parted company from Aln Boatyard, but soon afterwards was back in the Merlin Class, building boats on his own. Though this may be his swansong within the Class, Arnott Dobson should always be remembered as a talent that most of the Class has missed.

Rowsell Brothers, 1966 to present

As the 1960s were dominated by Bob Hoare and to an extent by Wyche & Coppock, it is undeniably true that the 1970s belonged to the Rowsell Brothers of Exmouth. The yard was set up by the eldest of four brothers, Brian, who became very famous in National 12s and more particularly Finns and International 14s. Peter "Spud" Rowsell, most well known amongst the Merlin Rocket fleet, first went to a Merlin Rocket National Championships in 1964, when it was held at Poole. That year he had come 3rd overall at the National 12's Burton Week, and had teamed up for the Merlins with the winner of Burton Week, to sail a Merlin called *Bobby's Girl*, No. 1507, a Savery design. They came 147th overall!

Having worked out that there was something wrong with the boat, they borrowed a "Mark IX" for one race and came 7th. Satisfied that it was the boat at fault, not themselves, they spent the last race on Brownsea Island with a crateful of beer where they were joined by David Robinson who hadn't had a successful Week either.

The following year, a meeting was held amongst the members of Exmouth Sailing Club, whereupon it was agreed that the Club would adopt the Merlin Rocket as one of its classes and orders for 8 boats were placed with Spud. Spud attributes much of the yard's early success to the refusal of Ian Proctor, then the top designer in the Class, to increase the number of licensed builders beyond the three then currently building, thus compelling Rowsells to look elsewhere for designers. Rowsell Brothers hit upon Martin Jones who had just designed the then daringly six-foot wide "Xpectant," which was the first to lead the fashion towards wider boats. With this design and the "Rage" - "Outrage" - "Courageous" designs which each year from Tom Booth for the heavier helmsmen (which Spud and other well-built members of the Class favoured), Rowsell Boats took an increasing share of the honours until, with the advent of the really wide boats, they established a near monopoly of the top places. Much of the success could be attributed to two factors. Firstly, Rowsell-built boats came from a small yard, in which work on all the boats came under Spud's own sharp eye and therefore any lapse in standards was quickly rectified before the boat left the yard, and secondly with lower overheads than yards in other areas, he could afford to put a finer finish to his boats than his then competitors, so that his boats looked even better. This made other builders improve their standards with the result that the Merlin Rocket Class has always attracted admiration from people in other Classes for superbly finished boats.

Conversely, this same factor has also been a possible criticism of the Class. In the continual spiral of seeking the immaculate Merlin, the fear of high cost has put off some potential newcomers to the Class. The cost incurred to produce these masterpieces is not in the planking up of the hull, all builders can do this in a week, but in the frames, decking and other, skilful joinery which goes to complete the package, often taking another three weeks. The side effect of this competition amongst the Class builders is that none of them are now prepared to produce "budget" hulls, which though it might avoid much of the high quality joinery, would result in a boring, dull-looking hull which could damage their reputation with the regular customers. Spud himself acknowledges that this problem has contributed to the reduction in the number of new Merlins built over the last seven years to well below that being produced by his yard in the peak years. In 1972, all the top 12 boats at the Championships were built by Rowsells and they had 72 Merlin Rockets on order. Five people were working for Spud and their aim was to produce one boat every fortnight. The yard was so totally committed to Merlins that they used to turn away repair work – an unheard of occurrence these days.

Aware of the drop in new Merlins being built each year, Spud decided to produce the foam sandwich "NSM" hulls which made their début at the 1980 Championships. The "NSM" design had proved very successful at the previous two Championships, and although Phil Morrison himself wasn't particularly enthusiastic about the project, Spud went to Omega, a local plastics moulding firm and commissioned the mould from his own "NSM" *Oliver*. History has shown that although 34 boats have been built from this mould, they never really proved popular, for a mixture of reasons. Structurally these hulls were superior, and the bare hull was noticeably stronger than an equivalent wooden hull. The problems were partly imagined and partly real. The real problems have been the fitting of the keel band and the strength of the bilge keels. The bilge keels were filled with a PVC type of foam which on some boats absorbed water, often after being locally damaged by the boat being poorly supported on the trailer, or from neglect when the hull was rolled over on the beach or shingle. Water has also sometimes entered the hulls through the screw holes for the keel band.

The other "problems" have been somewhat over accentuated. People have claimed that the hulls have a weight problem – a fact probably publicised by those boats with the problems already mentioned earlier. Another area of concern was the rise of floor measurement, which was found to vary somewhat between the boats. This apparently was caused by the length of time for which the hull was left to "cure" in the mould.

Perhaps the real reason for their apparent decline in popularity was the timing of the project. 1980 was the year when Jon Turner left Rowsells and set up on his own. The first boat he built was an "NSM II," which won the championships the following year, but Spud found himself with an apparently outdated design on his hands as well as an extra boatbuilder to compete with who knew as much about Merlins as he himself did. None

Prospect, the second Omega foam-sandwich "NSM" to be completed by Rowsells in 1980, and was originally owned by the Class Chairman, Robert Harris.

Photograph by John Bickford

the less, the Omega "NSM" was a brave try on Spud's part to increase the annual output of Merlin Rockets being built, and these boats are still excellent club and Silver Tiller competitors.

Spud himself is as well known for his racing successes in the Class as for his boatbuilding skills. With Jon Turner as his crew, this awesome duo have won the Championships twice, finished 2nd three times, 3rd once and 6th once, covering a span of eleven years. With Chris Owen from McNamara's Sail Loft crewing for him, Spud again came 2nd overall in 1983 which makes for an extremely successful career in Merlins.

It would have been very easy for a yard such as this, with proven Championship performers, to stick to well-known designs with which it was regularly succeeding and not move forward. This was something which Spud had never done and in the 1970s he always sailed a different design of boat each year and had been very willing to take a right-angled course to the current thoughts on hull shape. This process was started, for obvious reasons, when he was beginning with the radical Martin Jones and Tom Booth designs, and was followed by the first maximum beam Merlin Rocket and then the unusual "Ghost Rider," which went against everybody's idea of what a Merlin Rocket should look like, including his own. According to Michael McNamara, his neighbouring sailmaking, Spud should by now have eaten a considerable number of hats!

When Phil Morrison and Keith Callaghan produced their first really effective designs in 1971, these were built initially by Rowsells although the designs were made available to all other builders, a fact which opened up the Class to amateur builders and other

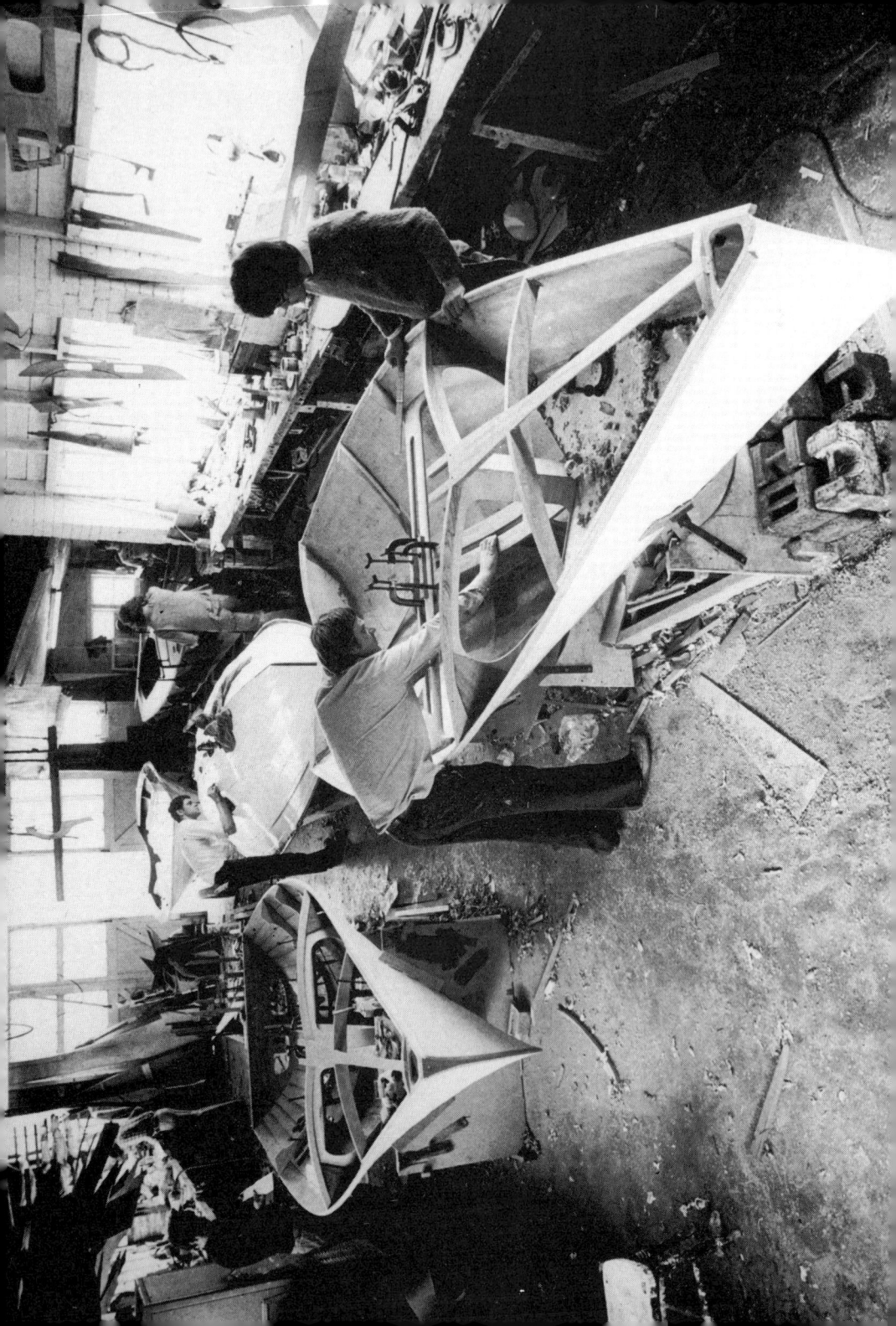

small yards in a way which had not been possible previously. Spud believes it to be wrong for people to think that they have to go to one particular builder to obtain a successful boat. This very generous approach from one who has had as much success as he has is very much in character with the man, as those who have raced against him and drunk gallons of beer at the bar with him afterwards will testify. However, Spud has always been in touch with the latest design thoughts, looking for interesting new hull shapes. Sometimes the new design did not gain the looked-for success but he always tried the design out himself and if people suffered from a new design it was because they were somewhat unimaginatively copying the boat which Spud would have himself for the next year, rather than thinking the changes out for themselves. The classic example was the experiments with the "Mustard Seed" shape, which Spud tried out before giving up and going back to trusty "Smokers Satisfaction." He has also kept up with new construction ideas, approving of the re-arranged bow tank, which substantially stiffened up the hull, by moving the aft bulkhead back to the shroud takeoff point, and was also the first person in the Class to use the new "West" system, building Jim Park's *Stringendo* with the epoxy resin at Jim's suggestion.

Stringendo, built by Spud Rowsell for Jim Park, co-editor of this book, was the first Merlin to be built using West Epoxy as the glue for bonding the planks. The design is a "Smokers Satisfaction."

Photograph by John Bickford

Spud has not blinkered his talents purely to Merlins. He has had a try at the Olympics in a Soling with Alan Warren and Barry Dunning, just as other notable Merlin sailors have, John Oakley in Solings, Phil Morrison in Stars, Warren most successfully in Tempests, before setting fire to the boat during the last race of his second quest for

◀ The Merlin Rocket production line at Rowsell Bros. with Spud Rowsell closely inspecting a new GRP foam hull.

Photograph by John Bickford

Gold, Rodney Pattisson, Jon Turner, Pat Blake and Lew Dann in Flying Dutchmen and Lawrie Smith in 470s (amongst almost every other type of sailing vessel possible to race in a span of thirteen years).

Following a few pints of beer, Spud agreed to build Phil Morrison's most adventurous design, the 54 foot Trimaran *Exmouth Challenge*, also known as *Marlow Ropes*, in which Spud has raced round Britain twice with Mark Gatehouse, and the boat itself, under some unpronounceable French name, won the Transatlantic Singlehanded Race.

A 1985 built Rowsell "Summer Wine," built with a stern buoyancy tank.

Photograph by Ian Holt

Now, in the 1980s, there are a number of boatbuilders challenging for the dominance of the top places in the Merlin fleet, but they will have to be very sharp in spotting a development which Spud has not noticed and be very capable builders to construct a better boat. Much of the yard's success is owed to the efforts of Nick Turner and Martin Handle, both of whom have been working for Rowsells for more than ten years and are more directly involved with construction of the Merlins than Spud himself. As befits one who has been so successful in the Class, Spud is a strong competitor and has no intention of losing his yard's influence and dominance in the Class. A warm outgoing personality, a Championship without Spud would be a much duller affair.

Jon Turner, 1980 to present

Much of Jon Turner's Merlin Rocket boatbuilding career overlaps with that of Spud Rowsell, as he worked for Rowsells throughout the 1970s during the "golden" days of Merlin Rocket building down in Exmouth. Jon left school in 1967 and started work at Souters, the famous boatyard in Cowes on the Medina River. There he spent the next twelve months trying to get into the small workshops set apart from the main area of work, in which the International 14s were built. This was the type of boatbuilding that really appealed to Jon, rather than the yacht repair and construction that the yard was more renowned for. Not being able to work regularly on building 14s, Jon applied to Rowsells for a job, having known of the yard from the time when they repaired the family's Albacore.

Joining Rowsells as an apprentice in 1968 enabled Jon to be involved with the Merlin Rocket Class just as it was approaching its peak in popularity and also to work for the boatbuilder who was producing *the* boats within the Class. The first Merlin Rocket that Jon worked on was No. 2131 *Bonnie Girl*, an "Xpectant" for Don Hearn and Keith Callaghan (just prior to Keith designing "Hotspur"). This boat stood out in Jon's memory as the first dinghy that he recollected having five coats of varnish, and looked extremely impressive. Initially, Jon crewed for Mike Davies in *Midnight*, the hull from which Bob Hoare took a mould to produce GRP "Mark IXbs," but the following year the famous Spud/Jon sailing partnership commenced with *Outrage*, the Tom Booth design which they built together in their spare time during weekends and evenings. Their successes are described in other sections within this book, but it should be realised that it was a true partnership on the water and Jon must be recognised for his part in the Championship successes which they achieved.

Throughout the 1970s Jon became steadily more involved with the construction and responsibility of the new Merlins at Rowsells until the time came when he felt a change in his career was necessary. Unable to progress further with Rowsells, Jon was faced with the option of trying to start up on his own or go to college to study teaching. Just when the latter option appeared the only way out, a chance arose to buy a bungalow out in the country, just north of Exeter, which had enough land for constructing a workshop large enough for building dinghies. The first boat to be constructed was *The Feet*, for Andy Street, and this was also the first "NSM II" to be built. Jon personally has always put a very high emphasis on symmetry, fairness of the planks and weight as being race winning factors, rather than radical hull shapes. His faith in the "NSM II" has been shown in the fact that the first 12 boats built by him were all to this design.

The racing successes of himself and his dinghies are outstanding. When Jon left Rowsells he initially teamed up and sailed with Phil Morrison, and in 1980 the pair borrowed *Summer Wine* from its latest owner, Chris Haworth, who had chosen to crew for Spud rather than sail his own boat. This was a typical Morrison Week, with controversial disqualifications and a broken rudder, but then faired somewhat better the next year. Whilst Phil and Jon could not quite manage to win the Merlin Rocket Championships Jon must have been well satisfied, as Andy Street won the Championships in *The Feet* which started a run of four successive overall Championship wins for Jon's dinghies. For 1982, Jon had arranged to borrow *Seventh Heaven*, the "NSM II" which he had built for Derek Hanrahan, and crew for Lawrie Smith. At the last minute his helm let him down, so Jon decided to helm himself and rented Richard Parslow as crew. Pat Blake won the Week in one of Jon's Merlins, but Jon came 3rd overall, being beaten by Phil Morrison who, as usual, had finished 2nd again!

1983 was even better. Jon was also by now building Scorpions and in one month succeeded in winning both the Scorpion and Merlin Rocket National Championships as well as finishing 2nd overall at the Inland Championships, and the sight of Turner and Parslow at the front of the Merlin fleet was by now to be expected. At the end of 1983 Jon was offered financial help to campaign a Flying Dutchman for the Olympics. After a ridiculously short tune-up period Jon came a close second in the trials to Jo Richards, but has subsequently followed this up by winning the Class National Championships and the Merlin Rocket Championships again, and at the time of writing, is the only obvious choice for selection for the next Olympics out of any of the classes. By

A set of photographs showing boats being built by Jon Turner. The first two are of a "NSM II" being built with the old style front buoyancy tank, the aft bulkhead being part of the jig. Jon's boats are easily distinguished by his construction of the area under the mast step, and how he stiffens up the centreboard case.

Photograph courtesy of J. Turner.

comparison, 1985 was a relatively poor year, failing to win the International 14 Championships ("We only built the boat for a bit of fun") and finishing 2nd at the Merlin Rocket Championships. However, Jon then turned his thoughts firmly onto the Flying Dutchman Class with the next Olympics as his goal.

His craftsmanship will however still be present in our dinghy parks and will continue to make the Merlin Rocket stand out in the midst of all the *plastic* boats that are ever increasingly taking over the sailing world.

Guy Winder, 1972 to present

Guy Winder is an unusual Merlin builder in two respects: firstly, he was not trained as a craftsman or joiner, and secondly he entered his second vocation at the age of 39! However, Guy's earlier years were not wasted, because he had the distinction of being an experienced production engineer, which has equipped him to bring new ideas into his building of Merlins. Some of the knowledge and skills learned during an apprenticeship in aircraft engineering with De Havillands and obtaining an H.N.C. in Mechanical and Production Engineering, with emphasis on strength of materials, are now being employed in boatbuilding.

The centrepiece of Guy's building technique, where he made use of his training in aircraft engineering, is his sophisticated jig. Whilst the basic idea was the same as that used by all Merlin boatbuilders, Guy refined his by making use of steel rods, which were run through the frames at each land. These had three advantages: firstly, they made the jig far more rigid, greatly reducing the chance of the hull distorting during the glueing stage; secondly, they supported and facilitated the clamping of all ply joints, and thirdly these rods acted as an instant guide to the fairness and shape of the hull that was about to be constructed. With any other builder, when a new design was commissioned the designer could never be too sure what it would look like until the planks were shaped and glued together. With Guy's jig, simply by fixing the rods onto the frames, a designer could instantly see what the finished hull would look like and from this three-dimensional full scale model of the boat, decide whether to make any last minute alterations.

Guy is an enthusiastic club sailor who competes regularly at local open meetings and National and Inland Championships. He had, in the past, regularly been seen at the front of the fleet, particularly in light weather and inland. His greatest hours of glory were in the last race at the 1984 Championships, which he won with Jenny King crewing for him in *Stilleto,* and the 1976 Inland Championships where he finished 2nd overall in *Late Night Extra,* this time with June Lloyd.

His sailing started as an apprentice at Maylandsea Bay in Essex with Merlin Rocket No. 272 *Pas de Deux,* which he sailed for about nine years, before buying *Windcheater,* No. 1825, a Proctor "Mark IX." He sailed at Hollingworth SC for nearly eight years before building first *Wide Guy,* No. 2778, and then *Late Night Extra,* No. 2887, which he owned for over five years. His record proved his theory that you do not need a new boat every eighteen months to be competitive. For many years he confounded his rivals with his dirty sails and unfashionable aft mainsheet system. In spite of his interest as a boatbuilder, Guy was a firm believer that our image of "pretty" boats was not only damaging but false. The aspects of our Class which he felt should be emphasized were that Merlin Rockets are good all round boats, structurally sound and therefore durable, which could be competitive on the sea, on a small reservoir in the Midlands or on the Thames. No stretch of water was too small or intimidating for a Merlin, nor any wind

strength too restricting, which was something that could not be said about all Restricted Classes in this country.

Guy was well known for his "Winder Box" design, which like his entry into full-time boatbuilding was more as a result of circumstances than an object of ambition or intent. In 1972 he wanted to build a "Phantom Kipper" for himself, but because he could not get in touch with Phil Morrison to ask for the drawings, he modified some "September Girl" plans and built *Wide Guy*. After a year in this boat, and deciding that he rather enjoyed building boats, he felt ready to have another go and so produced *Late Night Extra*, so named after the radio programme to which he frequently listened whilst he worked.

Then Mike Greenhalgh of Hollingworth SC asked him to build a boat. This boat became the first "Winder Box" and was a further modification of *Wide Guy* with more width aft and less sheer height. It had a very successful first season and Guy consequently received orders for five shells, to be decked by their owners. These he built in his spare time in his garage at home. At this stage Guy did not undertake decking, because this required more joinery skills than he felt he possessed. He could not see a way of simplifying this phase of construction. However, the demand for his boats from local Merlin Rocket sailors pressed him into building complete boats and he decided that the only way to accomplish this was to go full-time. This was not such a difficult step, because Guy admitted he liked the idea of being self-employed. The job of production engineer had not always been satisfying. Having responsibility for only a small area of the production operation and being sandwiched between operatives and management, both resistant to change and innovation, was often frustrating, and this was all in the contesdt of a declining textile industry, which had become Guy's career following his move to Bradford. Now Guy obtains particular pleasure from being able to see the whole job through from start to finish and having complete control of the decisions made at any stage.

Anybody who has seen Guy's recent boats will agree that even if he was not trained as a craftsman, he is now a self-taught one. He has now built more than 45 hulls and there can be no doubt that the increase in Merlin popularity in the North in the 1970s was due to Guy's existence as an enthusiastic boatbuilder whose heart was truly with the Merlin Rocket.

Laurie Smart, 1974 to 1984

Laurie Smart is an individualist, craftsman and Merlin Rocket enthusiast. His individualism showed in many ways. It was evident from his desire to work for himself, demonstrated by the fact that he started up on his own no less than three times. First after completing his apprenticeship as a boatbuilder at the age of 22, the second after five months repairing ocean going yachts on the Hamble and the third after working as a farmhand near Handcross, with the establishment and subsequent dissolution of Smartboats Limited. Laurie then lived at Handcross in a comfortable cottage and built boats in a converted agricultural shed at the bottom of his garden.

There was no truth in the popular rumour that Laurie used to hand-pick his customers. Orders were accepted on a first come first served basis, but at the end of the

◀ A sequence of photographs following the construction of *Diamond Smiles* by Guy Winder. The first photograph shows his rigid jig with the centreboard case already in position. The second photograph shows how Guy clamps the planks during gluing, and illustrates the tapered centreboard case. The boat was built without a thwart. The last photograph shows how the knee at this point has been built up and capped to strengthen the hull.

Photographs by Guy Winder

1970s, Laurie was only building around four Merlins a year. He found it unprofitable to employ skilled labour and did all the work himself. As a result, building four boats took half a year, but even without employed help there was little money in it and Laurie could not afford to build Merlin all the year round. He also liked a change of work during the summer. Over the past decade, many of Laurie's boats have achieved considerable success. In Merlin Rockets he built Pat Blake's *After Myth*, Phil Morrison's *Summer Wine*, Alan Warren's *After Burner* as well as his own *Sweet Charity* in which he won the Burnham Icicle in 1978. In International 14s he has built two Prince of Wales Cup winners and from a Bob Hoare shell he built Pat Blake's Flying Dutchman, which achieved notable success.

The cynic might be tempted to say that the success of his boats was attributable to the sailors who bought them rather than the quality of the boats. However, many of his distinguished clients went back to him for more and many of them were very particular and discriminating gentlemen. When his craftsman's pride was allowed to penetrate his modesty, Laurie would admit that he thought his boats were special. He attributed this to the great care he took over certain aspects of construction, which did not show but he nevertheless considered important. In particular, he would take as much trouble as possible to ensure that his boats were straight, perpendicular and not twisted.

Nothing spoke better for the durability of his boats than his decision to buy back, with his crew, Russell Bell, Jerry Rook's boat *ASP*. As for the superficial aspects of craftsmanship, his repair to one boat in particular, *Gold Dust*, was a good demonstration of his skills. Even though eight planks of this hull were replaced on the starboard side from amidships to the transom, it was impossible to tell which side had been repaired without locating and counting the scarf joints.

Whilst his skills as a boatbuilder were comprehensively acquired over such a wide range of boats as ocean racing yachts, gin palaces and skiffs, it was the woodwork which he enjoyed the most, and his preferred way was to supply a Merlin hull ready to paint and without fittings. Laurie was, of course, not just a respected builder of Merlin Rockets, he was also a highly competitive sailor of them. He began sailing at the age of 12 as a sea scout in cutters on the Thames at Marlow. Then at 17 he joined Henley Sailing Club and crewed for Geoff Keen, who was a pioneer of glued clinker construction in National 12. Next he sailed International 14s at Hamble before moving on to helm his own National 12 at Pevensey Bay, at which point he teamed up with Russell Bell. In 1974 Laurie had his first Merlin Rocket, *Satanita*, a product of Smartboats, of which he was the working director.

Laurie's enthusiasm for Merlins was genuine. He found the appearance, both shape and quality of materials, and the craftsmanship attractive. He thought they had the best sailing characteristics of any racing dinghy, and believed they were sensitive in light weather and sensational yet controllable in heavy weather by normal weight and sized crews. To Laurie, this made Merlin Rockets truly rewarding boats to sail.

CHAPTER 8

The Silver Tiller Series

All dinghy classes hold Championships, all have Open Meetings and many have an aggregate series for these events, usually confined to areas. None can compare with the Merlin Rocket Silver Tiller Series which has an unbroken history stretching from 1950 to the present day.

The idea for a series of Open Meetings came almost simultaneously to two very forward thinking classes, the then unamalgamated Merlin Class and the National 12s. This was in 1949, approximately the time that the sport of motor-racing was reviving the Grand Prix series after World War II and engineering firms were turning their attention to strong lightweight boat trailers which would enable dinghies to be more easily transported by road. The National 12 series only had a very short life, the trophy eventually being re-allocated for another purpose. Fortunately for the future of dinghy racing in this country, the Merlin Rocket Class (as it was to become in 1951) held firm.

One has only to look at much of the pre- and post-war housing built without garages to see that car-ownership was a minority privilege and thus dinghies were sailed mainly at their clubs. The idea of travelling to a series of Open Meetings needed a wider car ownership, efficient boat trailers and a Series which would make the whole exercise worthwhile. As England gradually struggled out of a period of austerity, the cars and trailers came. In 1950, Duncan Ferguson was persuaded by some Merlin owners to present the Silver Tiller for a national (rather than an area) series which would be a stern test of the versatility of boat and crew.

The advantage of a national series was that it encouraged helmsmen to travel outside their immediate area to interesting new venues in the search for points. In a local series, there would be no benefit gained by travelling outside the area, but when a club staged a Silver Tiller event for its Merlin fleet, the entries could come from anywhere in the country. This made the club look favourably upon its Merlin fleet which had brought this entry of good (and thirsty) helmsmen from afar. The whole sport of dinghy sailing benefitted as the cross-fertilisation of cultures brought together new ideas on fittings and sailing techniques throughout the whole season rather than just at the Championships.

One of the very early requirements of the Series (and oddly one which has hardly ever been copied by other Classes) was that helmsmen must count results both inland and on the sea. In most classes, helmsmen can count all their qualifying races in their favourite conditions and set their boat up accordingly. Merlin Rocket helmsmen, on the other hand, had for many years to count 2 races on the sea and 2 inland. The opening of large reservoirs has now split venues into a middle category of Open Waters, but the overriding principle remains that the Series is to be a rigorous test of versatility. In the course of a normal season, the Silver Tiller circuiteer will have to show boat handling skills in the narrow confines of a river or small reservoir, roll-tacking on the shifts upwind and snappy spinnaker work downwind, plan a tactical race on the larger reservoirs where decisions have to be made which side to go for the next shift – and where some races may be started in winds stronger than would be considered safe on the sea. Finally, racing on the sea will test not only ability to make the most of waves but also to gauge tides. It is not surprising that from the Silver Tiller circuit has come a number of the finest helmsmen of their era, at home in any conditions.

In a development class where boats can be designed for extreme conditions, the value of such a series is that while the boats must be able to perform well in extreme conditions, they must also be able to succeed in conditions at the other extreme, and anything in between. This has led to much greater thought amongst designers than would have been required to produce a boat which performs well at one venue, as was the case with the local one-designs which used to be found round the coast. The Merlin Rocket must be a "Boat for all Seasons."

Many experienced dinghy sailors feel that instead of the rapid increase of new dinghy classes in the '60s which so fragmented sailing talent, it would have been better for more helmsmen to join a smaller number of classes, including those such as the Merlin Rocket, where they could have chosen the appropriate design for their weight and favoured sailing conditions.

The Class spread to a wide variety of sailing waters and these were scrutinised by a succession of Silver Tiller Secretaries for inclusion in the Series. The intention was always to offer a challenging test, preferably differing from that offered elsewhere. The marvellous sea conditions on the South Coast were matched by the navigational decisions to be made at Lowestoft; to the river meetings on the Thames was added an extended river race of 18 miles on the Crouch estuary. The large "inland seas" of Grafham Water, Lake Bala and Draycote Water were quickly incorporated and provided a different type of sailing to the small gravel pits and canal compensation reservoirs which had provided much of the inland sailing after World War II. Eventually the series was expanded to count 5 races, at least one of which must be on the sea, one on Open Waters (the large lakes) and one on Restricted Waters (the smaller lakes and the rivers).

Because the best sailing waters often have clubs with the most expensive subscriptions, the Class sometimes dwindled at such clubs to such an extent that it was difficult to persuade the club to hold a Silver Tiller Meeting. However, if the venue was a good one, the circuiteers would respond and the Class was a popular guest. Connoisseurs of fine craftsmanship enjoyed examining the boats, those who understood racing appreciated well sailed boats making the best of their local conditions while the Committee welcomed visitors who were used to finding unaided a vacant spot in the dinghy park, rigging and launching in time and hardly ever needing the services of the rescue boats. Finally, the Bar Committee appreciated the well-known Merlin Rocket thirst.

The Class Handbook shows many famous names succeeding in the Series, from Jack Holt in the early days, Brian Southcott (who would have won many more series had he owned the boats he raced), Robin Judah (later Olympic Dragon representative at the 1968 Games), Brian Saffery-Cooper (Finn representative in 1964 and later a member of the Admirals' Cup Team) and Alan Warren (Olympic Tempest Silver Medallist in 1972).

Judah and Saffery-Cooper were great rivals. Pat Blake (later to win the Silver Tiller 4 times) recalls as a young boy, standing in the Cookham Reach SC bar one Saturday lunchtime on a weekend when there was, unusually, a Silver Tiller Meeting both at Cookham and at Bolton. Judah's Aston-Martin was seen to approach, stop near Saffery-Cooper's boat, reverse (all Silver Tiller circuiteers expertly reverse with trailer) and depart, clearly bound for Lancashire and a much-needed Inland win which he was more likely to achieve with Saffery-Cooper safely at Cookham. Brian had all the inland wins he needed, but was determined that Judah should not get one. Finishing his beer, he hooked up his boat and set off up the pre-motorway roads to Lancashire, arriving just as Judah emerged from a shop with a picture postcard of Bolton Town Hall, upon which he had penned a "wish you were here" message for Saffery-Cooper. Winning the Silver Tiller mattered and helmsmen were prepared to go to all legitimate lengths to do so.

The '60s were great years for the Silver Tiller. There were less events than now, but more helmsmen at each Meeting which lasted the whole weekend. The five-day week had liberated many from the tyranny of Saturday morning at the office and liberated wives had not yet started the tyranny of confining helmsmen and crews to one day's sailing per weekend. On the Sunday before Derby Day, most of the London-based helmsmen would set out along the A4 (no M4 then) to Cheddar Gorge for two days of racing for the Derby Bowl at Bristol Corinthian YC. Saturday evening would be spent getting through an enormous home-made steak and kidney pudding at the Bath Arms followed by draught cider by the pint and West-country skittles in the cellars. At the beginning of August, the circuit would move to Bognor Regis and after a race on Saturday for Queen Guinevere's Breastplate, there would be some very serious croquet played on the club lawn.

The tradition of helmsmen offering hospitality to visitors from afar made for some splendid house parties and a very much more leisurely atmosphere than now exists when events are confined to a single day during which one must travel, rig, cram in 3 races, de-rig, eat and return. The reason why the Class went over to one day events, or rather insisting that Silver Tiller points be taken on the Sunday results only, was due partly to a changing pattern in the Class. As there passed that "golden era" between the end of Saturday morning work and the harder times of the '70s, a newer type of helmsmen was emerging. Often self-employed (which in the new economic era meant working many more hours than if employed) and married to one of the new breed of wives who expected husbands to be at home at least one day of the weekend, the new breed had not built up a network of contacts with whom he could stay wherever the Meeting was held and who was finding the cost of overnight accommodation for himself and crew (who would frequently make the payment of his accommodation a condition of coming to a two-day meeting) more than he thought he could afford.

Many of the older generation passed on to the many keelboat classes, racing off the South Coast, regretting the high technology now required for a competitive boat and the way that the young engineers were taking over. This was, of course, due to the Class keeping a keen eye upon developments overseas as well as in England and the quality of information coming from improved yachting journalism and from the many members of the Class employed at Proctor Metal Masts and other companies involved in the dinghy racing industry.

Right at the head of this was David Child, whose feat of 4 consecutive Silver Tiller Series wins has never been equalled. In fact, he would probably have made it 5 had not Alan Warren entered into an arrangement with a local builder, John Freeman, then building the first of the really wide Merlins. Alan "ran in" each new boat of which he was a joint owner with the builder until a customer appeared. Offered the choice of a new untested boat or one which had been tuned by Warren, he usually chose the latter. Warren then had a new boat with new sails and went on to win the series with his 4th boat that season. A little hard on Child, perhaps, but within the rules.

Oddly enough, the nearest anybody came to equalling Child's feat was very shortly afterwards in the early '70s. In 1971, Pat Blake had a season-long battle with South Yorks' David Spiers which continued right up to the final Meeting at the Welsh Harp. Blake had a slight lead, but Spiers would win the Tiller if he won the Meeting. Competing for the first time at Wembley, was a father and son team from Nottingham who had progressed

David Child and Peter Morton, 1968 Silver Tiller winners.

Photograph by Guy Gurney

through the Midland Circuit and were now attempting the major events. Formerly a racing cyclist, Harry Haynes' boats were always very carefully prepared and his sailing techniques, in flat water anyway, were being steadily honed to a fine edge. The Haynes duly won all 3 races and effectively presented the Tiller to Blake.

The following year, Haynes was a serious competitor in his own right and had a slight lead at the start of the final Meeting, now established at Draycote Water, which could be overtaken if Blake won the Meeting. Also competing was Francis Williams, the 1971 National Champion but only occasionally seen on the Silver Tiller circuit because of the travelling involved from Exmouth. On a blustery day, Francis won all 3 races and effectively presented the Tiller to the Haynes. By 1973, Williams had decided that the Tiller was worth winning. Careful attention to tune of his rig had brought the first Inland Championship and the last 2 races in the Nationals in light airs supposedly unsuitable for his "Ghost Rider." In a critical race at the Welsh Harp from which he needed a Restricted Water win, Francis spent so much time adjusting his rig that he was not off the pontoon at the 5 minute gun and was disqualified. Blake did not win the race, but he found on returning, since Francis could not now win the Meeting, he had won the Tiller.

In 1974, the position was even more bizarre. Coming into the final Meeting at Draycote Water were 3 helmsmen who could all the win the Tiller – Blake, Haynes and the convincing winner of that year's Nationals, Spud Rowsell. The Force 5, gusting 6, favoured Rowsell, the lake conditions favoured Haynes; the most experienced Silver Tiller campaigner was Blake.

With everything depending upon the last race, Jim Park remembers coming up to the starting line and encountering Haynes, head to wind and being blown backwards at a rate of knots. Trying to avoid a collision with a potential winner of the Silver Tiller series, he bore away and put a dent in a boat belonging to another potential Silver Tiller winner, Pat Blake! Rowsell, happier on the open sea, had wisely kept clear of the favoured end and powered away upwind in a cloud of spray. Had Rowsell just carried on and played safe, he would almost certainly have won the race, the Meeting and the Silver Tiller. Completely confident of his boat, his crew and his sailing ability in a Force 6, Rowsell decided to hoist spinnaker on a reach which a shift had made a little closer than before. As Jonathan Turner was engaging the pole, they were hit by a gust and, with the weight forward, the bow buried. Had they capsized there was enough time to right the boat and enough wind to empty the water through the flaps without losing any more places than would easily be recovered on the next beat. However, Rowsell and Turner had not got where they were by capsizing, so they kept the boat upright – and the mast broke!

Somewhat emotionally disturbed by the dent in his boat, Pat Blake had the feeling that the fates, which had twice given him the Silver Tiller at the Welsh Harp in '71 and '73 but which had deprived him here at Draycote in '72, were going to deprive him again in '74. In consequence, Blake was sailing carefully round the course having given up the thought of winning. Haynes, on the other hand, had recovered well from his bad start and a morose Blake could see Haynes pulling through the leaders to take the race. Harry returned to shore to the applause of the local Midlanders, delighted that one of their number had broken the "Southern monopoly." Understandably tired and elated, Harry Haynes never got round to signing the declaration and, under the rules of the host club, was quite properly disqualified. While apologising for causing the dent and giving insurance details, Jim Park, as Silver Tiller secretary, was able to improve Blake's day by advising him that since Rowsell had not finished and Haynes had been disqualified, neither had finished high enough to upset Blake's lead and that he had won the Silver Tiller for the 3rd time.

The '70s continued to produce close-fought series. In '75, that long-time supporter of the Class, John Harris, had an incredible year in which he nearly won every Meeting he attended only to come second in nearly all of them. This was the year when he had only to finish better than 15th in the last race to become Champion and then was disqualified for being over the line. He kept in contention right up to the last race at Draycote. This time it was Harry Haynes, determined not to have the Tiller snatched from his grasp again, who secured the Series with a second place. For John Harris, there was not even the runner-up spot. David Liddington won the Meeting and snatched even this from him. No wonder John took up golf shortly afterwards. Happily, John still races Merlins, but has adopted a more relaxed attitude ever since.

Hectic action at Hamble Sailing Club Silver Tiller. The event is held in Southampton Water and counts as a sea event.

Photograph by Trevor Pountain

The first two places gained by Haynes and Liddington were achieved by counting results gained on the large lakes at Grafham and Draycote and ignoring the sea. Neither helmsman was really happy in waves and there was a strong body of opinion that the measures designed to make it easier for Midlanders to qualify had diluted the main principle of the Silver Tiller series, that it should test all-round ability. The Open Water classification was kept, but as a new category, and competitors would now have to count 5 rather than 4 events, with at least one on the sea, one Restricted and one Open Water event. This still meant that competitors would only have to go on the sea once, rather than twice as in the pre-1972 days, but could not get away with ignoring the sea altogether.

Having helped his father win the "Double" of National Championships and Silver Tiller in one year, Kevin Haynes decided it was time to do some helming at more than club level. Acquiring Harry's old *Phantom Rider* (a "Ghost Rider" design) he carefully restored it, signed up a fit young crew like himself and started the 1976 Silver Tiller campaign. He quickly won a few Meetings on Midland reservoirs, but was showing inexperience in the major events. However, with advice from Harry and a careful choice of Meetings, he started collecting points. Lacking only a good sea result, opportunity came when Arun YC, whose May Meeting had been blown off, decided to try again in October. Hearing about this from the Silver Tiller Secretary on one of Kevin's

◀ Andrew and Caroline McAusland sailing in the beautiful upper reaches of the Exe estuary.

Photograph by John Bickford

discreet telephone calls to see how he was doing, Kevin made the long journey down from Nottingham. Going the "wrong way" up the first beat, according to those who race there regularly, Kevin picked up a favourable shift and won the race to take the Silver Tiller in his first full season on the circuit – a remarkable achievement.

In 1977, there occurred the first, and so far only, "treble". Although this had been technically possible since the introduction of the Inland Championships in 1973, the strength of the competition had prevented anybody winning these, the Nationals and the Silver Tiller in one year. Pat Blake, who had virtually given up Merlin Rocket sailing after winning the '74 Silver Tiller in order to concentrate on his Olympic campaign in a Flying Dutchman, returned with a new "Smoker" called *Aftermyth*. In 1977, that boat was the fastest one around whatever the conditions and Pat Blake, crewed now by Dave Webster, needed no luck to win the Silver Tiller for the 4th time. He had already won the series well before the end of the season.

It will be seen that in the '70s, the engraver had only had to inscribe the name Blake or Haynes on the Silver Tiller. In 1978, he had to fit in another name. The extremely able ex-University team racer, John Patterson, had been around for some time, making the competition hot without quite winning the top prizes. Sailing a boat which he had put together very cheaply two years earilier, and in which he had enjoyed two seasons of decidely moderate success, John suddenly set the boat up differently and started to go. A good Nationals, spoilt by two disqualifications, a creditable 2nd place at the Inlands and ultimately the Silver Tiller crowned a career in Merlins which was just coming to the highest peak. Sadly, the demands of a medical career persuaded John to seek a Class where there was not such a regular weekly commitment.

By 1979, the Haynes had decided to pin their faith on Inglis designed boats which would exploit to the full their favourite lake conditions. Harry's experience took him into an early lead, but the debilitating effects of glandular fever which had affected him over the past three seasons, prevented him winning a Sea Meeting. Kevin stepped in to win on a blustery day at Lowestoft and this was enough to restore the Tiller to the Haynes' sideboard. Harry was second – a splendid family double and a proud moment for Beryl Haynes who contrives to be wife, mother and team manager. The following year it was Harry's turn to win with Kevin as runner-up. Harry took this opportunity to retire at the age of 53 as Silver Tiller winner for the third time. A remarkably fit helmsman for his age until weakened by glandular feaver, Harry's racing cyclist past was shown in the meticulous preparation of his boat and himself for each event. More than anybody else since Leslie Brain, he showed Midlanders that they need not confine themselves to their local meetings, but could go out and win anywhere.

Just as Harry had decided to take up sailing after cycling, Kevin thought he would go the opposite way while still young enough. As the sport is controlled by the professional side, Kevin may return to Merlins. His premature departure certainly indicated that the '80s would see as many new faces at the front as had the '70s. Pat Blake, deprived of an Olympic Games after winning the final Flying Dutchmen trials by the RYA's decision to boycott those held in the USSR in protest against the Russian invasion of Afghanistan, was still spending time on his 1984 campaign and seen but little on the circuit. The new names coming through were Phil King, emerging from an erratic decade, Chris Haworth and Gavin Willis. After Kevin Haynes had equalled his father's achievement in winning the Tiller for the third time, Phil King won the 1982 Series from Chris Haworth with the results reversed the following year. King won again in 1984, but in spite of small bonus points for winning in large fleets (a 0.1 reduction for every 10 boats in the fleet over 20) there was a tie for 2nd place between Bristol's Chris Haworth and Hollingworth

Lake's Roger Harris. This was the first tie in the top 3 places since the Silver Tiller started and showed the continuing commitment of competitors right through the season.

An example of this arose that very year, 1984. Phil King was closely challenged by Haworth and needed to win the final Meeting at Draycote Water in a fleet of at least 60 to score .5pts. When he counted the entry list, Chartered Accountant Phil made it only 58. Thoughtfully entering a couple of his friends whom he hoped would be coming, Phil lifted the entry list to 60 and enabled the winner to gain maximum bonus points. His plans, however, were thwarted by Roger Harris who, in true Silver Tiller tradition, came from a distance and, unfancied won all 3 races to decide which of two contenders would win the Tiller. In so doing, he achieved that first recorded tie for second place.

A very windy 1985 season saw that excellent Britol Corinthian helmsman, Gavin Willis, with his long-standing crew, Bob Taig, give some impressive displays of heavy weather sailing to win the Tiller from club colleagues Chris and Nigel Haworth. Third was Phil King, now crewed by his wife Jenny, who would keep going the tradition of excellent female crews in the Merlin Rocket Class.

Chris Haworth, winner of the Silver Tiller series in 1983, and runner-up in 1982, 1984 and 1985, sailing here with brother Nigel, in *Shadowfax*, the boat in which he has dominated the 1986 series.
Photograph by Ian Holt

Looking at the Silver Tiller Series after 36 years, a history almost as long as that of the Class, one can see that it has had a very decisive part to play in shaping the development of the Class as one where the members visit each other, compete on widely different types of sailing water and ensure that their boats and themselves are equal to every challenge put before them. The Series runs from the beginning of March to the end of October, stopping only for the National Championships (at the Inlands, one of the races is for Silver Tiller points) and Salcombe Holiday Week. Some may think the Series too long, but this is the price to pay for giving the Open Meetings of more clubs Silver Tiller status and making it easier for helmsmen to acquire the necessary 5 results in the correct categories without a vast amount of travelling.

For a brief period, between 1980 and 1983, the Class enjoyed sponsorship from Benedictine – and some very generous prizes. Older Merlin helmsmen may be amused to note the concern of this highly reputable company that it should not be thought to be encouraging otherwise teetotal helmsmen to drink! Withdrawal by the sponsors to back a different sport had none of the disastrous effects seen in lesser sports where the motivation of competitors is too closely linked to the financial rewards available. As the Series climbs towards its own 40th anniversary, still offering exciting sailing on the sea and on magnificent large lakes made from flooding valleys, and still providing tactical battles on small reservoirs, it could be said of the Silver Tiller series as Enobarbus said of Cleopatra, "Age does not wither nor Custom stale her infinite variety."

CHAPTER 9

Salcombe Week

Salcombe Merlin Rocket Week has been given a short chapter to itself in this book due to its compelling attraction to such a large number of the class. How many other regattas are held in this country where if your entry form is not returned immediately (i.e. within half an hour of collecting your mail off the doorstep – husbands tend to delay leaving for work around mid-January each year) then you won't get in? The entries for the Week are limited to 80, but there are usually over 100 applicants for these places, which currently make Salcombe Merlin Rocket Week more popular than the National Championships.

Why? Not for the prizes that is for sure. Key rings, playing cards, rule books and the like do not justify travelling hundreds of miles for and the event does not even count towards the Silver Tiller Series. It can be even worse when "unofficial" prizes are awarded. One year, the Week's winner overall, Phil King, decided that additional prizes were warranted to certain characters in the fleet. These included a toy yacht to Paul Seddon (because he had *not* ordered a new Merlin Rocket that year), a red bucket to Dan Alsop (because he lost his previous one, which was considered his lucky Salcombe mascot), a funnel for Nigel Appleton (so that his weekly alcohol consumption could be even further increased) and a plastic bin liner for Graham Pike (in memory of his attraction with the moored garbage barge during a race). No, Salcombe has a unique atmosphere which quickly becomes addictive (no matter how disastrous your results) and is compelling sailing for many Merlin Rocket sailors.

The large entries each year have a lot to do with the fact that it is very much a family week, somewhere and something to amuse most members of the family can be found. It is the combination of a number of unique characteristics of Salcombe that make the Week so entrancing to the dinghy sailor looking for a change of scenery. There is a superb beach where the boats are kept, which is in fact privately owned, situated on the opposite side of the estuary to the town, from where the beach support parties can obtain a good view of much of the racing. The beach alone can rival most comparable beauty spots in England – the fact that there are 80 Merlin Rockets parked on it is almost incidental.

The majestic clubhouse overlooks the start line (and often the first beat and run), and is perfect for bar supporters and armchair experts. There are many stories of daring overnight dashes through 7ft 2in wide Devon lanes to make the first start, attempting to avoid the milk lorry and the grockles.

The races themselves are interesting because they appear to actually "go" somewhere, as opposed to the more normal olympic courses. No two beats in the same section of the estuary are ever the same, as the tide will have changed and the gaps between the moored boats and the beach altered. Sometimes there are horrendous beats against the tide in amongst the swimmers and moored boats, then on the return leg having to gybe in a Force 6 off the ferry step in front of all the spectators peering down at you from the pub. The list goes on.

Certainly the races are never won until the final leg has been completed: you can meet more obstacles in one race at Salcombe than in a year's Silver Tiller racing. The number of people who have caught their rudders around anchor lines doesn't bear counting, the sight of boats sailing towards each other, all on dead runs, as a sea breeze slowly takes over from the land breeze, the "bag" that infamous half mile stretch of water that has very narrow exits and can usually catch out everyone except Jon Turner, yacht owners who produce wire cutters and threaten to cut your rigging, just because your boat happened to capsize underneath theirs, frightening death runs in heavy weather whilst sailing within ten yards of the shore. These kinds of obstacles should be enough to put most sane dinghy sailors off ever coming back to such an event, but for some reason, Salcombe has the opposite effect – they *love* it!

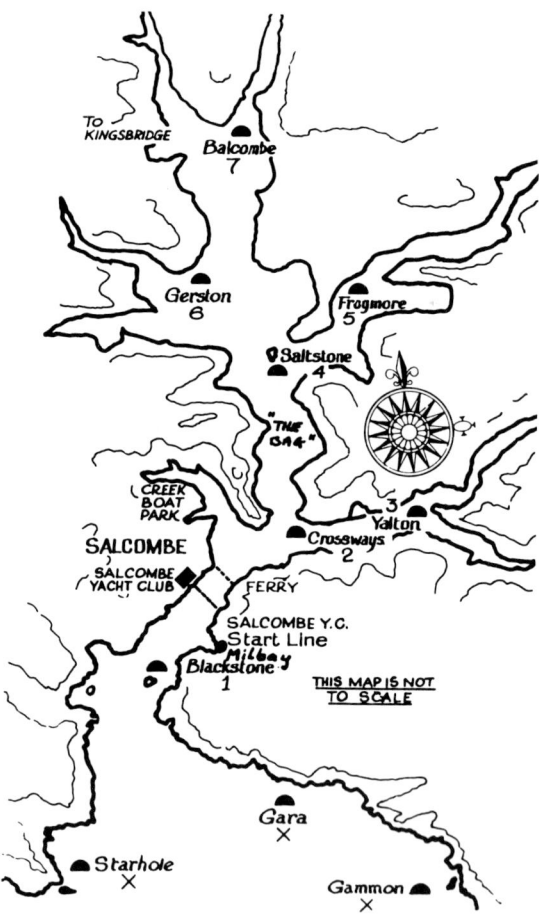

It all started back in the 1950's. Salcombe has two regattas each year, the Town Regatta and the Salcombe Yacht Club Week. The Town Regatta is very much a local carnival-type week, including rowing and raft races, whilst the Yacht Club Regatta is an open house for just about every dinghy class. The first Merlin Rocket sailor to venture down to the area was Guy Pearce sailing his dinghy in the local club races. He invited friends from London down to the Salcombe YC Week and gradually the word spread around the London-based Merlin Rocket fleets that this was an extremely enjoyable way to spend a week's holiday (must have been mad!).

Gerry Britton was one of the early participants, sailing a Proctor "Mk IX," No. 1729. He subsequently retired from competitive racing and moved permanently to Salcombe to become the SCYC sailing secretary. During the next few years he played an important role, along with Alan Chaplin, representing the MROA, in moulding Salcombe Merlin Rocket Week into the form it is today.

Over the years, the number of Merlin Rockets participating, increased to such an extent that it became clear that something had to be done. Serious discussions took place in the meeting rooms of the Victoria Inn bar, and many pints were consumed in the various attempts to reach a solution. In 1971 the Merlin Rockets, along with the Solo class, were given a separate week. In 1972 and 1973 it was shared with the Fireballs and finally, in 1974, we were given our very own week. Entries that year were well over 100 and have stayed around that figure ever since, though due to the harbour authorities limit of 40 boats maximum on the starting line at one time, the participants have been limited to 80 for the week.

There was a time when the prizes consisted of money – £2 for first place in each race. In those days, bed and breakfast was around 12s. 6d. a night for double room, and the better helmsmen were aiming to recoup their accommodation bill for the week. Nowadays, accommodation for the competing crews, their families, camp followers and groupies consists of a wide mixture of tents, rented houses or flats or just plain bed and breakfast, or for the elite Porsche owners club, an exclusive hotel, virtually on the start line. Back in the good old days everyone was bed and breakfast, and before the days of wet suits, the entire flock of landladies at Salcombe would be inundated with piles of soaking wet clothes all week, steaming out their kitchens.

With the vast majority of accommodation available being located on the "Town" side of the estuary but the boat being kept at Mill Bay on the opposite side, there are always logistic problems concerning how to transport the launching trolley, mother, deckchairs and the windsurfer across on a daily or weekly basis. Ingenious methods have been used to transport trolleys inside Merlin Rockets, which have proved to be far more successful than the few attempts at towing them. With only one commercial ferry service across the estuary, which then leaves you with a 15 minute walk to where the Merlin Rockets are beached, most crews arrange the hiring of motor boats for the week. Indeed, the Wembley crowd have recently been so well organised that they bring their own driver for the launch. Again, times have changed over the years. Previously, only rowing boats could be hired which were nowhere near as much fun. It is quite a long row to Mill Bay.

The only way to understand the attraction of Salcombe Week is to compete in it. To actually witness Paul Seddon ploughing up Mill Bay beach with his fixed rudder still attached to his transom, but not to the boat. To suffer the whales at the end of "Vernon" and "Peter's" *"Old MacDonald had a Farm."*. To witness John Harris charging along the start line on port and see the entire fleet get out of his way. It is hoped that the photographs of Salcombe that are included in this book will help in some way to capture the magic of this very special week.

▲ The start of a race is never easy, but at Salcombe there are a few additional problems: the start line isn't quite long enough, there usually only two routes to the first mark (up one of the shores), and the tide causes more than a few headaches. With the starting line raised up on the sea-wall, and observers looking down from the woods, it is very rare to have general recalls – early starters are ne always caught!
Photograph by Robert O'

Old-timers of Salcombe Week, Chris Andrews in *Fantasia*, being chased by John Harris in *Tobacco Road*. Whilst the estuary i wide in many places, there is usually only "one way" to go between marks, giving very close-quarters racing. *Photograph by Robert O'*

I

II

III
The Class is indebted to Mike and Mandy Fowler for their ability to perform in front of the camera at Salcombe. In their first act, one of the perils of sailing at Salcombe is brought to light. Fixed rudders and anchor lines don't go together!
Photographs by Robert O'Neill

Barry Dunning and Bungy Taylor approaching the windward mark in *Substitute*. Beyond is the "bar" and then the English Channel. In strong wind against tide situations a large swell can build up in the estuary mouth, giving very testing conditions.

A typical race at Salcombe. Five boats racing neck and neck, only yards from the shore so as to cheat the tide. In the foreground is Harry Haynes in *Spring Fever*.

◄ Mike Fowler's second performance is more specialised. All apears well in the first photograph, but the gybe that follows would be very difficult to repeat and will never be found in any sailing manual.

Photographs by Robert O'Neill

CHAPTER 10

The 1970 Championships at Pwllheli

Just as the tide turns at different times in different places, it is difficult to place one's finger on when the Merlin Rocket changed from the conventional 14ft dinghy which Jack Holt first designed to the modern wide power machine we know today. Those seeking such a turning point might start with the success of Alan Warren in winning the Silver Tiller in 1964 with a centre mainsheet system which was the key to modern power sailing. Others might choose the resolution at the 1965 AGM to allow transom flaps, which gave designers the confidence to design a wide hull in the knowledge that, although it would hold more water if it capsized, the boat could be speedily emptied. Some might point to the 1970 rule changes which, *inter alia*, allowed the spinnaker chute. Everybody, however, would agree that all these came together in 1970 at the Pwllheli Championships.

At the opening of the '70s, the Class Committee had resolved to recognise the growing strength of Merlin Rocket racing in the North by holding the Championships in the North West. Hitherto, the Championships had almost invariably been held on the South Coast or at Whitstable. The one occasion the Class had gone elsewhere (to Gorleston in 1961) the low entry and East Coast mists had produced no call to repeat the experiment and northern helmsmen themselves had preferred the warmth of the South Coast. The Lancashire coast is singularly inhospitable for dinghy sailing (no doubt the reason why so many clubs sail on reservoirs) and the Class has never been strong in the North East. The ultimate choice was an almost unknown bay on the Lleyn Peninsular of North Wales, with no record of dinghy sailing at even serious Open Meeting level. The moving spirit was Vincent Blake (father of Pat) who claimed that Pwllheli Bay, where he owned a holiday flat, was the best place in the North West to hold a National Championship.

Vincent Blake's choice proved amply justified, for during the course of the week, Pwllheli produced every wind strength from Force 1 to Force 7 and provided one of the most memorable Championships on record.

The news that the Championships had at last "come North" brought out from every little pond and river Merlin Rockets of all shapes and ages. Enthusiastic helmsmen bought or borrowed boats whose masts had been up so long that old fashioned rigging screws had rusted in, new boats were hastily ordered, deals were done on old ones. The resulting championship entry became the largest ever recorded in any British dinghy championships – 227 boats. The entry had, in fact, closed at 226 when Olympic Gold medallist Rodney Pattisson caught the fever of the time and turned up with a boat belonging to the builder of his famous Flying Dutchman and asked if he could join in. His entry, needless to say, was welcomed as a splendid opportunity to see how one of the best helmsmen in the world would cope with a Merlin Rocket Championship.

Pwllheli is a small and unpretentious Welsh holiday resort, brought to minor prominence by the railway and a Butlin's holiday camp. It was the almost limitless capacity of this holiday camp which persuaded the organising Class Committee that the unexpectedly large entry would not cause accommodation problems. In the event, most of the fleet stayed at the camp.

The small harbour at Pwllheli dries out at low water and race times rather depended upon when the Committee Boat could be launched. The boats were berthed on a separate privately owned beach situated among picturesque sand dunes and heather. The small car-parking fee each day was a small price to pay for privacy from the holiday makers who thronged the popular "free" beach. Although the weather was colder than usual on the South Coast and there was not so much sun-bathing after racing, the unspoilt surroundings were much appreciated by the competitors' families. The mild conditions of the first race on Sunday, Force 1 just reaching 2 at its strongest, gave little indication of what was to come.

David Child, sailing in his last Championships before starting his Olympic campaign in the Flying Dutchman class, led in a manner befitting one who had captured the Silver Tiller four times in the past five years. Determined to win a Championship which had always just eluded him, David would have won the first race had he not suffered one of those unaccountable lapses which so often snatched victory from him. He had forgotten to put a key ring on the clevis pin of one of his shrouds. The clevis pin came out and was apparently lost, the shroud shook itself free, thereby endangering the mast. Child had no spare clevis pin or key ring and the race was lost. The winner was Alan Warren in *Superwot*, a modified version of the "Wotnot" design in which he had won a fairly heavy weather Championships the year before and supposed only to be competitive in strong winds.

It is at the end of the first Championship race, when competitors have sorted out their boats and the conditions, that they start noticing who has done well and why. Before the Pwllheli Championships, helmsmen of narrower boats who sailed on rivers or small lakes tended to believe that the new wide designs were all very well in strong winds at sea, but when it came to "really skilful" conditions, a loose translation for light variable breezes where a lucky shift could sometimes bring anyone up among the leaders, they would show the South Coast boys a thing or two. Yet in conditions which were ideal for their boats, one of these "lumbering monsters" had triumphed. The atmosphere back at Butlins that evening was by no means one of jollity, frivolity or "Hi-de-Hi." There was some serious thinking going on.

From a design point of view, the Class was at a most interesting crossroads. The long period of domination by Ian Proctor's designs had ended the previous year and there were many challengers for his throne. Proctor's immediate successor in the National 12s was the talented engineer Mike Jackson. His "Superstition" design, as well as the flared out version, had tremendous reaching speed, but were thought suspect punching to windward through steep waves. The Haworth brothers from Blackpool owned one of each type, with the wide version also supported by Neil Henderson from Leigh, sailing with 17 year old Jilly, now Mrs. Pat Blake. They were to come 7th, 8th and 11th. Another highly successful National 12 designer was Martin Jones, who was represented by his "Xpectation" design, responsible for the imposition of the maximum beam rule, which was sailed by Chris Andrews and David Spiers, who both made the top 12. The previous year's runner-up, sailmaker Mike McNamara, had also bought an "Xpectation" but could not make it point to windward, so had borrowed a "Courageous" from designer-naval architect Tom Booth. With a win at the major pre-Championship Silver Tiller meeting at Arun only a fortnight before, Mike was a verious serious contender. Another strong contender in a "Courageous" was builder Spud Rowsell, 3rd the previous year, while Tom Booth also had supporters in Graham Pike and Francis Williams, each sailing his narrower "Outrage" design.

Two of the Class's radical thinkers had come to opposite conclusions. David Child considered that the wide boats would not succeed unless the wind blew above Force 4 and had opted for Martin Jones' original "Xpectant" design at just over 6ft beam. David

Robinson, also small in stature and even ligher, had looked to a man who had never designed a Merlin Rocket before, but who had a respectable record in the New Zealand Cherub class, Greg Gregory. Robinson also was the first to incorporate into his Merlin the then new-fangled idea which was to revolutionise spinnaker handling, the spinnaker chute.

The traditionalists amongst new boat owners were represented by sailmaker Graham Leech, whose "Northern Light" was a continuation of the "Surf Scooter" theme which had been so successful in the mid-'60s, and who was a firm believer in the traditional transom mainsheet, and by Pat Blake and Guy Gurney who both remained faithful to Proctor's last production design, the "XVII".

After the first day of light winds, which had shown that wide boats were competitive below Force 4, there came an opportunity to see whether anything else would be competitive above it as the fleet was greeted on Monday morning with a Force 5.

When you have a large fleet on a starting line, including those without much experience of championship starts, it is generally considered wise to lay a fair degree of port bias on the line. The reason is that, while the inexperienced tend to start at the starboard end, the pundits will choose the other end to benefit from the bias, which will avoid the fleet bunching in the same area. It also leaves clear the middle of the line where it is most difficult to see who is over.

On that Monday morning, however, there was so much starboard bias that boats that end were able to luff round the Committee Boat after starting. There was considerable bunching in heavy seas and many collisions which a better laid line might have avoided. Rowsell and his crew Jonathan Turner, punched away from the start. Anybody who had any doubt about the value of wide boats in heavy weather could see that they were using their extra leverage to keep the boat upright with everything pinned in. Others were spilling wind or trying to luff through the puffs, but in each case losing the drive needed to punch through the waves.

As was to happen on other occasions during the week, Rowsell was first to the weather mark and still in the lead at the end of the first triangle. Because of the large entry, the Race Committee had decided (since copied by many other Classes) to separate boats hoisting spinnakers at the start of the run from those still beating into the weather mark. An extra mark was laid 100 yards to port of the weather mark to which boats must beam reach before starting the run. This separated the fleet as anticipated, but Rowsell was to forget this innovation while leading in 3 races. As will be seen later, this would make a significant difference to the overall results. The person to take advantage of this error on each occasion was the reigning champion, Alan Warren. Alan's laconic manner hides a shrewd brain which rarely makes any mistakes about a course and was, two years later, to win him a Silver medal at the Olympic Games. Sailing *Superwot*, a modification of the Watts "Wotnot" design with which he had won the previous year's championship, Alan and Barry Dunning, one of the most successful partnerships in the Class's history, were revelling in the heavy conditions. They took the winning gun with Rowsell and Turner, another partnership to become of equal stature, second.

The enormous speeds achieved on the reaches by some boats were due to them using the spinnaker in risky capsizing conditions. The advent of the spinnaker chute, whereby the spinnaker could be lowered if the boat was getting out of control without the crew having to stand up, was encouraging the use of the spinnaker in much stronger winds. Although the first chute had only been seen that Spring on David Robinson's boat, every new boat was now coming equipped with one and many older

boats had been hastily converted. Most of the boats with chutes came from the South coast where the owners were closer to the latest ideas. Clearly this one was a winner. There was even more serious talk at Butlin's that night.

Tuesday morning saw the Butlin's flags flying stiffly to the north-east, indicating another strong blow. This was to be one of the windiest days in which a Merlin Rocket championship race has ever been held. There was a long run off the beach to the leeward mark where the startling line was laid and many capsized on the way. It was dawning on many inland sailors that their "sensitive" designs with their circular sections, so effective on small lakes and rivers, were difficult to control in a strong wind across tide.

That day the line was good with enough port bias to enable the canary yellow *Gigolo* of Graham Pike and Patrick King, another famous partnership, to cross the fleet on port tack soon after the start. The reaches which followed still live in the memories of those who sailed them. The gybe mark showed the superiority of the centre mainsheet in such conditions. While those with transom mainsheets may have felt more confident of their ability to spill wind in the gusts, the ability of the helmsman with centre mainsheet to cleat it with his top batten aft of the mast and gybe in the knowledge that it would remain aft on the other side was crucial. Further, the ability to cleat the mainsheet gave the opportunity to rest aching arm muscles and reduce fatigue.

Once again, Warren benefitted from Rowsell's error over the dan buoy used to separate the fleets at the start of the run, to win the race. Notable, however, was the performance of the 9½ stone David Robinson in his radical V-shaped "Ghost Rider," the boat they said that would never plane. Visitors from One-Design classes were impressed by the fact that design flexibility enabled such a lightweight to keep up with the leaders in the Force 7 conditions. Rather less happy with his borrowed boat was Olympic gold medallist, Rodney Pattisson. Bob Hoare had lent him his own "Kingsize" which he had designed for the calmer waters of Poole Harbour. Pattisson was as prepared to set spinnakers as the leaders and showed considerable speed on one reach before trying to set a world record for submerged sailing.

The beach that evening told its own story of the race. Boats were being rebuilt, bent masts straightened, fittings replaced (some rudder stocks had cracked under the unusal strains), while many competitors just lay, too tired to move.

Help was to come from an unexpected source. The wind next day blew even harder and the Race Officer decided that in such conditions, the rescue boats were insufficient for the huge fleet. After initial postponements, the race was left over to be sailed at the end of the week. This gave the repair parties much-needed time. The wind strength increased and boats had to be lashed to their road trailers to prevent them being blown over on the beach. One fascinating sight was *Ghost Rider,* tied down with only a strongback on an open trailer, swinging into the wind like a giant weathercock.

Thursday brought as strong a wind as Wednesday and again the Race Officer signalled a series of postponements, delaying the start until 6 pm. There followed a most attractive race in the evening sunlight. Rowsell and Turner once again led the fleet round the first triangle and once again started off down the run without remembering the new dan buoy after a gap of nearly two days. Once again it was Warren and Dunning who profited to win with Rowsell second. Some years later the Race Officer, Robert Lee-Warner, told Warren that he should really have disqualified the entire fleet for

◀ One of the very few photographs taken in the difficult conditions. Spud Rowsell and Jon Turner sailing *Courageous,* in which they so nearly won the Championships at Pwllheli in 1970.

rounding the wrong weather mark! Apparently, soon after the start, a local fishing boat came in and found the weather mark a very convenient place to anchor. In so doing, the boat completely masked the mark and Alan Warren led the fleet to a similar mark nearby, round which every subsequent boat passed without complaint. The Race Officer sensibly let this be treated as the proper mark and none were the wiser.

As the fleet assembled for the last day, Friday, the wind had moderated to Force 3, gusting 4. Two races were scheduled for the day to complete the programme. At this stage the Championships should have been a foregone conclusion, Warren having won all 4 races sailed. However, apart from a 7th place in the first race, which would probably be discarded, Rowsell had 3 second places and a win. If Warren was poorly placed in the morning this could leave the Championship open until the final race.

The first race started bright and early. At last Rowsell got his navigation right, leading from the start to win. To make the long awaited victory taste even sweeter, Warren could only manage 5th place. Allowing for a discard, Warren now had 3pts and Rowsell 6¾pts so, if Rowsell won the last race and Warren finished lower than 4th (exactly that which had happened that morning), the latter would lose the Championships despite having won the first 4 races! This would not have been so likely under the Olympic scoring method where there is a steep curve in the graph, but the Merlin Rockets use the "straight-line" graph of a point per position with a quarter point bonus for the winner.

Having had to endure comments about starting lines with insufficient port bias, the Race Officer put some 20 degrees of port bias into the line for the final race and this increased in the last minute and a half as the wind backed. Realising what was happening, Jim Park and Guy Gurney sailed at speed for the port end of the line, tacked alongside the craft marking its end and enjoyed the rare experience of crossing in front of the entire fleet at the gun.

At the first mark it was Gurney in the lead, determined to leave the Class in style. However, a backing wind converted an already close reach into a fetch. Those behind did not bother to set spinnakers and, from the confusion, there emerged another helmsman also determined to go out with a win, David Child. Child was one of those helmsmen whom one could never ignore when he was behind, but who always gave hope however far he was ahead. Having lost a lead the year before with a trivial capsize only to discover that he had not replaced a bung in his front buoyancy tank, and another lead in the first race at Pwllheli by omitting to tape up the key-ring on his shroud clevis pin, Child's position at the front did not cause his pursuers to resign themselves to a battle for second place. Gurney showed his characteristic flair for winning back places which his equally characteristic inconsistencies lost him while, climbing through the fleet after an unusually bad first beat, came the menacing grey hull of *Courageous*. Twelfth at the end of the second beat, third at the end of the next triangle, Rowsell was stretching out for his first Championship, with Warren nowhere in sight.

This time David Child was not going to throw away his lead and, benefitting from the lighter wind, kept ahead of the advancing Rowsell to take the gun in the last race of a distinguished Merlin Rocket career. Rowsell's hard-earned 2nd place left him with an overall score of 8¾pts. If Warren finished lower than 5th, the Championship would still be his.

Alan Warren's relaxed manner not only conceals a shrewd brain but also determination. Too far behind to know whether Child or Rowsell would win, he knew he needed to finish at least 4th, to guarantee his four earlier wins were not going to be ruined by a disastrous Friday. However, between him and that 4th place on the final beat were three tough competitors, his Sussex Motor YC clubmate Chris Andrews in the maximum beam *Xpectation* and Rowsell's Exe SC clubmates, Francis Williams in *Kraken* and Paul Seddon in *Acapulco*.

Seddon had actually started the week in one of the original "Xpectations" and had not been doing as well as he had expected. On the Thursday evening, the owner of *Acapulco*, a "Courageous" design identical to that of Rowsell, had come ashore in an irritated mood saying "If someone gives me £400 for this b----- boat he can have it!" Seddon had coolly produced a cheque book, written out the sum of £400 and politely asked the owner to whom the cheque should be made payable! Spending the morning sorting out the boat to his satisfaction, Seddon was now up with the leaders, back where he felt he belonged.

Nobody was going to let Warren through. It was not a matter of Rowsell's Exe clubmates helping him, they were determined to finish the week with the best result they could achieve. Warren and Dunning had to make that 4th place on their own. Calling upon their last reserves of stamina after an exhausting week, they kept their boat more upright than their competitors and found enough speed to gain 4th place and the Championship with 7pts.

Spud Rowsell's 4 second places and one win would have been enough to win the Championships in most years, but at Pwllheli he had to settle for second place. As a boatbuilder, his disappointment was tempered over the winter by a large number of orders for the "Courageous" design, which competitors thought the fastest boat of the Week and, from those taking a look into the future, the new "Ghost-Rider."

Third place could have gone to a number of helmsmen – to David Child had he not lost his shroud clevis pin while leading the first race, who had to settle for 4th place by ¾ of a point; to David Robinson in the prototype "Ghost-Rider" (which was to prove such a popular design over the next few years) had he not twice broken a rudder – replacing one just before the start of a race, or to Mike McNamara had he not for the second year running scrupulosly retired after a collision he knew to be his fault when well placed. Would that all helmsmen were as honest as Michael! In the event, 3rd place was won by some extremely consistant sailing from Hamble's Graham Pike and Patrick King in *Gigolo* with countable positions of 5-3-5-2-9. With two inland and one sea Silver Tiller wins before the Championships, Graham and Patrick might have gone on to win the Silver Tiller had they not accepted an offer to crew Rodney Pattisson's new Soling with a view to campaigning for Olympic selection. Selling *Gigolo*, they enthusiastically started crewing the Soling, only to have Pattisson return to his Dutchman in which he was to win another Gold medal. The opportunity lost, Pike and King were never to get near winning the Silver Tiller again.

The names which came to the top at Pwllheli may not win so often these days, but after 16 years most are still loyal to the Class. Alan Warren still competes in the Championships trying, with difficulty, to keep ahead of his son for which purpose he has now bought a new boat to a radical Holt design. Spud Rowsell, the Class's largest boatbuilder, was to win the Championships twice and be runner-up as recently as 1983 before relaxing and enjoying his sailing. Jonathan Turner would take up helming and achieve a 3rd, two 2nds and two wins in his first 5 Championships. Graham Pike kept it up for many years before choosing his events more sparingly in the mid '80s. David Robinson was to weave in and out of the Class returning to win a heavy weather Championships at Shoreham in 1985. Francis Williams was to win the following year's championships and to campaign an Olympic Tornado successfully, while Michael McNamara was to damage a tendon and retire to dinghies requiring less sitting out.

Of those lost to the Class, David Child vanished without trace after two reasonably successful years in Flying Dutchmen, while Guy Gurney skippered a 12-metre in America's Cup trials before becoming a major yachting photographer in the USA.

The effect of the Pwllheli Championships spread rapidly throughout the entire Class. Not only were wide hulls essential on the sea, but they would be made to go fast inland and narrow boats would not be built again. The largest ever number of new boats was registered in the next three years as helmsmen decided that they must join the new age. No boat would be built without a spinnaker chute and not many with transom mainsheets.

The Class was to return to Pwllheli in 1974 and enjoy excellent sailing in slightly less winds, but by then there would be a greater proportion of modern well-built boats, better prepared with strong fittings and with helmsmen and crews who better understood the rig and what was expected. The older boats, which had come so joyfully to the first northern Championships, would now confine their aspirations to the new Inland Championships.

The North Wales connection continues every four years, coinciding with the World Football Cup. The venue has changed to the more sheltered waters of Abersoch, not because of any complaint about the superb sailing conditions enjoyed in Pwllheli Bay, but more because of a splendid relationship which has built up between the Class and Abersoch's South Caernarvonshire YC. Despite one or two attempts to run a Silver Tiller Meeting, the Merlin Rockets have not been seen at Pwllheli and, sadly, it seems unlikely that the Class will return.

But if there was a time when the Class paused at the crossroads and saw where its future lay, it was in that week at Pwllheli. To some, the old days when the Merlin was just a big National 12 with a little running spinnaker were the best. To others, the wide hulls (to compensate for the absence of a trapeze) and the spinnaker chutes represented the way the Class had to go if it was to keep ahead of the rash of similar sized boats, built with cheaper methods, which had become popular in the '60s. Certainly, the Class has never been the same since, and much more than an exhilarating week's sailing is owed to that first championship at Pwllheli.

CHAPTER 11

Where Merlin Rockets sail

The Merlin Rocket Class has been described as pursuing a somewhat erratic course along the A6 road. Starting in the London area where there are over a dozen clubs, the next concentration is in the Midlands and moves in a North-westerly direction to Lancashire, and from thence to the Clyde.

If one starts in the North, the real northern outpost lies in the Orkney Isles. The Merlin Rockets started there in the 1950s when some local boatbuilders acquired plans and built in the traditional clinker method to which they were accustomed. The demand had come not only from the occasional dinghy sailor posted to the Isles, but for an efficient means of transport from one island to another without wasting valuable whisky money on fuel for outboard engines. Wind is in plentiful supply up in the Orkneys, so why not harness it for transport?

A former editor of the Class Association Newsletter, the late Bill Vaughan, had to visit the Orkneys in the '70s to examine the effect of seals upon the local fishing industry. He found the Merlin Rocket class in a healthy state, because they had kept a voluntary embargo on newer boats which might outclass the still strong old ones. This was, of course, long before the North Sea oil bonanza had brought money to the Isles. To help the local fleet, Bill enlisted the help of that splendid Northumbrian character Maxie Dunn, who did so much to promote the Class in the North-East. Boats of the approved vintage, up to No. 2000, were acquired, and shipped to the Orkneys when a sufficient number had been gathered and there was a cargo ship going there with space to fill.

The deep and cold waters of Scotland have always given excellent keel boat sailing but have deterred people from the sort of boats which capsize, so dinghy sailing has never been as popular a sport as in warmer English waters. There were a few Merlins based at Holy Loch and other isolated spots in the '70s and they would occasionally make the long trip to the South Coast for the Championships. However, few have been seen in the last decade.

Moving South, Berwick at one time offered sailing, and one of the original Rockets, No. 301, after amalgamation with the Merlins, has been preserved for posterity after a serious collision. She was cut in two down her length and one half used as the counter for the Club bar!

The Royal Northumberland YC used to have Merlins, but they have all moved up the coast to Newbiggin which is now the northernmost Silver Tiller venue.

THE NORTH

Newbiggin SC holds its Silver Tiller event over the Spring Bank Holiday weekend and traditional northern hospitality offers a warm welcome to those who make the long journey up the A1. Launching is from one of those sandy beaches you can usually find in Northumberland. However, the sea coal makes the water rather dirty and it is inadvisable to capsize.

Leeds SC is a misnomer. It is situated in the heart of the Yorkshire Dales between Harrogate and Skipton. Look for the Washburn Valley and you will find Thruscross Reservoir. Like all these lakes formed by flooding valleys, the sailing is good if the winds blow up or down its length, but somewhat variable if they blow across. Access to this splendidly large lake set amid beautiful scenery is via a steep ramp and help is needed to pull the boat up at the end of the race. Such difficulties however, always seem to have a beneficial effect upon the friendly spirit in a club. If you want people to help you, you must help them. The Silver Tiller event is a good place to take the family, for there are many square miles of countryside and a feeling of being away from civilisation. This is now the only Merlin Rocket club on the East side of England between Newbiggin and Oulton Broad.

Moving across the Pennines, the Merlin Rocket class has thrived in Lancashire. The unsuitability of the Lancashire coast for dinghy sailing and the shallowness of Lancashire rivers made the county one of the first to develop the use, for water sports, of the canal compensation reservoirs one finds so often in the north. Drinking water reservoirs, have Water Boards, and their officials took much longer to convince that dinghy sailors were not going to pollute a city's water supply.

Hollingworth Lake SC might justifiably describe itself as not only Lancashire's principal Merlin Rocket club, but that county's leading club for any Class. Started just after World War 2, the Club very quickly established itself as a place where the top Northern dinghy sailors were racing, and this attracted more. The Merlin Rocket connection has a long history here and has been strengthened by recruits from the Club's very successful Firefly Class. A large club fleet ensures good class racing for local members and its Silver Tiller meeting is one of the best attended. Approximately 120 acres of navigable water may not be large by present day standards, but it offers a variety of courses. Launching is down a concrete ramp. Access by road to Littleborough (near Rochdale) has been made easier by completion of the M62.

Leigh SC sails at Pennington Flash, a local name for a flooded open-cast pit. It has probably the largest inland sailing area in Lancashire. As at Newbiggin, a capsize may be looked upon positively as a coal-gathering exercise but, also like Newbiggin, locals will encourage you to wash away the memory with gallons of local ale. Silver Tiller status just makes the Open Water category and the club has a number of very good helmsmen to provide competition.

Bolton SC sails on Belmont Reservoir just off the A675 north of Bolton. A long connection with the Merlin Rocket Class and the Silver Tiller series has survived a reputation for snow at its Open Meeting, and an island which divides the sailing area into two. Class racing is maintained by a strong local fleet.

Dovestone SC is situated at the edge of the Peak district, not far from the villages of Delph and Diggle, just off the A635. Unlike many reservoirs which can dry out in a hot summer, Dovestone tends to keep its water level. The sailing can be bedevilled by a wind which spirals down vertically, but at least the sailing continues. The feeling that one is sailing at the bottom of an inkwell can be dispelled by the sight of an opponent sailing too close to the bank and finding a cow contentedly chewing his spinnaker!

WALES

Bala SC is one of those clubs sailing on a flooded valley. Excellent winds if blowing up or down, not so excellent if blowing across. Marks have to be laid at the side of the lake, otherwise you would need rather a lot of chain! A shingle foreshore should be treated with care, as should the shallow shelving shore. A lifting rudder is an asset. In addition to an Open Water Silver Tiller Meeting, the club has also run the Inland Championships three times. A popular venue, with Lancashire and West Midland owners. Bala also has a strong local fleet and offers good Class racing.

Abersoch is situated at the end of the Lleyn Peninsular and is a popular Championship venue. Because the South Caernarvonshire YC and the Merlin Rocket Class have forged a good relationship, we also have a valuable northern Sea event there. Beach launching and a clubhouse which caters for all needs makes this the Class's most popular Championship venue away from the South Coast.

THE MIDLANDS

The choice here lies between river sailing on the Trent or lake sailing on the many reservoirs which have opened up in the last thirty years. The reservoirs vary enormously in size, but it is a peculiar feature of the area that while the large ones obviously have the best attended Open Meetings, the smaller ones often have much bigger home fleets.

Nottingham SC is situated on the Trent, near Trent Bridge and adjoins the Holme Pierrepoint National Water Sports Complex. The river is deep and wide here with a slow current. A bend ensures courses giving all points of sailing, so that the Nottingham Club can claim substantial advantages over more historic river clubs. Silver Tiller status is usually granted to its Open Meeting.

Trent Valley SC is the complete antithesis. An historic club with a fine old wooden clubhouse located near Long Eaton on a bend of the river near its confluence with the River Soar. This is the place where Dick Wyche and Digby Coppock first tried out their ideas of an International 14 inexpensively built of clinker construction, which was to become the Rocket. Although the Open Meeting still retains Midland Circuit status, the narrow (and at times shallow) river has meant that it has lost status to newer clubs, such as Nottingham, where the sailing conditions better suit large visiting entries. However, there are those who will positively enjoy getting more out of tricky conditions than others in a delightful, unspoilt area, where narrow boats are at no disadvantage. Sailing with Trent Valley SC, and enjoying the facilities of sleeping cabins ashore and stewards to serve meals, is being part of dinghy sailing history.

Notts County SC is different again. Situated 2 miles downstream from Nottingham near Stoke Bardolph, those many members of the Class who have never quite embraced the aims of the Teetotal movement will welcome the idea of a pub (where everyone changes) built right on the starting line. The narrow river means that narrow boats which tack well are in their element. Midland Circuit status only for the Open Meeting, but there is a splendid New Year's event.

Draycote Water SC stands out in this area as offering the best sailing and clubhouse facilities. The lake is one of those very few which can offer an Olympic triangle with a one mile beat for the visitors, and a similar triangle for the club racing. The well-equipped modern clubhouse is reached via the end of the M45, just south of the village of Dunchurch. The club has several times hosted the Class's Inland Championships and, since 1972, has been the venue for the final Silver Tiller Meeting of the year.

Burton SC took the brave step of moving an old-established Merlin Rocket club in the town of Burton from a lake which had been overtaken by the opening of large reservoirs, to a magnificent 128-acre reservoir set high on a hill overlooking the River Trent near Repton. Beware of trying to find Foremark Reservoir on any maps printed before 1980. Look for the grid reference SK3223.

Blithfield SC is located near Abbots Bromley, Staffs. A large open water lake with a roadbridge across the middle is occupied by a club with strong Merlin Rocket leanings and has a popular Open Water Silver Tiller Meeting. The location is convenient for both Midland and Lancashire owners so the event is usually well-attended. A small but modern clubhouse with hard standing for boats and cars makes for sound facilities which are attracting more and more members.

Banbury SC is a small club on a small kidney-shaped lake situated nowhere near Banbury (which has a totally separate club) but near the village of Upper Boddington. A long connection with the Merlin Rockets and a truly rural location has made this a popular Silver Tiller meeting for owners from the Birmingham area. This is another club where older designs are still competitive.

Midland SC is another club where the Class has been established for many years. Situated at Edgbaston in the Birmingham suburbs, the club usually has a large local fleet for club racing and its Open Meeting has Restricted Water status in the Silver Tiller series.

Earlswood Lake SC is situated 6 miles south-west of Solihull. The small lake is surrounded by trees which make for attractive surroundings but tricky windshifts. Old boats are competitive here as long as they know which way the wind will shift next!

Redditch SC sails on a triangular lake with an island in the middle set in parkland in the town of Redditch.

Sutton SC also sails on a small lake set in parkland, this time in Sutton Coldfield. The clubhouse is inaccessible for visitors' cars so you must sail across to get a drink, and presumably back afterwards. Much safer!

Shustoke SC sails on an oval 100 acre lake about 3 miles east of Coleshill which is north of Birmingham. A newish club which adopted Merlin Rockets at the end of the '70s, quickly won Silver Tiller status by efficiently organising Open Meetings and showing how the lake is open to the prevailing wind. This club has won a reputation as a young club going places.

Tamworth SC is one of those gravel pits which introduced so many people to dinghy sailing during the boom years. A staunch member of the Midland Circuit, the islands in the lake call for interesting tactical decisions although they may also be the reason why the Open Meeting no longer has Silver Tiller status.

EAST ANGLIA

The Broads area was a strong supporter of the Merlin Rocket Class in the early days. However, just as the boatyards of Jack Holt, Chippendale and Wyche & Coppock had a beneficial effect upon the spread of the Class in the London, River Trent and Sussex areas respectively, the building of cheap hard-chine One-Designs in Norfolk inevitably led to fragmentation of fleets. Although there are several Merlin Rockets sailing in handicap fleets on the various Broads, the Class's stronghold is on one of the finest stretches of water, Oulton Broad.

Waveney & Oulton Broad YC has a small but beautifully situated clubhouse overlooking the Broad. With a harbour where boats can moor after sailing round from a delightful dinghy park, the club offers two major events in conjunction with the Royal Norfolk & Suffolk YC, a couple of miles away at Lowestoft. Over the Spring Bank Holiday, there is a fascinating Meeting comprising one race on the Broad, one up a splendid river course (which is worthy of Silver Tiller status on its own), and one race at sea, with all 3 to count. You must really be an "all-rounder" to win this trophy. The other event, which attracts a larger entry, is the August Bank Holiday Double. This comprises a Restricted Water Silver Tiller event on the Broad (3 races) on the Sunday and a long race at sea off Lowestoft on Monday. This is a great exercise in navigation, finding the buoys and judging the tides, together with a test of ability to sail through waves which can be long in deep water and short in the shallows. A friendly local fleet makes this one of the clubs for which all visitors have a strong affection.

Great Yarmouth & Gorleston YC sails on the sea near Yarmouth at Gorleston, the venue for the 1961 Championships. There is a small fleet of Merlin Rockets, some of whom sail also at Oulton Broad and some of whom go inshore to Horning in the winter and sail as the Snowflake SC. The Open Meeting has Broads Area, but not Silver Tiller status.

Grafham Water SC is one of the largest man-made reservoirs in the country and its Open Meeting is one of the best attended in the Silver Tiller year. Situated just off the A1 from Buckden, Hunts, and clearly marked on all maps, the sailing waters and clubhouse facilities are probably unmatched anywhere. A regular venue for the Class's Inland Championships. Launching is easy, if a little muddy.

THE LONDON AREA

As with the Midlands, the choice is river sailing on the Thames or the reservoirs. The river clubs tend to be old and well establiished in delightful surroundings but with many obstructions to the wind, whereas the reservoirs offers excellent sailing but without the same sense of history.

Starting at the mouth of the Thames and moving upstream, the first club is:

Whitstable YC. Situated on the south side of the Thames Estuary not far from the end of the M2 and close to the famous oyster fishing boat harbour, the Whitstable Club is one of the fishing port's main social centres. The club has been the scene of many memorable Championships and Silver Tiller Meetings. The Thames Estuary is so wide here that you might be on the open sea, were it not for the short chop kicked up by the flood tide (on which you usually race) against the prevailing south-west wind over the shallows. Launching is over a shingle beach (big trolley wheels help) on to a shallow shelving shore (a lifting rudder helps). There is now once more a strong local fleet and the Silver Tiller is not to be missed.

Ranelagh SC. This club, situated at Putney near the starting place for the University Boat Race, celebrates its centenary in 1989. The club where "Merlin" was conceived, runs racing throughout the year, for Ranelagh was always a pioneer of winter sailing. Boats are kept under the grand old clubhouse, which means that masts must be stepped and unstepped at the end of each race. The whole life of the club revolves round the tide tables. The racing programme is organised so that in the lighest of breezes, the flood tide takes you down to Hammersmith Bridge and the ebb tide brings you back. Trees and buildings obstruct the wind, but the river is wide to give a variety of options. The Silver Tiller is well supported and the Club is a second home for the flat and bedsit dwellers of that part of London. Class racing is strong because the Club restricts its boats to Merlin Rockets and National 12s.

Tamesis Club is situated just above Teddington Lock and therefore in non-tidal water. The river is narrow here and the current strong. The techniques here depend upon quick tacking to get out of an adverse current and to take marks neatly. The sailing conditions themselves resulted in the club losing Silver Tiller status for over 10 years until the revival of the Merlin fleet inspired its return. The club has a strong family reputation because the area of river sailed is fairly small and almost the entire course can be seen from the clubhouse. Access by road is easy and launching merely involves tipping over the side.

Ranelagh SC – "Where it all began."

Photograph by J. Lowden

Thames SC has a marvellous clubhouse at Surbiton and has a considerable reputation for off the water social life. The beautiful tree-lined stretch of river near Hampton Court may be very pretty but the resultant wind-shadows make for very tricky sailing and it is no coincidence that this is the home of the Thames Raters with their enormous high masts.

Hampton SC sails on the Thames at Hampton Wick, close to the old Hurst Park racecourse. The clubhouse is on the north side of the river. Trees on that side can restrict the wind but there are less obstructions to the south from whence comes the prevailing wind. There is Class racing for Merlins and although the Open Meeting does not have Silver Tiller status, the club regatta attracts Merlin support.

Cookham Reach SC provided a home for Merlins in the early days when their more famous neighbours, Upper Thames SC, would not adopt any Class which did not have National or International status. Set in attractive, but tree-lined surroundings with simple but sufficient accommodation and dinghy parking space, Cookham has always set out to provide the basic necessities for good racing at low subscription. In this way, not only has it ensured that there is always a large fleet in the adopted classes, of which the Merlin is one, but it has encouraged those pundits who spend their summers away from the club at Open Meetings to maintain their membership. The Open Meeting usually has Silver Tiller status in alternate years.

Upper Thames SC is situated at Bourne End near the ferry. Although early development was stunted by the presence of a strong International 14 tradition, the suitability of the Merlin Rocket for one of the finest reaches on the Thames has ensured a healthy home fleet and a well attended Silver Tiller Meeting in April. In addition, the Club puts on a most civilised Week in June, Bourne End Week. This consists of racing, sipping chilled white wine on the lawn and enjoying dinner in a different Thames-side pub each evening.

Turning now to the reservoirs:–

Queen Mary Reservoir SC is the largest of the reservoirs in the London area. Opened in 1972, it held the first Inland Championships in 1973 and has seen its Merlin Rocket fleet grow steadily ever since. Although the club offers racing for over a dozen different classes, the Merlin Rocket fleet entries are usually about the third largest, a remarkable feat when one considers that the other classes are very much larger in size both nationally and locally. As with the other large reservoir clubs, it is easy to feel that you are a small part of a major business, but this is small price to pay for magnificent sailing conditions, Olympic triangles with one mile beats available for club members throughout the year whatever Open Meetings may be on, and excellent facilities ashore. The launching ramps are rather steep and assistance is needed to recover the boat. The Open Meeting (which has Open Water status) is held in the smaller reservoir, separated by a central peninsular, and the open meeting fleets have this section to themselves.

Wembley SC sails on the Welsh Harp, a canal compensation reservoir on the North Circular road, close to the southern end of the M1 and within sight of Wembley Stadium. The "Harp" is a mile long by a quarter and is open to the prevailing winds. Launching is easy, down shallow ramps to large pontoons where boats can be left moored between races. Because the club restricts the adopted classes to three, there is always a large Merlin fleet in the racing throughout the year. The Silver Tiller Meeting in October has Restricted Water Silver Tiller status and the club runs the SE Area Team Championships each year. There is a large dinghy park and a clubhouse orientated towards the racing members.

Aldenham SC sails on another canal compensation reservoir at Elstree close to where the A5 joins the M1. This small reservoir is situated in attractive surroundings, although the trees restrict the wind and the shape of the lake does not allow for very long legs. Clubhouse facilities are limited by the lack of running water. The club has a very long connection with the Merlin Class although the number now sailing at club level is small. The Open Meeting occasionally has Silver Tiller status.

Broadwater SC sails on a small gravel pit just off the North Orbital road between Rickmansworth and Denham. Mainly older boats sailing, some class and some handicap racing.

Harlow (Blackwater) offers estuary sailing on the Blackwater near Mayland, Essex. Although the small clubhouse is situated at the end of a little creek, and there is therefore less time either side of high water when you can launch and return, the splendid launching ramp covers a wide tidal range and the creek gives some very interesting sailing out on to the Blackwater. A sheltered dinghy park makes this not only an excellent Silver Tiller venue (very much more easily reached from London now the M25 has been completed), but a good club for Merlin owners wanting to join a club based upon one of the best sailing estuaries in the country.

Up River YC sails on the River Crouch upstream from Burnham at Hullbridge. A small but modern clubhouse is set in a field. A launching ramp leads to a creek which dries out at low tide. A small Merlin fleet enjoys some excellent sailing and a large Silver Tiller fleet enjoys an interesting Long Distance Race. This consists of a race downstream, past Burnham to the mouth of the River Roach and back again, a total of 18 miles. Often there are strong winds, always there is a tide to be watched. This is an unusual Meeting well worth attending.

THE SOUTH COAST

Starting from the east and working westwards, we start with an inland club in the Sussex Downs.

Bewl Valley SC sail near East Grinstead on a large lake amid beautiful South Downs scenery. This large reservoir gives excellent sailing conditions and the family element has produced a large membership in a very short time. Silver Tiller status has recently been given to the Open Meeting and the club has a most promising future.

Rye Harbour YC sails at the ancient Cinque Port of Rye. From the small modern clubhouse you launch into the narrow river and sail out to the sea, or trail down the coast road to the mouth of the river and launch down a steep shingle slope. Once you are actually out on the sea, conditions are easy and the Open Meetings have always been well run. The event lost its Silver Tiller status in the early '80s but this was probably only due to complaints about the launching. Many feel that Silver Tiller status ought to return.

Pevensey Bay SC sail in the Bay itself. Strong winds and waves have made for some excellent Open Meetings and have inspired a number of Phil Morrison's designs when he lived there. Launching can be difficult if the wind is in the wrong direction, but the club has always a helping hand for visiting boats.

Sussex Motor YC. Don't be put off by the title! This is a highly organised racing club on the south-west (and therefore, most importantly, the windward) side of the Adur River at Shoreham. The old Sussex YC on the other side always had trouble launching from what was usually a lee shore, so the dinghy sailors moved across and took over the Motor YC. A large clubhouse and a large lawn for a dinghy park make for comfortable facilities. The ramp leads down to the sheltered harbour where you can organise your boat before sailing out on to the sea. The prevailing conditions at Shoreham seem to be strong winds and huge rollers. You quickly realise why Sussex Motor helmsmen have done so well in heavy weather Championship races. People such as Alan Warren got regular practice here. The Silver Tiller event is always well supported.

Arun SC sails at Littlehampton. Situated just downstream of the roadbridge over the Arun, there is a large clubhouse with a changing room apparently designed for midgets. The Silver Tiller has always been well attended and was always put considerably early in the season to help inland sailors prepare for the Championships. There is an interesting sail down to the sea (watch the bar at low water) and usually a vigorous sail when you get there. As with all the Sussex venues, the tide is a set and you can go for the windshifts rather than worry whether you are in the right part of the tide.

Bognor Regis YC has a very long connection with the Merlin Rocket Class. Many memorable Silver Tiller meetings have been held from that little clubhouse at the west end of the promenade. There have been some equally memorable croquet matches on the club lawn as the fleet waited for the tide to come in. Watch out for the lobster pot lines catching your rudder!

Hayling Island SC was the venue for the Class's first two Championships, those held in 1977 and many Open Meetings in between. A splendidly improved clubhouse with sleeping cabins faces north-east, overlooking Chichester Harbour and easy launching.

Too many classes quickly meant an insufficient number in each and the Merlin Rockets suffered along with the rest. As a Championship and occasional Open Meeting venue, the opportunities of exciting sailing out in the Bay, or tactical sailing inside the Harbour, are excellent.

Hamble River SC has an unrivalled reputation in the Merlin Rocket Class. This has built up by a combination of factors: a succession of top class helmsmen and crews, excellently run races by Nicholas Robinson, a river event in the March winds for the Hamble Warming Pan, and a Silver Tiller event in August down at the mouth of Southampton Water, both attracting every year the fastest boats in the Class. The home fleet always provides enough competition to test any newcomer. Launching from the shingle "hard" is into the river. The waters tend to be a little flatter than out at sea and therefore even higher speeds can be attained. This is a very good place to find out how well your rig is tuned, for the many Merlin owners in the marine trade who are members here usually have extremely well tuned boats against which you can measure yours.

Parkstone YC sails in Poole Harbour from Parkstone. A well appointed clubhouse with a lively social programme and a large concrete dinghy park is the home of a fairly large Merlin fleet. This may be due, partly, to the membership of the celebrated boatbuilder Bob Hoare whose boats won the Championships 8 times in 9 years between 1960 and 1968. Shallow launching conditions (a lifting rudder is helpful) lead out to the racing station, on stilts in the main channel. Sailing conditions call for an appreciation of both windshifts and tides as affected by the large islands. The Silver Tiller Meeting has Restricted Water status at times and Open Waters at others. The narrow channels in which one can safely sail at low water call for one category while the large expanses of water and the strong winds you can get at the top of a Spring Tide call for the other. The surrounding countryside and the further reaches of the Harbour are deservedly popular. Poole Week at the end of August attracts many Merlin owners seeking a more enjoyable week's sailing than the highly competitive National Championships.

Weymouth SC has long been known as one of the clubs running excellent Championships in Weymouth Bay, the same Bay considered by the RYA as the best place to have the preparations for and the final Olympic trials. The Merlin Rockets have enjoyed several Championships in this Bay, but not until 1984 did the local club suddenly adopt the Merlin Rocket as a racing class, apparently impressed with the performance of the Class at its Championships and the way in which the competitors made so little call upon the rescue services. Silver Tiller status was quickly given to the Open Meeting and the Class is keen to support the growth of the home fleet in this most attractive bay. A charming old-world clubhouse overlooking the river which runs into the harbour together with sheltered launching conditions, make this a very welcome new addition to the Merlin Rocket family.

Exe SC sails at Exmouth, Spud Rowsell country. A modern clubhouse replaces the old one which fell into the harbour when, it is rumoured, Spud got locked in one of its smallest rooms and nobody knew he was there. A large well-filled dinghy park shows the enthusiasm there is for sailing on one of the loveliest of estuaries. Cruising up to Topsham is but one of the delightful options open to members of the club. The Merlin Rocket fleet, which once contained six of the top dozen helmsmen in the Class, may have dropped in numbers recently, but with Rowsell building boats just round the corner and a choice of sailmakers in Morrison and McNamara, this state should not last. The Open Meeting at Spring Bank Holiday is a good opportunity to spend a long weekend in a lovely part of England and enjoy either some tactical racing in the estuary or some glorious uncomplicated planing out on the sea. The Bay was a most popular venue for the '81 and '84 Championships and without doubt the Class will return to a spot where the sun seems to shine more often. If your boat should be damaged, you have only to sail it into Rowsell's yard and it will be returned as good as new.

Bristol Corinthian YC sail just in from the Severn estuary at Axbridge Reservoir near Cheddar Gorge. This club is the Class's stronghold in the west and has one of the most competitive Winter Racing Series anywhere. Over the May Bank Holiday, the club runs a splendid Silver Tiller Meeting which is rated as one of the hardest to win every year. Launching is down a short ramp to a patio on which boats are rigged and then tipped or sailed over the edge into clean deep water. Without rain the water level drops and launching and recovery can be so difficult that racing stops in high summer. This has had the effect of pushing Bristol men out on the Silver Tiller circuit and at one time there was a sensible tradition of spending the summer with Exe SC which is only a short distance down the M5.

This probably combines the best of both worlds and is a suitable recommendation upon which to end this brief description of places where Merlin Rockets sail. The views are bound to be personal impressions and intending members or Open Meeting competitions should, of course, check to see whether the information is still correct. These impressions are intended to give some idea of the large scope of places where Class racing is offered or there is a good Silver Tiller or Championship venue. There are many more places where Merlin Rockets are happily sailed in a Handicap fleet but, with the type of support which the Class has given to clubs on interesting stretches of water, some of these may in time be offered Class racing and even pressing for Silver Tiller status.

The Merlin Rocket Class has been greatly strengthened by the Silver Tiller series and has become a Class which travels to find not only good competition, but also good sailing waters.

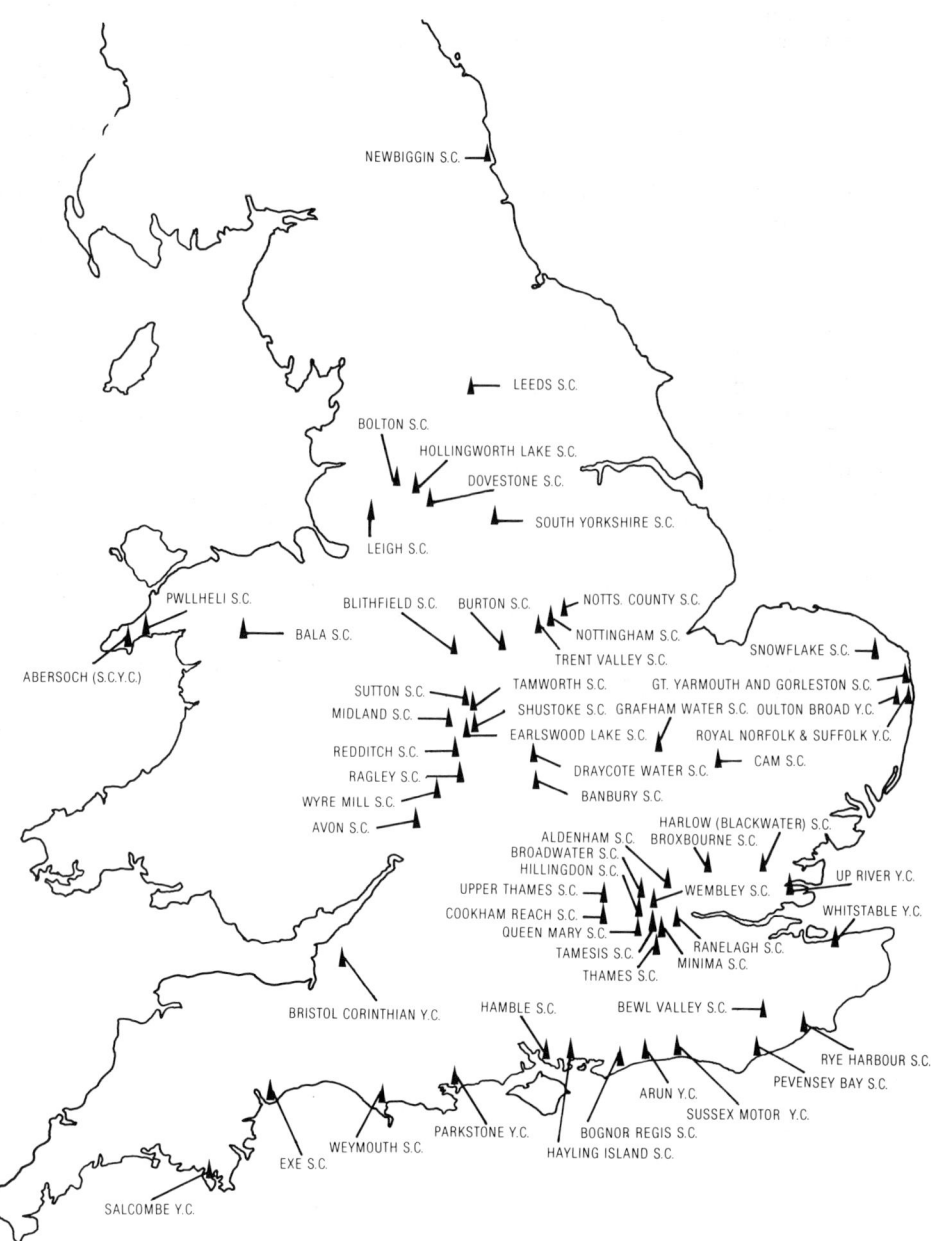

Where Merlin Rockets sail

ABERSOCH (SCYC)	Cardigan Bay
Abersoch, Gwynedd, N.Wales	
ALDENHAM SC	Aldenham Reservoir
Aldenham Road, Elstree, Herts.	
AVON SC	R. Severn (W)
Chaceley Stock, Tewkesbury (SW), Gloucestershire	
ARUN YC	S.E. Coast
Riverside West, Littlehampton, West Sussex	
BALA SC	Bala Lake (NE)
B4403, Bala, Wales	
BANBURY SC	Boddington Reservoir
Nr. Byfield, Banbury, Oxfordshire	
BEWL VALLEY SC	Bewl Bridge Reservoir
Lamberhurst (S), Kent	
BLITHFIELD SC	Blithfield Reservoir
Abbotts Bromley, Rugeley, Staffordshire	
BOGNOR REGIS SC	South Coast
Victoria Road South, The Esplanade, Bognor Regis, West Sussex	
BOLTON SC	Belmont Reservoir
Belmont Village, Bolton (NW), Lancashire	
BRISTOL CORINTHIAN YC	Axbridge (Cheddar) Reservoir
Axbridge, Nr. Bristol (S), Somerset	
BROADWATER SC	Broadwater Lake
Moorhall Road, Harefield, Uxbridge, Middlesex	
BROXBOURNE SC	Broxbourne
Meadgate Road, Nazeing, Essex	
BURFIELD SC	Burfield Lake
Station Road, Theale, Reading, Berkshire	
BURTON SC	Foremark Reservoir
Milton, Nr. Repton, Burton Upon Trent, Derbyshire	
CAM SC	River Cam
Clayhythe, Waterbeach, Cambridgeshire	
COOKHAM REACH SC	River Thames
Berries Road, Cookham, Berkshire	
DRAYCOTE WATER SC	Draycote Water Reservoir
Dunchurch, Nr. Rugby, Warwickshire	
DOVESTONE SC	Dove Stone Reservoir
Banks Lane, Greenfield, Oldham (E), Cheshire	
EARLSWOOD LAKE SC	Earlswood Lake
Malthouse Lane, Earlswood, Birmingham (S)	
EXE SC	River Exe Estuary
Estuary Road, Exmouth, Devon	

GRAFHAM WATER SC	Grafham Water
West Perry, Huntingdon, Cambridgeshire	
GT. YARMOUTH AND GORLESTON SC	East Anglia Coast
Gorleston on Sea, Norfolk	
HAMBLE SC	River Hamble
The Hard, Hamble, Hampshire	
HAMPTON SC	River Thames
Hampton, London	
HARLOW (BLACKWATER) SC	River Blackwater
Nipsells Chase, Maylandsea, Chelmsford, Essex	
HAYLING ISLAND SC	South Coast
Sandy Point, Hayling Island (SE), Hants.	
HILLINGDON SC	Hillingdon Sail Base
Bews Lane, Harvil Road, Harefield, Middlesex	
HOLLINGWORTH LAKE SC	Hollingworth Lake
Lake Bank, Littleborough, Rochdale, Lancs.	
LEEDS SC	Thruscross Reservoir
Pateley Bridge (S), Nr. Harrogate, North Yorkshire	
LEIGH SC	Leigh Flash
Sandy Lane, Lowton Leigh, Lancashire	
MIDLAND SC	Edgbaston Reservoir
Icknield Port Road, Edgbaston, Birmingham, West Midlands	
MINIMA SC	River Thames
48A High Street, Kingston, Surrey	
NEWBIGGIN SC	NE Coast
Bridge Street, Newbiggin by the Sea, Northumberland	
NOTTS COUNTY SC	River Trent
Stoke Bardolph, Nottingham (E), Nottinghamshire	
NOTTINGHAM SC	River Trent
Adbolton Lane, West Bridgford, Nottingham, Nottinghamshire	
PARKSTONE YC	Poole Harbour
Pearce Avenue, Poole, Dorset	
PEVENSEY BAY SC	South Coast
Old Martello Road, Pevensey (W), East Sussex	
QUEEN MARY SC	Queen Mary Reservoir
Ashford Road, Ashford, Middlesex	
RAGLEY SC	Ragley Park Lake
Ragley Hall, Alcester, Warwickshire	
RANELAGH SC	River Thames
Embankment, Putney, London SW15	
REDDITCH SC	Arrow Valley Park Reservoir
Redditch, Nr. Birmingham (S), Worcestershire	
ROYAL NORFOLK & SUFFOLK SC	East Anglia Coast
Royal Plain, Lowestoft, Suffolk	

RYE HARBOUR SC	Rye Harbour
Rye Harbour, Rye, East Sussex	
SALCOMBE YC	Salcombe Estuary
Salcombe, South Devon	
SHUSTOKE SC	Shustoke Reservoir
Reservoir Drive, Shustoke, Birmingham (E), Warwickshire	
SNOWFLAKE SC	Rive Bure
The Street, Horning, Norwich (NE), Norfolk	
SOUTH YORKSHIRE SC	Moor Hall Reservoir
Bolsterstone, Stocksbridge, South Yorkshire	
SUTTON SC	Powells Pool
Sutton Park, Monmouth Drive, Sutton Coldfield, W.Midlands	
SUSSEX MOTOR (SHOREHAM) YC	South Coast
223 Harbour Way, Shoreham by Sea, Sussex	
TAMESIS SC (Nr. AERIAL SC)	River Thames
Trowlock Way, Broom Road, Teddington, Middlesex	
TAMWORTH SC	Kingsbury Water Park
Kingsbury, Birmingham (NE), Warwickshire	
THAMES SC	River Thames
Portsmouth Road, Surbiton, Kingston, Surrey	
TRENT VALLEY SC	River Trent
Trent Lock, Long Eaton, Nottingham, Nottinghamshire	
UPPER THAMES SC	River Thames
Wharf Lane, Bourne End, Marlow, Buckinghamshire	
UP RIVER YC	River Crouch
Pooles Lane, Hullbridge, Essex	
WAVENEY & OULTON BROAD YC	Oulton Broad
Nicholas Everett Park, Lowestoft, Suffolk	
WEMBLEY SC	Welsh Harp (Brent) Reservoir
Birchen Grove, Wembley, Middlesex	
WEYMOUTH SC	South Coast
Nothe Parade, Trinity Street, Weymouth, Dorset	
WHITSTABLE YC	Thames Estuary
Sea Street, Whitstable, Kent	
WYRE MILL SC	River Avon
Wyre Mill, Wyre Piddle, Pershore (NE), Worcester	